W9-BNF-472

INSIGHT-IMAGINATION

INSIGHT-IMAGINATION

The Emancipation of Thought and the Modern World

DOUGLAS SLOAN

Cataloging-in-publication Data

Sloan, Douglas.
  Insight-imagination : the emancipation of thought and the modern world
  p. cm.
  Bibliography: p.
  Includes index.
  1. Knowledge, Theory of. 2. Imagination.
BD161.S55 1993
ISBN 1885580002

Insight-Imagination was originally published in hard cover by Greenwood Press, an imprint of Greenwood Publishing Group, Inc., Westport, CT, 1983, under the auspices of the Charles F. Kettering Foundation. Copyright © 1983 by Charles F. Kettering Foundation. This edition by arrangement with Greenwood Publishing Group, Inc. All rights reserved.

In memory of my father
Leland Milton Sloan

Contents _____

Preface

This book is written out of the conviction that the world we live in, and that lives in us, is far richer and more meaningful than we can begin to realize, given the conceptions of knowledge and ways of knowing that dominate the modern age. For many people, it seems, knowing is simply knowing and knowledge is knowledge, and, the more we do of the one and have of the other, the more we will understand of the world and the better things will be. It is widely conceded, to be sure, that modern efforts to know the world have shown it to be exceedingly complex, and that the applications of knowledge through modern technology, while they have made the world more comfortable for many, have also made it for all of us an increasingly dangerous place to live.

And, rather than yielding to our attempts to solve them, the problems that threaten to engulf us on every side actually seem to multiply and to grow worse with every new advance in knowledge and its applications. The spoliation of nature; the continuing suicidal buildup of nuclear weapons; a spreading illiteracy, apathy, incivility, and violence among the citizenry; the breakdown of personal relations; a miasma of low-level depression; a haunting sense of futility in all that we do; signs of a deepening cynicism in individuals and society—the problems range from the global to the excruciatingly personal, and we become daily more familiar with them.

As the problems mount, there frequently appear to be only two choices in coming to grips with them: Either to plunge ahead in the faith that we will surely, though it must needs be soon, make the ultimate discovery and devise the final technology that will undo and turn around all the major problems our old knowledge and its applications have created or failed to solve; or, for those to whom this faith in new knowledge and technology appears more an act of superstition than of rational faith, the only alternative frequently is to abandon the pursuit of knowledge altogether and in its place to call for an emphasis on values, personal commitment, and human relationships. Either way, and the dilemma is often posed in just this form, the choices are not especially attractive. Knowledge without meaning, purpose, human commitment, and values becomes trivial or destructive; but an emphasis on commitment, purposes, and values that has no grounding in our perceptions and knowledge of reality soon becomes sentimental, wishful thinking, and ineffectual—or crazy and deadly.

Our conceptions of knowledge and ways of knowing, the grasp of reality that these make possible, and the values that follow thereon are all intimately connected. One of the chief problems of the modern world is that our conceptions of knowledge frequently give rise to views of reality that provide little place and support for the values and personal-social commitments necessary for a rich, whole, and life-enhancing existence. What might be called an orthodoxy about how we know and what we can and cannot know, a kind of epistemological orthodoxy, has settled over the modern mind. This orthodoxy has adopted a narrowly quantitative, materialistic, and functionalist view of knowledge with such zeal that it tends to exclude feeling, imagination, the will, and intuitive insight from the domain of rationality—or to accord them only the most limited importance—and to deny any place for mind, meaning, and persons as constituent of reality. In its extreme forms, which are by no means rare, this orthodoxy maintains that we can know only that which we can count, measure, and weigh. In this view, all things having to do with the qualitative dimensions of experience are regarded as having little or nothing to do with knowledge and are frequently even disparaged as sources of irrationality. And in this view, there is often an undisguised contempt for the possibility that the kind of world we are able to know and experience may be integrally bound up with the ways of thinking and knowing made possible by the kinds of persons we are.

Within education today the consequences of this narrow and dominant conception of knowledge have perhaps been most apparent precisely at those points where genuine efforts have been made to come to grips with the central problems and purposes of modern life. In recent years, the relations between education and issues of meaning and value have received considerable attention. Programs for moral education and citizenship training, for example, proliferate in schools and departments of education. General education, ignored for some years, is once more a burning issue as leaders in higher education seek ways of reunifying and of introducing questions of value into the curriculum. Consideration is being given as seldom before to the teaching of ethics, from the elementary through the college and professional years of education. And the problems that threaten the future of the earth have turned many to look to education for help, calling for broad biological, ecological, and agricultural education—for peace, world order, and disarmament education.

From one perspective, this turning to education can be seen as the latter-day expression of a long-standing, venerable American tradition of faith in the power of education to do what nobody and nothing else are succeeding at. The faith in this instance seems to be misplaced. For one thing, much of the current discussion of values in education and the solutions proffered—values clarification, some new courses in ethics, more general education and interdisciplinary work—all seem too easy and superficial when compared with the complexity, depth, and tenacity of the problems they are meant to address. Moreover, the fragmentation, the confusions of modern education, its lack

of wholeness to which many critics have pointed, and its frequent ineffectuality in carrying out even the most rudimentary
undertakings, suggest that perhaps education—and not only in
schools, but education also in the family, in public cultural institutions, in the media—has itself been a major victim of the
very problems it is being asked to solve, and in the process has
sometimes become a prime contributor to them.

Most important, however, amidst all the "value talk" in education, the connection between knowledge and values is seldom dealt with. That knowledge and education are connected
seems obvious enough to everyone. That values and education
ought to be connected is being widely remembered. But that
knowledge and values must be integrally connected is often
denied, when the issue is dealt with at all. And so there exists
a fundamental inner contradiction at the heart of education, a
contradiction that seems all the more insurmountable to the
extent that education is itself—in the university, the school, the
media—dominated by the modern orthodox view of a knowing
that excludes on principle any connection between values and
knowledge. Educational reforms have time and again foundered
on failure to engage this primary question of what counts as
genuine knowledge about the world—and the continuing failure
to address this basic issue permits only the dimmest of hopes
for most of our present educational reform enthusiasms. Within
education and elsewhere, most calls for an increased emphasis
on values ignore this central issue: in them, all knowing is usually still conceived in line with the canons of the dominant orthodoxy, and values accordingly become synonymous with those
irrational aspects of experience, which are thought, by those
concerned with them, nevertheless, to be that which makes life
worthwhile. Despite the genuine concerns that give rise to it,
such value talk thus serves often to reinforce the contradiction
between the two worlds of knowledge and of values. And, in
any event, it is easily sidetracked by all manner of secondary
questions about these values, where they are to be found, what
their status is, whether they are unchanging and absolute or
relative and mutable, and so on and on. If wholeness in knowledge, education, and human values is to be achieved, if the
circle connecting the three is to be truly closed and the inner

contradictions that now separate them is to be dissolved, it can only come through a transformation in our ways of thinking and knowing such that meaning, qualities, and the value of persons are seen as integral to our knowledge and to the reality we seek to know. Our primary focus, therefore, must be not upon values as such but upon the adequacy of our ways of thinking and knowing. A thinking that is fragmenting, detached, and rigid will continue to give us a world that is increasingly broken, alien, and dead. The possibility of a living, harmonious, and meaningful world can only be grasped and realized by a thinking and knowing that are themselves living, whole, and engaged. To speak of a transformation of knowing in this sense is at the same moment to contemplate a transformation of the knower, of ourselves, and of the society and world in which we live. What at first glance may appear to be abstract and arcane questions of interest to only a few actually touch the lives of us all because they bear directly on the major issues and problems of our times. The beginnings of such a transformation are to be found in an adequate grasp of Insight–Imagination understood as the involvement of the whole person—thinking, feeling, willing, valuing—in knowing (a conception much different from the modish, and basically trivial, notions of "imagination" which currently abound). It is the possibility of just such a transformation of knowing and of its place in our wider life experience—from a knowing that is more than a doing and having to a knowing that is also participation and being—that we will explore.

Chapter One examines the destructive consequences in every sphere of life that flow from the narrow conceptions of knowing and reality that dominate the modern mind set and its scien*tistic* and tech*nicist* world view.

Chapter Two looks at alternate and more adequate ways of knowing in what are described as the radical humanities and in the great religious and wisdom traditions of humankind. A consideration of the importance of human language and a new approach to the old question of the relation between science and the humanities, and especially to the currently much-discussed question of "scientific literacy," are undertaken. The crucial need for a renewed, though critical, appreciation of the religious and wisdom traditions is explored. Particular attention, however, is also given to the problems involved for the modern mind and modern society in attempting to reappropriate the traditions.

Chapter Three distinguishes genuine science from scientism, and locates the scientific enterprise within a larger context of values and meaning. This chapter also examines in some detail new vistas opening in science, which reveal the importance of Insight–Imagination, which recognize the importance of the human being and the centrality of human experience in our understanding of the world, and which point to the potential unity joining science, religion, and the humanities. At the same time, the real dangers of the rise of a new scientism resulting from an uncritical enthusiasm for the discoveries of twentieth-century science are taken fully into account (dangers sorely neglected by many who now champion the religious significance of the new science).

Chapter Four is the pivotal chapter of the book. This chapter develops the conception and reality of Insight-Imagination as the involvement of the whole person in knowing—thinking, feeling, willing, and valuing. The work of the physicist David Bohm and of the philosopher and philologist Owen Barfield figures centrally in the discussion of this chapter. Their thinking, converging from the side of science and from the side of the humanities, helps to make clear that the development of Insight-Imagination is essential for the future of the earth and of human civilization.

Chapter Five explores, both in educational theory and in actual, specific, curricular and classroom practice, the thoroughgoing implications for education of a transformation in our consciousness and ways of knowing. The larger personal and social dimensions of an education of Insight-Imagination are integral to the discussion.

Those thinkers on whose work I have drawn will recognize the large debt I owe to their insights and wisdom; they will also be the first to recognize that any misunderstandings to which I may have subjected their views and arguments and any shortcomings and weaknesses in the development of my own are entirely my own doing and responsibility.

My special gratitude is to Robert F. Lehman, General Counsel and Director of Exploratory Research of the Charles F. Kettering Foundation. It was Robert Lehman who first conceived a symposium, subsequently sponsored by the Kettering Foundation and held at Woodstock, Vermont, in June 1980, to explore the topic "Knowledge, Education, and Human Values: Toward the Recovery of Wholeness." As a result of the symposium, it was Robert Lehman who proposed that I write this book, and his personal encouragement and thoughtful reflections have been indispensable in seeing it through. My deep thanks also go to Frances B. Simon, Mary Lindamood, and Kathy Heil for their help in typing and preparing the final manuscript.

I also want to express my appreciation to the Charles F. Kettering Foundation for its support in the writing of this book. However, the views and ideas set forth in it are solely my responsibility and do not represent those of the Kettering Foundation.

INSIGHT-
IMAGINATION

1
Fragmented Thinking, Broken World _____

Scientism

If we are to plumb the deepest connections between knowledge and human values, it is imperative that we look closely at the conception of knowledge and knowing that has come to dominate our modern world: namely, the scientific and technological. Since the beginning of the scientific revolution some four hundred years ago, the tendency has become firmly entrenched to regard science as the only valid way of knowing and the only real source of genuine knowledge. As it has become increasingly dominant, this view of knowledge has made extremely difficult any considerations of values other than those already embedded in natural science and its technological applications. The overwhelming tendency has been to equate all genuine knowledge with scientific and technological knowledge and to consign everything else to the irrational or the ephemeral. The result for society, for culture, and for all educational endeavors has been momentous.

In order to prevent serious misunderstanding at this point, however, it is important to stress at the outset that the discussion of science that follows is not to be construed as a criticism and rejection of science as such. The intent of this discussion is quite other. In the first place, it aims to uncover the limited and mis-directed tendencies in our thinking that have led to a twofold distortion of science in the form of (a) inflated claims that have been made for science, both as a method of knowing and as a view of reality, and its overextension into realms in which it does not apply, and, hence, does not belong; and (b) the mis-apprehension of science itself as non-human, and its consequent vulnerability to humanly destructive forces and uses. The ulti-mate focus of the criticism that is developed is, therefore, not science itself, but deep, underlying forms of thinking and con-sciousness which are prior to science and which reach into every realm of human endeavor. But, because of the dominance of science in today's world, a look at its misconceptions, misap-plications, and inner limitations becomes an obvious and all-important—though in principle not the only—point of departure for such criticism. The discussion thus aims, in the second place, to clear the way for a genuine appreciation where fitting of the achievements of science as it now exists, and for the recognition, which an out-and-out rejection of science could never give, of the promise, now apparent at many points within science itself, of a fundamental change of premises and transformation in our ways of knowing. This potential for transformation is always in danger of being overlooked, or dragged down and over-whelmed, as long as inadequate, unexamined assumptions about our knowledge and ways of knowing are accorded a false sanc-tion and standing by a misconception of science.

In order to grasp the full consequences of the dominance of science as the way of all knowing, it may be well to recall some of the fundamental assumptions that have been part and parcel of modern science since its early development in the theories of Copernicus, Galileo, Kepler, Newton, Descartes, Bacon, and others. A basic assumption has been that knowable reality is quantitative, that which can be counted, measured, and weighed. At the beginning, Galileo established that, in order to carry out observations based on measurement and calculations, it was necessary to distinguish between *primary* and *secondary* qualities in experience. The primary qualities included size and extension in space, number, weight or mass, motion, and time; these were regarded as belonging to the world, and to be the only proper objects of investigation and knowledge. Color, taste, smell, form, and tone were regarded as secondary qualities in that they were held to exist only in the mind of the observer, not in the world observed; and hence, being also tied up with feeling and sensations, were taken to be purely subjective and ultimately unreal.[1]

Modern science has taken the further step of getting rid of all qualities except motion, number, and force, and even these are often regarded as having only pragmatic value. Thus, from the beginning of modern science there has been a systematic effort to eliminate from the domain of genuine knowledge all qualities that pertain to the knowing subject, including not only those qualities bound up with feelings and sensations, but consciousness itself.

Closely related to this is what might be called the reductive-analytic assumption of scientific inquiry. This is the view that every whole can be reduced to more fundamental and smaller parts. If we want to get at reality, we must break it down into its smallest elements or entities. These smallest units are themselves conceived in quantitative, physicalist, materialist terms. A third related assumption is that the world-parts, the quantitative facts, are related solely by physical cause and effect. Any other postulated relationship would remain by definition unobservable and experimentally unverifiable.

A fourth assumption is that the goal of science is increased control over nature. By measuring, by calculating, by reducing everything to its ultimate microconstituents, nature is to be made amenable to manipulation and redirection. In Francis Bacon's words, the purpose of science is "to put nature to the rack, to torture her secrets from her." As Bacon clearly saw, such knowledge is power; indeed, a standing temptation arises to rely not on a concern for truth as the touchstone for what is to be accounted knowledge, but on that which offers power and the means to control.

Underlying these assumptions, almost as their presupposition, has been yet a fifth. This is the assumption that the knower stands detached, apart from the world, and looks upon it as something to analyze and to dissect into its component parts. The world exists "out there," as object, with no integral, essential relation to the subject as knower. It is this sense of separateness from nature, what Ernst Lehrs has called the "onlooker consciousness" of modern man, that has been the characteristic mode of the scientific consciousness.[2] It is just this sense of detachment and separateness of the knower from the world that undergirds the dichotomy erected between the qualitative dimensions of experience as purely subjective and the world "out there" as at bottom the only reliable and knowable reality. It is also this very onlooker consciousness that has made it possible to regard nature as itself void of feeling and inner-relatedness. Hence, nature has become fair game for being broken down through experimental manipulation into its parts, which can then be reassembled to yield great technological power, but for purposes totally alien to nature's own requirements.

Over the centuries these assumptions have been extended, refined, and qualified (and by some today are being subjected to fundamental criticisms in ways that we will have occasion later to consider). In their own domain they have proved immensely valuable, giving rise to a science, a way of knowing, that has been unsurpassed in human history in revealing the quantitative and mechanistic dimensions of reality. The truly impressive development of modern technology and of its many benefits have been eloquent testimony to the power of science to explore the quantitative realm.

During the nineteenth century, however, there began that tendency, noted earlier, to claim that science is not only one specific, if powerful, approach to a limited part of reality, but the sole way of knowing all reality. Positive scientific knowledge was to replace what were regarded as other inferior, in fact, mistaken, claims of knowledge. Beginning with Auguste Comte, from whom the doctrine first originated, scientific positivism was to have many variants, but all have maintained in common that the only genuine knowledge of any kind is that attained through the methods of science applied to what are considered in quantitative, physicalist, and reductionist terms to be the positive data of experience. Positivism in whatever variety (scientific materialism, scientific naturalism, logical positivism) thus makes three all-encompassing assertions (a) that science provides our only way of knowing and our only source of genuine knowledge about the world; (b) that science provides the only way of understanding the human being's place in the world; and (c) that science provides the only trustworthy approximation of a total picture of the world—the so-called scientific and technological world view. Again, while there are minor variations in the world views drawn from science, all agree in portraying a mechanistic, atomistic, materialistic model of a universe connected in its parts only through physical cause and effect. In some versions of this view, the universe is governed by immutable laws of iron determinism; while in others more recent, it is governed by pure chance. In both cases, because with the elimination of qualities has also gone purpose, it is a universe without significance, without point. Alfred North Whitehead, a main critic of the positivistic world picture, described well the kind of world it presents: "Nature is a dull affair, soundless, scentless, colourless; merely the hurrying of material, endlessly, meaninglessly."[3]

The twentieth century began with high hopes in the promises of science to usher in a world of peace, plenty, and universal enlightenment. Scientific positivism, with its all-encompassing threefold assertion about knowing, the human being, and the world, has been aptly described as an expression of scientism—at once an unwarranted extension of science beyond its proper limits and an unquestioning (hence, ironically unscientific) assumption that science can solve all of humankind's problems. Now, with two decades remaining in the century, there is no denying that the achievements of science have been remarkable, that our knowledge and control of the physical universe have exceeded even our parents' most extravagant imaginings. But the earlier naive faith that science and its technological applications contribute ultimately to the universal benefit and enlightenment of humankind has been badly shaken.

The involvement of science in the great human catastrophes of our century—Verdun, Auschwitz, Dresden, Hiroshima, to list only the more staggering—no longer permits an unquestioning faith in scientific progress. Moreover, there is a growing realization that science and technology are deeply implicated in the rampant exploitation and dismantling of the environment and in the relentless invention and buildup of ever more terrible means of military destruction. Nearly half the world's scientists, it has been observed, are engaged in military—"defense"—projects, and most of the remainder are supported by the state and industry, with their less than universal interests and concerns.[4] Nor has the promise of science to enlighten and educate been unambiguously fulfilled. Indeed, as science has become increasingly abstract and mathematical, it has also become farther and farther removed from general understanding and from the possibility of the public's informed participation in scientific decisions and policies that directly affect the public. This increasing abstraction has brought great technological power, but even as scientists pursue their inquiries into one field after another there is a sense of powerful and destructive forces being unleashed over which we have less and less control. The physicist Paul Zilsel wrote a number of years ago: "With all our mushrooming know-how and frenzied hurry to transform the world out of all recognition—if not indeed out of existence—we are increasingly helpless and confused in the face of the world we are creating."[5] Many, nevertheless, continue to call for a more assiduous application of science and technology to bring under control the social, political, economic, ecological, psychological, and other problems that threaten to overwhelm us. Others, however, are beginning to ask whether there is not something fundamentally irrational in ceaselessly seeking to solve our problems mainly by doing more of what has helped to bring them about. If the patient has been poisoned by the wrong medicine, does it make sense to think that we can cure him by more doses of it?

The public uneasiness, nevertheless, remains inchoate and largely inarticulate and has done little to loosen the hold of scientistic premises and categories on the modern mind. At a deeper and more significant level, however, the scientistic, positivistic world view is being directly challenged and the way charted for moving beyond it. From within a renewed appreciation of older religious and philosophical traditions, from within a radical re-visioning of the humanities, and, perhaps most importantly, from within science itself, small but growing numbers of outstanding thinkers are beginning not only to demonstrate in detail the failures of positivism, but at the same time to develop alternate ways of knowing and thinking about the world and the place of human beings within it. Our primary task here is to begin to explore these new conceptions of knowledge and views of reality and their implications for education in its broadest sense. This is the essentially positive (not positivistic!) task set before us. If there is to be any hope for its success, however, this task must be undertaken with a full awareness of the obstacles in its way.

A first step, therefore, must be an unflinching look at the continuing force and dominance of scientistic attitudes and assumptions, and at their consequences. As Frederick Ferré has written, "The scientistic worldview, eventually accepted in gross form as the common sense of modernity, has structured the consciousness of the modern world."[6] And this world view continues to hold sway, providing the basic framework within which we perceive and interpret ourselves and our world. Because they operate as accepted common sense, the assumptions of this world view remain largely unexamined, and efforts to bring them to consciousness often invite incomprehension, ridicule, and anger.

At the popular level we encounter the scientistic world view at every turn: in the science and daily-living supplements of our newspapers and journals, in school textbooks and classrooms, in television space spectaculars, in everyday conversation. At a more sophisticated level in the university disciplines, its hold is no less tenacious. In the social sciences, reductionism and functionalism are the favored modes of explanation; and in schools of education, behaviorism and mechanistic models of human development and learning flourish.[7] Because they have time and again failed to engage the issue of what counts as genuine knowledge, the humanities, thought to be the main guardians of human values, have been unable to offer effective resistance to the scientistic world view. Indeed, humanists have often been enthusiastic collaborators in their own undoing, at one moment seeking to out-science the scientists, and at the next acquiescing in the notion that they deal only with inspiring and entertaining fancies. In the physical sciences when the adequacy of mechanistic models are called into question in one field, they are reasserted with renewed vigor in others.[8] So tightly and pervasively have the premises of scientism battened on the modern mind that even those thinkers most committed to finding more adequate perspectives have repeatedly had their attempts to do so vitiated by what Owen Barfield has humorously called the presence of RUP, a "residue of unresolved positivism," in their own unconscious outlook and thinking.[9]

The deep, unexamined assumptions of scientism constitute what Huston Smith has aptly characterized as the Modern Western Mind Set.[10] This mind set, Smith argues, is one that focuses upon one domain that it takes to be reality; namely, the quantitative, material domain that the methods of modern science have brought to view. For the modern Western mind set all else that does not fit this view of reality, when it is not denied outright, is called into question, if only by neglect. With its emphasis on objectivity, analysis, number, and control, modern science has proven extremely powerful in its own realm but in the process has omitted certain things essential to the human experience. These things that modern science does not and cannot deal with, Smith points out, include: (1) normative and intrinsic values—science can deal only with descriptive and instrumental values; (2) purposes—the question of "Why?"; (3) global and existential meanings—ultimate questions and the problems of life; and, above all, (4) qualities—qualities that involve feeling, awareness, and life. For Smith this modern Western mind set is one in which the extension of a particular and limited way of knowing to all of reality has produced a world view that has no place for the quintessentially human. The consequences of this mind set for modern culture in general and for education in particular have been devastating.

The Reign of Quantity

The most immovable of all the assumptions of the modern mind set is that which holds that the qualities of experience reflect only subjective preferences and emotional states. The tendency of the past four hundred years has been to regard only that which can be dealt with by science—quantity—as objective and real, and all else—qualities—as purely subjective, and thus, ultimately, as non-existent. "Look closely and you find there is today," Owen Barfield has written, "a widespread assumption, sub-conscious for the most part, but raised to the level of consciousness in the philosophy of a value-free science, that there is really no such thing as quality. There is the useful and the useless, the desirable and the undesirable, and that is all."[11] In order to prevent misunderstanding, it may be worth repeating that this is not to denigrate the importance of the quantitative approach of science—nor of its mechanistic models—within their proper and limited domain. It is to stress, however, that the unwarranted extension of the purely quantitative to encompass the whole of experience is eventually to create a dead universe in which quality, meaning, and life have no place. "The exclusive preoccupation with quantity," Lewis Mumford has written, has "disqualified the real world of experience," eliminating all that makes human life worthwhile and driving the human being "out of living nature into a cosmic desert."[12]

Barfield has noted the paradox that the more hesitant people are to talk about the actual qualities of things, the more readily they resort to the terms "values," and especially to "human values." "One of the things I have particularly noticed in the course of my life," he writes, "is the ever-increasing vogue of that word *value*, and especially its plural, *values*, as well as of relatively modern concepts like *value judgments* and *value free*, in philosophy, psychology, sociology, journalism and elsewhere."[13] The popularity of such value talk, he suggests, is that it seemingly reintroduces the possibility of dealing with the centrally important human concerns without challenging the quantitative presuppositions of the dominant modern conceptions of knowing. "People used to talk," Barfield writes, "about the beautiful and ugly, noble and beastly, right and wrong; but that could only go on as long as there was confidence that qualities are objectively real. The current preference for 'values' has come about because the term is one that neatly avoids any such ontological commitment."[14] This shallow reliance on value talk is illusory; by leaving untouched the deeper question of the reality of qualities, it reinforces the modern propensity to regard all that is not quantitative as purely subjective, unrelated to our knowledge of the world, with no grounding in it.

Once qualities are excluded from the world, and from our knowledge of the world, with them go also the reality of human values, purpose, and meaning. Statements about value, meaning, and quality come to be viewed and treated as merely expressions of subjective feelings and preferences or as manifestations of folk traditions and social habits or as ideologies masking group interests. Ultimately, they come to be regarded as unreal, epiphenomena, to be ignored in favor of what can be empirically measured and manipulated or to be explained away in terms of what are seen as more basic biological, social, and economic factors.

Science owes much of its success to the clarity and power of its method of analysis. The reductive-analytic approach assumes that all larger phenomena are to be understood in terms of simpler phenomena that are considered the real constituents of the universe. A living being is viewed as a composite of different chemical compounds, each of which can be broken down further into yet simpler components, into molecules, atoms, and finally the subatomic units that are thought to be the ultimate particles making up all that exists. The aim is to provide a mechanical model of the universe that reduces the complexity of the whole to the functioning of a relatively few simple parts. Thus, one assumption of the reductive approach is that living processes and living substances are ultimately explicable in terms of non-living physical components. And even the *life sciences* beginning from these methodological assumptions must bring living substances into the realm of the inanimate by analyzing them chemically, crystallizing them, x-raying them, and so forth in order to pursue their investigation.[15] The method of reductionism has enabled man to intervene in nature, and to predict and manipulate aspects of nature's processes with a good deal of precision. As a limited method, reductive analysis is highly useful and essential.

When the claim is made, however, that reductionism provides a final and total vision of reality, then destructive consequences follow. Wholeness and unity are dissolved away; only the parts remain. Rather than the primary reality that makes all thinking and meaningful experience possible, wholeness itself is regarded as an artificial construct, a sometimes useful abstraction of the mind. With the disappearance of wholeness, meaning also vanishes. The connective tissue of experience, the network of intricate qualitative relationships that constitute the whole of life and make meaning and significance possible, disintegrates. Reductionism as a total view goes hand in hand with a universe in which only quantity is acknowledged, for qualities inhere in meaningful relationships which are ruled out by definition in a universe consisting of only physical cause-and-effect interaction among its constituent units. A disqualified universe falls to pieces—if it is not taken apart first.

Again it needs to be emphasized that specialization and analysis in themselves are valuable and not to be rejected as such. Moreover, specialization is not the result of reductionist analysis, since it is a necessary concomitant of all careful and serious scholarship. An unfettered reductionism, however, not only adds impetus to the drive toward an ever greater narrowing of focus, by denying or ignoring the larger and prior meaning of the whole, it also undercuts any basis for communication among specialties. Each discipline begins to claim to be self-sufficient, each advancing its particular explanations as the final truth, specialists no longer are able to talk to one another, and the world of learning is fractured, seemingly beyond repair. The widespread desire manifest during recent years in American higher education to promote interdisciplinary studies points to a perception of the need for the integration of knowledge and of the curriculum. The failure of many of these interdisciplinary endeavors to sustain themselves for long has been testimony to the strength of the reductionist perspective and its fragmenting effect.

Ironically, even the most extreme reductionism, if it is to make significant observations and draw meaningful conclusions, requires at least some subsidiary awareness of a larger, prior, and interrelated pattern of meaning. "Before we begin to analyze an interesting whole," Frederick Ferré points out, "we must first be able to recognize the whole as interesting. Any consciousness operating by analysis alone could never recognize the difference between the atoms of the frog and of the fly and of the air and water surrounding them. We must—logically must—move *from* holistic awareness of significant unities, *then* to the detailed parts that find their meaning and importance in the wholes within which they function, if we are to understand the universe as it is."[16] It is the sense, however vague, of a more comprehensive, coherent whole that directs and gives significance to the most precisely focused analysis.

Without the whole, without a prior *gestalt* of meaning, the parts by themselves—the particular observations and pieces of data—when put together would never amount to more than chaotic congeries of unrelated details. The scientist Michael Polanyi has argued that "real discovery in science is possible for us because we are guided by an intuition of a more meaningful organization of our knowledge of nature provided by the slope of deepening meaning in the whole field of potential meanings surrounding us. We are then able to know (in some anticipatory, intuitive sense) enough of what we do not know as yet in any explicit sense (because we have not yet discovered it) to enable us to locate a good problem and to begin to take groping but effective steps toward its solution."[17] When reductionism asserts that the parts are prior to the whole and ultimately more real, it chops away at the foundation on which its own usefulness and significance rest. Reductionism then becomes, to use another metaphor, parasitical and like the parasite ends by destroying itself along with the source of its own life and potential.

A fragmentary view of the world is probably rooted in attitudes and habits of thinking that go much deeper than science itself, and that are no doubt as old as mankind. As long as the dissecting and separative mentality did not dominate our view of reality it could be criticized, countered, and complemented by more holistic modes of thinking. Once the method of reductionism, however, had been extended—in what Polanyi has called "an aberration of the imagination; a fantastic extrapolation of the exact sciences"[18]—to a total and exhaustive vision of the world, integrative, holistic thinking was consigned to secondary status, if not ruled out entirely. "The prevailing tendency in science to think and perceive in terms of a fragmenting self-world," the theoretical physicist David Bohm has written, ". . . tends very strongly to re-enforce the general fragmenting approach because it gives men a picture of the whole world as constituted of nothing but an aggregate of separately existent atomic building blocks, and provides experimental evidence from which is drawn the conclusion that this view is necessary and inevitable. In this way, people are led to feel that fragmentation is nothing but an expression of 'the way everything really is' and that anything else is impossible. So there is very little disposition to look for evidence to the contrary."[19]

Although there are intimations within science itself (at which we will look) of a growing dissatisfaction with an exclusive reductionism, it continues to pervade the public mind and the scientific outlook. Indeed, Bohm remarks, "One might in fact go so far as to say that in the present state of society, and in the present general mode of teaching science, which is a manifestation of this state of society, a kind of prejudice in favor of a fragmentary self-world view is fostered and transmitted (to some extent explicitly and consciously but mainly in an implicit and unconscious manner)."[20] Enjoying the prestige of science, and thought to be the product of the only valid way of knowing anything, the atomistic, reductionistic world view itself serves as a kind of writ for treating the world in a piecemeal and fragmented way.

The loss in our ways of knowing of a sense of a prior and undergirding wholeness has provided a lease for the unrestrained dismantling of nature. The biochemist Erwin Chargaff writes that

> the overfragmentation of the vision of nature—or actually its complete disappearance among the majority of scientists—has created a Humpty-Dumpty world that must become increasingly unmanageable as more and tinier pieces are broken off, "for classification," from the continuum of nature. . . . The wonderful, inconceivably intricate tapestry is being pulled out, torn up, and analyzed; and at the end even the memory of the design is lost and can no longer be recalled. What has become of an enterprise that started as an exploration of the *gesta Dei per naturam?*[21]

But the reductionist world view does more than produce and certify fragmentation. Because its only recognized categories are quantitative and mechanistic, the world view itself is unable to recognize and account for the full richness and complexity of life and its accompaniments—feeling, consciousness, and purposeful striving. To be sure, few scientists are so consistent in their adherence to the world view that they suppress their own wonder at the marvels of life. Most scientists, in fact, seem to be motivated by a deep desire "to unravel the mysteries of life" (a frequently used and revealing expression) in order to enhance life's satisfactions. But the world view itself provides no ground for pursuing such concerns. It offers no support for the scientists' own value commitments and idealism; it provides no basis for dealing with human concerns as rooted in genuine knowledge of the world.

The Narrowing of Reason

The tendency has been to count as genuine knowledge only that which is derived from empirical observations of sensory data, and the logical and mathematical inferences drawn from these observations. The result has been a drastic curtailment in our conception of reason itself. This narrowing of reason has proceeded relentlessly from two directions. On the one side, reason itself has been cut off from its own deep sources of imagination, intuition, and insight in the mind of the knower. It has become customary, it is true, to speak of the importance of the imagination in science. And a few persons, to whom we will give much attention later, are beginning to point out that to do so requires a fundamentally new look at the entire process of scientific discovery, and an understanding of the imagination as involving a good deal more than its usual portrayal as the re-shuffling of patterns and relationships among the empirically given. Even when the important role of the imagination is acknowledged, however, seldom is any account of it as the source of new meaning and new perception actually attempted, and almost no provision is made for its development and strengthening. Both the most familiar experiences of consciousness and the deepest activities of the knowing mind are systematically neglected, or are consigned by definition to the unknown and unknowable—in short, to the irrational.

On the other side, reason loses touch with the intelligibility of the world it would claim to know. A reason that is limited to dealing only with sense experience and the logical relations among observed phenomena cannot speak of any non-empirical dimensions or structures in reality. It cannot even speak of those other dimensions of non-sensory experience that, as Alfred North Whitehead never tired of pointing out, even our most ordinary conscious experience, including sense experience, must always presupppose. It certainly cannot speak of any non-material, qualitative, and unitary dimensions of reality on which all apprehensions and affirmations of meaning and purpose depend. Instead, a reason based solely on the primacy of sense experience deals only with the logical and instrumental relations among empirical phenomena.[22] Severed from its roots in the processes of consciousness and at the same time denied access to non-empirical intelligible connections in reality, reason thus becomes identical with logical, technical reason—that is, with only one very limited aspect of all that reason, or perhaps, better, rationality, was once supposed to encompass.

Such a twofold narrowing of reason has made it almost impossible to understand the sources of new knowledge and the place of insight in human thinking; it has exalted technical and instrumental manipulation at the expense of understanding; and it has played havoc with attempts to generate and pursue values other than those already imbedded in the scientistic and technological world view.

This drastic curtailment of the meaning of reason, this epistemological narrowing, helps to explain some of the major intellectual movements and theories of knowledge of the twentieth century. When reason is conceived in such a way as to deny it access to any intelligible, objective meaning in reality, one alternative is to interpret all statements and affirmations of larger meaning as referring to the subject who makes them. Such affirmations of a meaningful world, whether coming from poetry or art, philosophy or science, are interpreted as forms of the individual's life, as expressions of the individual's attitude or emotional state. If such statements arise from the experience of the subject as observer, they are taken not as referring to the world as it is, but to what state of mind or attitude it arouses in the subject as observer. This has been the existentialist response to the limitations imposed in the modern world on our concepts of rationality. It is the response that says that the purpose of all statements of larger meaning is to promote or provoke deeper self-understanding, but the connection with the world beyond the self is cut away.

Existentialism has represented an attempt to salvage the human being in a universe thought to be indifferent to human meanings. In this, existentialism has rendered an important service. It has shown that, apart from the values and qualities of life associated with subjectivity, no meaningful conception of the human being is possible. It has established that the human being is not a thing and cannot be treated as a thing without being destroyed. It has shown that the very substance of the human being is to seek and live in meaning. It has demonstrated that self-understanding involves acts of free choice, assumptions of responsibility, that make illusory the notion of any value-free rationality in the realm of human affairs. But this emphasis on the human has been purchased at an enormous price, for in remaining unabashedly subjective, in attempting, in fact, to make radical subjectivity a virtue, existentialism has only served to underwrite and perpetuate the dualisms that modern thought has erected between subject and object, mind and matter, quantity and quality.

Deprived of and undirected by any direct cognitive access to a larger intelligible reality, the existentialist act of choice itself becomes arbitrary and absurd (which the existentialists have been the first to acknowledge, absurdity being one of their favorite notions) and in the end is unable to give any account as to why human values ought to be preferred to anti-human values. Or (and this they have been more reluctant to admit), the act of choice itself becomes indistinguishable from willful expediency and is thus always in danger of merging with the very kind of manipulative, technological reason and calculative intellect the existentialists originally set themselves to combat.

Another major response to the limitations imposed on our ways of knowing has been that associated with the various forms of linguistic analysis or language philosophy. The language philosophers simply ignore any affirmations of larger meaning and restrict themselves to the analysis of the interrelations of statements to one another, and to the clarification of grammatical, logical, and syntactical meanings. The language philosophers appear at the most to have been forced to derive any human meanings they wish to affirm from the internal logic of language systems peculiar to some actual community of discourse, which is to say they ground human meaning in some form of social and institutional convention beyond which, on their own principles, there is no appeal. The end result of linguistic analysis has been to provide a philosophical sanction for dualism and its denial of genuine knowledge either of the person or of the larger order of reality.

The form of reason that today has become dominant, what I have dubbed more generally as a narrowed—and narrowing—view of reason, has various specific names. We speak of analytic reason in describing the process of breaking larger entities into simpler components. We speak of discursive reason in indicating the articulation of statements or propositions that carry information gained through analysis. We speak of critical and logical reason in describing the processes of constructing and relating propositions and of drawing out their implications in a way free of contradictions and other internal fallacies. And, we speak of calculative and technical reason in depicting the rearranging and manipulation of information so that it becomes a tool for concrete action in and on the world. What each of these has in common with the others, however, is that all are partial and reductive, and all require for their guidance and ultimate significance an antecedent and more fundamental awareness of a larger context and whole. The narrowing of reason, with which we have been concerned, does not result from the rigorous development and refinement of analytic, discursive, and technical reason but rather from the tendency not merely to refuse the name of reason to that primary and more fundamental awareness of the whole, but more drastically, to ignore it altogether.

The exclusive emphasis on a limited expression of reason has led to a growing contradiction in our lives. We extend our powers over nature and social organization seemingly without hindrance and with great potential benefit to humankind. We solve problems that hitherto have mocked our every attempt in dealing with them. We bring within our ken new realms of exploration and research. At the same time, however, the increase of knowledge goes hand in hand with a mounting uncertainty, anxiety, and often skepticism about our ever understanding the world and our place in it. It is in calling attention to this contradiction that Philip H. Phenix has distinguished between what he describes as the "anxious uses of reason" and the "faithful uses of reason."[23] The anxious orientation arises from the assumption that all knowledge, and, hence, the "security, quality, and meaning of life," depends on the information we garner from rational analysis and discourse. Since such knowledge is always partial and contradictory, however, total reliance on it can only produce anxiety and the anger bred of discord between those who represent conflicting views.

The faithful uses of reason come not from discarding analytic and informational knowledge, but from grounding it in a prior and primary grasp of the larger whole. This requires a sense of reason that includes but extends well beyond the boundaries of rational calculation and discourse. "I refer," writes Phenix, "to the knowledge that consists in the immediate awareness of other beings and events in their unanalyzed integrity, together with consciousness of our own being as persons. It includes knowledge of oneself or of another person as a singular, total subject and the perceptual knowledge of an object, such as a work of art, apprehended as a complex presented unity. One's knowledge of such beings in presentational immediacy can never be duplicated or exhausted by any number of informational statements."[24] He goes on to say: "Anxieties arise when thinking is divorced from the realm of the whole of being and is erected into an autonomous activity by which the meaning and direction of existence are determined. This happens because all conceptual structures are in their very nature partial and have validity only when understood as dependent, for specific purposes, upon the truth of the integral being of which they are particular aspects."[25] The backbiting and feuding of academics; the rise of contending ideologies that vie with one another, often violently, for political and social dominance; "the attempt," as Phenix puts it, "to substitute for the fullness of concrete existence a world of fabricated intellectual abstractions";[26] the spurious hope that more information, more research efforts, if not the artificial heart, then interferon, and if not that, space colonies, or, perhaps, all taken together, will finally turn the corner on human misery and uncertainty—all testify to the desperate anxiety that feeds on and drives an illusionary reliance on a limited sense of reason.

A total reliance on a narrow conception of reason abolishes wonder and mystery and leads to the thinning and flattening out of the actual richness and complexity of life. A sense of wonder and mystery comes to be viewed as a source of confusion and obfuscation, an obstacle to clear thinking and efficient implementation of policy. A sense of wonder and mystery is dismissed as characteristic of an earlier, childlike stage of human development, but ill-suited to an age bent on the achievement of unambiguous exactitude and the unrestrained application of the technological solution. It is true, Einstein is often quoted in his repeated affirmation that, whoever is incapable of wonder, "whoever remains unmoved, whoever cannot contemplate or know the deep shudder of the soul in enchantment, might just as well be dead for he has already closed his eyes upon life."[27] But due recognition of genius having been granted, we then proceed as though what for the great thinkers is essential to all important discovery is for lesser minds dispensable as, at best, a bit of educational piety which can be emotionally uplifting for those who have the time and inclination to indulge it.

For the ancients, a sense of mystery and wonder was the source of all significant knowledge. Wonder before nature and civility to fellow human beings are akin, and both prompt a way of knowing guided by reverence and respect. Cultivating and strengthening the awareness of the wondrous quality of nature as an inexhaustible font of delight and discovery is the capacity that seems to be least fostered by our generation. "The aim nowadays," writes Charles De Koninck, "seems to be to show, over and over, that Nature is 'no more than. . . .' "[28] And the attitude toward the human becomes increasingly what the English have quaintly called "nothing buttery": the human being is nothing but a "bundle of reflex behavior," nothing but a "complex computer," nothing but an "intelligent animal that secretes symbolism." On the face of it, there appears no good reason not to try anything with or do anything to that which is "no more than," and "nothing but."

Perhaps indifference and outright hostility toward a sense of mystery stem from an unwillingness and inability to confront the complexity and ambiguity of actual living experience and the life decisions it demands. For mystery, there is substituted, as Gabriel Marcel pointed out, the problem; for vision, the technological fix. The lengths to which this can reach are to be seen in those schools of thought that hold only those questions worth asking for which there are unambiguous answers. "The principle now reigning," observes De Koninck, "is that anything debatable is not worth debating."[29] Thus, mystery is lost, and with it eventually all that is truly interesting.

A limited conception of rationality also leads to a false divorce between reason and emotion. No longer is there any place for the traditional understanding of one of the primary tasks of education as the "schooling of the emotional life." Any relation between feeling and reason is seen as a pollution of the sources of knowledge and to be avoided. But feelings do not disappear: they surge thick and furious, in an indiscriminate welter, above and below the surface of all we do and think. As long, however, as the view of reason as value- and feeling-free holds sway, neither the destructive nor the creative forces of the emotions can be dealt with. Both the notion of an education of the emotions and of an education through the emotions become unknown and foreign. The idea that reason has roots within the feelings and that it is therefore a primary task to discriminate between those feelings that help lead to knowledge and an enhancement of life satisfaction, and those that are destructive and sources of confusion, is lost.

The appearance within modern education of what is sometimes called *affective learning* as opposed to a purely *cognitive learning* represents an attempt to reclaim the emotional dimensions as essential to education. Unfortunately, the distinction itself perpetuates the split. Both sides share the dominant modern assumption that reason and feeling have nothing to do with one another. They differ only in their estimation of the value of the affective, emotional domain. Partisans of the affective recognize the intrinsic value of the emotions, but their failure to link feeling and reason leads them frequently to deride the importance of careful, rigorous logical thought and to condone the worst excesses of sentimentality and undisciplined self-expression. From their side, champions of a feeling-free rationality are unable to understand the power of reason that flows from feeling. Reason at its most fruitful is grounded in interest in the subject; in commitments to the importance of knowledge; in the capacity to persevere in the face of difficulty; in the anticipation of satisfaction and enjoyment in the discovery attained; in an appreciation of the beauty, intricacy, and mystery of the totality that sustains inquiry and from which all meaningful discovery proceeds.

The task is not to separate reason and feeling but to learn to discriminate between those feelings that conduce to knowledge and those partial and misdirected passions—hate, anger, jealousy, ambition, and so forth—that distort and obstruct knowledge. "The trick," as David Ehrenfeld has commented, "is to get rid of contamination without getting rid of soul." And, he adds, "It is not easy."[30] An adequate understanding of reason will recognize that love, compassion, trust, and faith are feelings that lead to knowledge. They are the fundaments of character that make integrative perception and holistic knowledge possible. In the fullest sense, love, compassion, trust, and faith can be properly described as "organs of cognition." They ultimately inform and sustain the calculative and technical intellect, and require the same sensitive and careful cultivation in the knower. It is here that the schooling of the emotions—the discrimination and disciplining of the feelings—can become a positive "schooling through the emotions."

The desiccated world views and the drying up of interest, which issue from reason separated from feeling, inevitably elicit reactions in the opposite extreme—reactions for which a narrow reason and an education erected upon it are unprepared and incapable of dealing with. "The dominating influence of science and technology has so overstressed the rational aspect of the world," the physicist Werner Heisenberg has written,

> that a reaction against this overemphasis seems quite unavoidable; or to put it in Nietzsche's words, that in desperation at the emptiness and suffering of such a world the god Dionysus should again make his appearance. In all these irrational doings there is probably an unconscious expression of longing for that world in which mind is more than information, love more than sexuality

and science more than the collection and analysis of empirical data. Let us therefore be thankful that life itself is constantly giving rise to movements that have not been preprogrammed in Huxley's brave new world.[31]

As Heisenberg intimates, the reactions can be salutary, but if a reinstatement of rationality in its largest sense is not effected, the reactions will more likely be an upwelling of blind and destructive passion. Indeed, an exclusive emphasis on a narrow reason invites those whose deliberate intent is to exploit peoples' unformed and undirected emotional forces. "By starving the sensibility of our pupils," writes C. S. Lewis with explicit reference to the responsibilities of educators, "we only make them easier prey to the propagandist when he comes."[32]

The truncation of reason in its fullest sense leads to the curious and extreme irony that we become saddled with a rationality that in its monomaniacal drive to control everything loses control over itself and becomes deeply implicated in all those things that threaten chaos.

The Tyranny of Technicism

Developing a critical understanding of the full dimensions and limitations of science and technology is one of the most important and neglected of modern educational tasks. Far from being a rejection of science and technology, the nourishing of such critical awareness is an indispensable step toward any clear conception of what is technologically appropriate to the needs of humanity and of the earth. It is requisite to any possibility of a science and technology that do not ultimately lay waste. Yet the development of such a critical awareness must be undertaken with care. The temptation of many cultural critics to blame all the ills of modern society on science and technology as such must be avoided. Such a blanket criticism remains at only the most superficial level. It can do justice neither to the potential of science and technology for serving human and humane purposes nor to the achievements of the human mind they represent. Most important, in not probing deeply enough, such a criticism misses the real source of the problems in which science and technology are, indeed, involved. The heart of the problem, as Michael Polanyi has striven repeatedly to demonstrate, lies not in science and technology but in the distorted images of the world that have come to supply the context within which they are pursued and employed.[33] And these deficient images of the world themselves spring from limited and fragmenting ways of thinking that have lost touch with the fullness of both reason and reality.

In an effort to provide a more adequate analysis of the misuses of technology, some writers have distinguished between technology itself and what they have called *technicism*. By technicism they wish to denote the mind set that seeks a technological solution for every life problem regardless of the actual situation and its demands. Thus, as scientism is to science, so technicism is to technology—a destructive distortion of a basically creative human undertaking. While technicism is a cumbrous and somewhat obscure term, it does help, along with the notion of scientism, to underscore that our characteristic modern problems do not stem from science and technology as such. It suggests, furthermore, that these problems are rooted in forms of consciousness and perceptions that acquire concrete embodiment in the world in which we live. They are not to be undone, therefore, by mere changes in attitudes or acts of will, political or other, that leave untouched our deepest perceptions of that world and our engagements with it.

In his studies of technology, Jacques Ellul has developed two concepts that are particularly helpful in understanding what he has called the *technological phenomenon*. One is the notion of *technique*; the other is what Ellul has described in the title of one of his most recent works as the *technological system*.[34]

The word *technology* is itself of ancient lineage, not at all to be identified with modern industry and industrialization as popular literature often assumes. Earlier generations associated technology with "the practical arts" of a craft or a discipline or a method of thinking. With the industrial revolution, technology was broadened to include also the apparatus of industry, the machines, the tools, the factories, and their many products. In the twentieth century the meaning of technology has been further changed. On the one hand, technology has come to include, as Langdon Winner has observed, an incredible diversity of things and concepts—tools, instruments, machines, organizations, methods, as well as their multitudinous combinations and effects.[35] On the other hand, despite the diversity of its references, technology, at the same time, has acquired nuances and connotations that imply the emergence of something very specific, almost palpable, something peculiarly characteristic of the modern world.

Technique

For Jacques Ellul, the term *technique* supplies the unifying element that also identifies the specifically modern. All peoples and cultures have had their own techniques for doing and making things, but previously these were shaped by the crafts and customs of tradition, were subservient to larger purposes, and remained "tentative, unconscious, and spontaneous."[36] What distinguishes modern technique, Ellul argues, is precisely that the method is made central and explicit, conscious, and deliberate. The method itself is that of breaking down any complex task or problem into simple units and rearranging these in such a way that they can be handled in the most efficient, logical, and orderly manner possible.[37]

Ellul's conception of technique helps us to understand how the meaning of modern technology seems to become ever broader and more inclusive and still continues to make sense. Every area of human life becomes fair game for technique—science, sports, speed reading, sex, advertising, psychotherapy, religion, and so on. All life becomes "technicized." "Wherever calculative intelligence intervenes to design a methodology," Ferré has written, "there is technique. Technique is present in the carefully thought out organization charts of our great corporations; it is present in the scientific methods of breeding and animal husbandry used in our great agricultural industries; it is present in the minutely considered lesson plans and behavioral objectives employed in our most advanced schoolrooms. The 'machine,' therefore, need not be made of metal, it may be social or bioogical or even psychological."[38] Ellul himself has delineated at least four kinds of modern technology: mechanical, economic, organizational, and "human" (in which he includes such activities as advertising, propaganda, group dynamics, psychoanalysis, and so forth). "It is now possible, I believe," Ellul writes, "to say that in the Western World, no activity of any sort whatsoever can claim to be nontechnological."[39] In short, modern technology, seen in the light of the concept of technique, can be described as the reductive-analytic method raised to conscious intention, made explicit, and extended to every conceivable field of human activity.

Technique proceeds by first separating and reducing natural complexity to simpler components, and by rearranging these in strict rational order. Step must follow step in logical sequence, since the aim is organization, prediction, and control. Technique, furthermore, focuses on the problem at hand. This does not mean that in principle broader goals and values are unimportant, for presumably the technical solution is sought with some larger purposes in mind. But technique itself is concerned only with means, and the most efficient connections among means. Technique stresses means, rather than meaning; process, rather than purpose; efficiency, rather than the richness of experience. Such emphases are proper to technique, and therein lie its powers. Guided and checked by broader goals and purposes, technique can be of immense value.

In cultures and situations, however, where a more encompassing conception of reason than the purely technical itself is lacking, a concern with integrating and guiding purposes will be increasingly regarded as lying in the realm of the irrational—for by definition such larger ends fall outside the logical step-by-step organization of method. In such situations technique tends to become its own end, and only the technical values of efficient method and control remain. Unrestrained by a pre-vailing sense of overall reality and governing purposes, technique, precisely because of its great reductive powers, acquires a corrosive and damaging, if not utterly destructive, impetus.

The task of maintaining a proper balance between technique and human purposes would be difficult under any circumstances. The balance is upset, however, and the possibility of directing technique, rather than being determined by it, is made immeasurably harder by the development of what Ellul has called the technological system. Not only does technology multiply within separate fields to produce interlocking networks of great complexity and interdependence. It becomes impossible to regard one technology and its products as separate and in isolation from other technologies and their sub-systems. The computer and its related (though not identical) electronic communication technology has furthered the drive toward the integration of various technological systems in ever larger patterns of coherence and interrelationship. And this interlinkage itself fosters the further extension of technique into still other, hitherto untouched sectors of human experience.

The growth of the technological system makes the question of how to control technology both urgent and vexing. Many writers have spoken of *autonomous technology* and the *technological imperative*, pointing to the tendency of technology to develop its own momentum and requirements irrespective of the needs and purposes of society, and even of the designs and guidance of the experts. This phenomenon of technological self-propulsion is a main reason why much talk about the need to "master technology" or to "take control of the technological levers" often rings shallow and sentimental. While it is possible to redirect, redesign, or even to eliminate a particular technology, the larger patterns of interaction either continue unaffected or, more likely, react in unanticipated ways, often creating worse problems than existed before. The complexity of technological linkages and their interdependence more and more inhibit the shutting down of a particular technology that everyone may agree is malfunctioning or has outlived any rational purpose for fear that to do so could cause the collapse of other systems on which we have come to depend. The internal momentum of the technology once employed thus often builds unchecked and undirected.

Moreover, what it might mean to exercise control over technology becomes increasingly vague as the size and complexity of the system grow. As long as a particular technique or system of techniques exists within a non-technological context, the meaning of control is relatively clear and its exercise a genuine possibility. As the technological system becomes its own context and environment, however, the points at which control might be executed become nearly impossible to specify.

None of this is meant to suggest that modern technology does not involve impressive feats of human ingenuity, nor that it has failed to bring significant benefits to humankind. The catalogue of technological achievements—in medicine, agriculture, industry, transportation, communications, and so forth—is long and growing. At the same time a parallel list of technological abuses, mistakes, unintended side effects, and possibilities for disaster in every area also multiplies. The dark underside of modern technology becomes increasingly manifest.

It is in this under or shadow-side of technology that the direct connection between our ways of knowing and the kind of world we prepare for ourselves—and ourselves for—can perhaps be seen most clearly. A closer look at it can help to make clear the issues at stake.

The Dogmas of Technolatry

Such is the hold of technology on our consciousness that to raise serious questions of it often evokes the same kind of fearful and angry response that in earlier ages might have greeted the breaking of a religious taboo. There is accuracy in describing a good part of our attitude toward technology in religious terms. Frederick Ferré, in fact, has coined the word *technolatry* to describe the modern worship of technique, which, he says, is becoming "the dominant religious reality of our culture."[40] Technology elicits feelings of awe and veneration once associated with a sense of the sacred. Technology has its own priesthood and initiates—the scientific-technological elite—and its own temples and cathedrals—research institutes and universities. And it is to technology that millions in the world look for ultimate salvation—a kind of "second coming" in the next breakthrough of medical science, genetic engineering, or space colonization. It is fitting then that from the fruits of technology also derive our most vivid images of apocalyptic finality—a disaster in genetic engineering or a nuclear catastrophe.

The worship of technique carries with it certain fundamental and unquestioned beliefs that serve almost as religious principles or dogmas. Here, perhaps, the usefulness of our regarding technique and technology for a moment as religious phenomena is most apparent. Technolatry has, as Ferré, Garrett Hardin, Chargaff, and others have suggested, three central dogmas.[41] The first is the Dogma of Logical Order and Control: Only that which can be logically organized and technologically manipulated is real; the rest is illusion and can be safely ignored. All problems are technological problems; all solutions, technological solutions. This belief has no place for the possibility that life may have more richness and greater dangers than can be encompassed by technological reason and logic. Consequently, it has no way of coping with the observation that the vaunted technological solution to one problem has again and again created other new, unanticipated—and often more serious—problems than existed before. To what has become almost a litany of point/ counterpoint of technological solutions that in turn spawn new problems, the call remains for still more technology. Non-technological considerations become excluded on principle and the proliferation of problems ad infinitum guaranteed.

The second dogma of technolatry is the Dogma of Non-Restraint: If we can invent it, we must implement it. This is the inner side of the technological imperative: as existing technology builds a momentum of its own, so too does technological possibility—and the latter seldom brooks restraint. If we can alter the structure of living matter, then we must. If we can alter the delicate balance of the earth's climate, then we will. The maxim, "What can be done must be done," Chargaff calls "the Devil's doctrine," since, as he points out, "it abolishes with one stroke all problems of conscience and free will."[42] "For the modern world," Langdon Winner writes, "the fact that something is technically sweet is enough to warrant placing the world in jeopardy."[43]

The third dogma, and the one that underlies both the others, is the Dogma of Progress: Technology moves ineluctably toward the creation of a better world. There may be setbacks, there may be false turns, but there is no need to worry, for in the end all will work out for the best. Those who question the dogma of irresistible progress are frequently dismissed out of hand as anti-science and non-growth people. If they persist with their questions, they stand to be branded as cranks, pessimists, ecofreaks, environmental extremists, neo-Luddites, doom-sayers, and Cassandras (though it is usually overlooked, curiously enough, that in the end Cassandra turned out to be right). The raising of uncomfortable questions is seen by the devotee of technological progress as unethical, irresponsible, and nihilistic. Despite thermal pollution, non-disposable atomic wastes, the threat of uncontrolled genetic engineering, the leveling of forests, the exhaustion of minerals, the depletion and poisoning of the aquifer, the extermination of plant and animal species, and so on, we can plunge ahead without worry. The Dogma of Non-Restraint is undergirded by faith in the Dogma of Progress and its assurance that the gods of technology will ultimately "make all things new."

Technolatry is a useful concept to the extent that it helps us see our own collusion with the technological system and the technological imperative. It is misleading, however, if it is taken to suggest that we can put the situation right merely by a change of attitude. The roots of the problem lie much deeper, in forms of consciousness and perception that have been all-encompassing and given concrete embodiment in the space and time organized by technique. An overweening faith in technology is itself not a cause but a symptom of a deficient and distorted way of knowing. What technolatry does is to enshrine the exercise and embodiment of this narrow way of knowing, exalting it above all else and insulating it from criticism at the same time.

The Irreversibility of Technological Change

A potential for violence resides in the reductive approach of modern technique (in the methodological necessity to take things apart). The high-intensity energies available in modern technology make this potential a reality and give a force to reductionism that almost nothing can withstand. No longer is it necessary to live with nature and to indulge her ways in order to win her favors and gain her riches. Nature now can be assaulted—directly and violently—and, in Bacon's prescient phrase, "forced to yield." Entire mountain ranges are laid open and eviscerated by the giant shovels of the strip miner. The methods of modern agriculture force an abundance of crops from lands where none would grow before. Even the rhythms of nature are attacked and overwhelmed. The hen that normally lays thirty eggs a year is forced in her factory-farm, light- and feed-intensive cubicle, to "produce" one hundred eggs a year. At the microscopic level, physical matter is itself subjected to high energy bombardment (even the language is violent) until it begins to disintegrate into substances that occur rarely or never in nature.

It is becoming increasingly apparent that many of the changes we are bringing about are irreversible. The fragility and delicate balance of many plant and animal communities are vulnerable to permanent disruption. It has been estimated that, at present rates of destruction, by the end of the century nearly one-fourth of all living species now inhabiting the planet will have been obliterated, never to appear again. Normal topsoil erosion from America's choicest farmlands has worsened dramatically as a result of intensive chemical farming and the use of heavy machinery, which enable farmers, and, because of their high cost, force them to abandon conservation practices in favor of continuous planting of high-yielding row crops. In many farm states current rates of erosion threaten complete eradication of topsoil within twenty years—topsoil that takes 1,500 to 2,000 years to replace (at one inch per century).[44] And this is to say nothing of the millions of acres of cropland buried annually beneath highways, factories, housing developments, and military installations.

We have known for some time that the relentless pouring of herbicides, pesticides, and organic compounds from the chemical and petrochemical industries into lakes, rivers, and oceans is causing untold damage to fish and birds. Now evidence is emerging that many of these lethal and carcinogenic substances have begun to contaminate the aquifer, the deep groundwater strata, in many industrial and metropolitan areas. Expert witnesses before the House subcommittee on environment, energy, and natural resources have recently referred to groundwater destruction as one of the worst environmental problems of the 1980s. And the pollutants, as they reach the deep recesses of the aquifer, do not go away. "Once contaminated," the Federal Council on Environmental Qualities has pointed out, "ground water can remain so for hundreds or thousands of years, if not for geological time."[45] In relation to even the whole of recorded human history, geologic time is a long time indeed. Many of the aquifers that have escaped pollution are themselves being rapidly depleted by the demands of heavy-technology agriculture, so that today many high plains and Southwestern states face the prospect of catastrophic, permanent water-source shortages.[46]

Nothing has become more emblematic of the potential for irrevocable damage to living beings than the production of nuclear wastes. Once created, there exists no known method for their disposal. Radioactive wastes such as plutonium, the exceedingly toxic product of the fastbreeder reactor, will remain to threaten all exposed life for tens and even hundreds of thousands of years. Such an epochal time scale—sufficient to provide for the rise and fall of all known human civilizations over and over again—beggars the imagination. The drive to expand reliance on nuclear energy, which rests on the energy extravagance of one passing generation, threatens utterly permanent consequences.

Perhaps even more far-reaching in the long run, and certainly as illustrative of a way of thinking that has lost touch with the wholeness of life, are the technical interventions contemplated in genetic research. Beyond the questions of disease, guidelines, and control, writes biochemist Erwin Chargaff, whose own research was crucial in the discovery of the structure of DNA,

> there arises a general problem of greatest significance, namely the awesome irreversibility of what is being contemplated. You can stop splitting the atom; you can stop visiting the moon; you can stop using aerosols; you may even decide not to kill entire populations by the use of a few bombs. But you cannot recall a new form of life. Once you have constructed a viable *E. coli* cell carrying a plasmid DNA into which a piece of eukaryotic DNA has been spliced, it will survive you and your children and your children's children. An irreversible attack on the biosphere is something so unheard of, so unthinkable to previous generations, that I could only wish that mine had not been guilty of it. . . . This world is given to us on loan. We come and we go; and after a time we leave earth and air and water to others who come after us. My generation, or perhaps the one preceding mine, has been the first to engage, under the leadership of the exact sciences, in a destructive colonial warfare, against nature. The future will curse us for it. . . . I am being assured by the experts that nothing untoward can happen. How do they know? Have they watched the web of eternity opening and closing its infinite meshes?[47]

Unfortunately, too often we discover nature's complexity and the fragile intricacy of her interconnections only after the damage has been done. A moving illustration of this is provided by David Ehrenfeld who points to the recent discovery that the last few survivors of an ancient tree, the *Calvaria major*, on the Island of Mauritius in the Indian Ocean, are no longer producing saplings. The reason is that, in order for them to germinate, the seeds, which the old trees still produce without difficulty, must pass through the gizzard of a dodo. "And," Ehrenfeld reminds us, "the dodo, one of our earlier victims, became extinct in 1691."[48] The systematic, indiscriminate application of technique can be counted on to produce large-scale, irrevocable change, the extent of which we will only begin to realize when it is too late to make repairs. Is it possible to cultivate a way of knowing and perception that, while it does not jettison technique, is able to participate imaginatively in the living wholeness of nature? A way of knowledge that reveals life, nourishes life, and makes it possible?

The Disintegration of Community

What a fragmenting way of thinking does to nature, it does also to human culture. It dissolves that sense of wholeness essential to the growth of persons in community. The fascination with "the dazzling parts," Werner Heisenberg, the physicist, has written, not only "eclipses the connections of the whole in the consciousness of the individual," but has as its further consequence that "the living coherence of the human community also suffers and is threatened with decay."[49] A sense of place, of fidelity to others within a shared past and common purposes, what Wendell Berry has called "communal memories and traditions of care," the very integuments of every whole and harmonious culture, are eroded and destroyed. Communities, like the bulldozed forests and strip-mined earth, are torn apart, dispersed, and with great waste and casualties reassembled in the artificial, rootless, monotonous aggregates that increasingly make up modern civilization. Natural and social rhythms, the carriers of significant activity, are themselves assaulted and assimilated to technique, to the demands of efficiency, cost-benefit accounting, and the consumer pleasures of the moment: no longer any family farms, but in their place, agribusiness and strawberries in winter. "We disregard the necessary persistence of ancient needs and obligations, patterns and cycles," writes Wendell Berry, "and assume that the human condition is entirely determined by human *devices*."[50] Even holidays, for example, are detached from their calendar moorings, by which alone they celebrate the events that nourish community, and are reduced by fiat to providing mere moments of necessary respite from the technological round.

True, the small, closed culture can be smothering and stultifying. There are probably few who on leaving the confines of the small town or village of their childhood and entering the anonymity and stimulation of the city have not felt a sense of release, even of exhilaration. The modern experience of personal emancipation from the confines of tradition and custom is frequently connected directly with the "distancing" of oneself made possible by modern technique and technology—both in actual possibilities of physical travel and in the attitude of detachment from the other which technical control entails. That technique has the potential to serve human freedom ought never to be denied (and it is well to remember that it is the dark side, the underside, of science and technology that we have been concerned to bring to view). But it is precisely here, in distinguishing the experience of genuine emancipation from the fracturing of meaningful communal commitments, that great care is demanded. As Heisenberg goes on to note in the words to which we have just referred, "With the replacement of the natural condition of life by technically contrived processes, there also enters an estrangement between the individual and the community that produces dangerous instabilities."[51]

These instabilities and the damage they cause must be recognized for what they are. The modern world is skilled in disguising as personal freedom and emancipation that narcissistic emotional detachment of its own casualties, of personalities forever crippled in their abilities to sustain deep commitment and responsibilities. More important, when genuine emancipation requires the breaking or escape from the confines of community that no longer nourishes, it is necessary that new community and human relation be reestablished. Freedom, to be real, is situated freedom; personal identity grows in fidelity to others; privacy finds its authentic underpinnings in community where the uniqueness of persons and their idiosyncrasies are cherished, not in the standardized, mechanized influences of mass society and of mass culture. An unrestrained technology and its underlying mechanistic view of the human being and society prevent just this—the constant building up and replenishment of genuine community.

Reporting on a research project on American social mores he is currently directing, the sociologist Robert Bellah has recently observed that while white, middle-class America is as free and materially comfortable as any group has ever been, there is mounting evidence that the patterns of many daily lives are without meaning, that workplaces are places of boredom for growing numbers of people, and that few have any sense of purposeful engagement with the larger society. His research group is finding increasing evidence of the emergence of a private world having great intensity—he notes in this regard the voguish use of such words as *creativity, excitement, energy, zing*—but with no real content and substance. We live more and more in a world, he writes, in which egalitarianism is conceived as mechanistic uniformity, in which we "maximize individual choice beyond what any traditional society has ever done and then deny all standards of choice as being any more than purely private." Nothing has authority for us or demands commitments from us; there are no significant differences between political parties, private individuals, or public issues: there are no shared commitments—people are isolated, the public world loses meaning, everything retreats into private experience or pure utilitarianism; and there are no longer religious commitments calling for sacrifice and a sense of wonder and awe. All is equal, all is indifferent.[52]

Yet, it is this that industrial society commends to the traditional world cultures for their emulation as "modernization," "progress," and "development." The allure of power and the more often than not illusory prospects of emancipation combine to make "development" nearly irresistible to those traditional cultures to whom it is proffered. The emergence of a Western (or Soviet) trained technocratic elite in the underdeveloped or modernizing country and the modification of the environment to accommodate the beginnings of a new industry—supported jointly by the state politicians and technocrats and by transnational business attracted by cheap native labor—signal that development is well under way. Once the process is begun, the entire society is drawn into it and transformed. W. W. Rostow, a major spokesman for the imperative and desirability of unrestrained modernization, is brutally clear about its demands: "Psychologically, men must transform or adapt the old culture in ways which make it compatible with modern activities and institutions. The face-to-face relations and warm, powerful family ties of a traditional society must give way . . . to specialized functions in the society . . . men must find a partial alternative for the family, clan, and region. And new hierarchies, based on function, must come to replace those rooted in land-ownership and tradition."[53] That with the ripping apart of entire cultures something priceless may be lost in the bargain is not usually pointed out by the proponents of development. Meanwhile, with spreading bureaucratic organization, "the sacrifice of independent intelligence, the sweeping away of individual differences, local customs, local diversity, and all the infinite branchings of humanity that enrich life," the slide toward a pervasive cultural uniformity continues without check.[54]

Wholeness as a living unity that connects and integrates individual entities and at the same time sustains them in their particularity is a difficult conception for many people in our times. It is much easier, and for that reason, perhaps, more congenial, to think of wholeness either as (a) an abstract combination of separate, self-existent parts, something put together by aggregating units, or as (b) monolithic uniformity in which the parts have no intrinsic worth whatsoever, except as they function to serve the collective. The latter, the exaltation of the collective, has been familiar to us in various sorts of twentieth-century totalitarianism, whether of the Communist or Fascist types (despite their important differences otherwise). The former is more commonly associated with the social organization of the "individualistic" West. But individualism conceived of in purely quantitative, mechanistic terms turns itself inevitably toward authoritarianism. The demands of large-scale modern production, trade, and consumption and the consequent drive for the most efficient use of science together encourage the growth of large, centralized organization and collective planning, as well as a heightened readiness to rely when necessary on propaganda, surveillance, and military coercion.[55] It is as though genuine wholeness, destroyed by a fragmenting thinking, returns, nevertheless, in the authoritarianism of our times as a travesty and mockery of itself. The recognition of wholeness as the living, creating, and complementary manifestation of variety challenges our habitual ways of thinking and the images of reality we are accustomed to. It calls for a thinking, a way of knowing, that is itself alive, creative, and integrating—a living thinking.

The disintegration of community and the authoritarianism of special interests all conspire to make impossible the consideration of public values that can lead to a just, participatory, and sustainable society. Modern society that depends increasingly on technology requires more, not less, public deliberation concerning its value commitments. The choice and employment of energy technology offer, as Richard J. Barnet has demonstrated, a case in point. Energy choices are not merely technical, for the energy system employed will itself inaugurate a certain path of development, which must be followed rigorously all along the line, if the system is to function as planned. A rational selection of energy technology depends, therefore, on an equally rational and constant consideration of values and ends: How much energy is enough? What economic policy is desired? Who is to benefit? Who is to control the economy? Is democracy to be preserved at the sacrifice of some efficiency? Who is to decide? What kind of political and economic control is to be exerted? By whom? These are value questions, not questions of method alone, and at bottom they are educational questions of vital importance to the public. Often, however, as Barnet points out, energy choices are made explicitly on other grounds based in large part on the immediately available technology and vested corporate and bureaucratic interests. And the value questions, he observes, "are decided implicitly without public discussion or even public notice."[56]

Where such public discussion and the education of the public it requires—something quite different from indoctrination—are lacking, technology will inevitably align itself with the most powerful social and economic forces in society. The sole business of technique, taken by itself, it to generate and focus quantitative power. This gives to technique and its technological elaborations not a neutrality vis-à-vis power, but rather a natural affinity for the accumulation of power in all its forms. Technique, despite frequent assertions to the contrary, is not value-neutral: it moves ineluctably in the direction of power. And the development of costly high technology provides both the means and the incentive for the centralization of power. It perhaps made sense to speak of the value neutrality of the old technique that existed in traditional cultures within a context of recognized social values and qualitative realities. This context provided the grounds for guiding and checking technique and resisting its abuses. In a *disqualified universe*, however, where only quantity counts as real, technique, the marshalling of power, becomes allied directly with the drive for power. As C. S. Lewis once pointed out, the idea of gaining unlimited scientific and technological power over nature will be apt to mean that some persons (those who control the science and technology) gain increased power over other *persons*.[57]

Reductionistic, fragmented thinking is vulnerable to capture and monopolization by those who would use knowledge not for enlightenment but for the consolidation of their own privileged positions. The decimation of nature and the disintegration of community are mirrored and reinforced by the parcelling out of knowledge. Jonathan King, professor of molecular biology at the Massachusetts Institute of Technology, in asking the question, "Who shall science serve?" has described the present tendency to pursue knowledge selectively according not to the dictates of the search for truth but of the desire for power. Consequently, he writes:

> Some areas of knowledge are developed, others are left in a primitive state . . . chemical companies that manufacture pesticides or drugs are not interested in supporting research on whether these chemicals are the cause of human kidney disease. The oil monopolies have a vested interest in the suppression of the technology of solar energy, unless it involves huge capital intensive

projects that would stay in their ownership. A military/industrial complex profitting off the manufacture of ever more powerful nuclear bombs does not support research on how radiation damages our genes. Transnational corporations reaping their income off the exploitation of agricultural labour do not fight for universal education, or for research on forms of early education that encourage the fullest development of human potential. However, they may be quite happy to support sociobiologial theories that argue for the intrinsic social inferiority of the poor and working classes of the population.[58]

Far from being merely academic matters, the central questions concerning knowledge and our ways of knowing have the most far-reaching political, economic, and cultural consequences.

The Eclipse of the Person

In a disqualified universe, the reality of persons and the world of the personal become ever more problematic and difficult to affirm. The world of quantity—the world of physical properties, mechanical cause and effect, predictive measurement and control—is the world of the non-personal. That of persons is a world of quality, meaning, purpose, value—and, indeed, of all those things that go with these, imagination, insight, love, beauty, comedy, tragedy. Within a positivistic and scientistic world view human values and concerns may be still considered important, but because they are regarded from that perspective as having nothing to do with knowledge, they can at best be merely asserted as matters of belief. They cannot be dealt with rationally as something of which and through which we can have real knowledge, on a par with that of science, of the world in which we live.

The eclipse of the human person in a quantitative world view may be glimpsed in two areas of current concern, both having a direct bearing on education in its fullest sense. The first example comes from the field of computer science and the work of Joseph Weizenbaum, professor of computer science at the Massachusetts Institute of Technology. As a leading computer scientist and creator of a number of important computer programs, including the well-known counseling simulation program, *ELIZA,* Weizenbaum has at the same time been a foremost critic of the misapplication of computer technology. He has been particularly forceful in his critical analyses of the artificial intelligence movement and of its leaders, whom he has dubbed the "artificial intelligentsia." There are some problems, Weizenbaum has written, that can be solved logically and for which techniques and mechanisms for arriving at final solutions can be devised. There are others, he writes, that "cannot be 'solved' (by man *or* by machine) in the sense that 'answers' can be found that forever dispose of them and all their consequences." These latter are those that are the uniquely human problems, and Weizenbaum gives some examples of such human problems: "How to serve truth and yet be a university professor; Maintaining good relations with one's children; The world pollution problem; How to reduce tension in one's neighborhood; etc."[59] Such are examples of the central human problems that can be "solved" only by maintaining the tension between polarities—between freedom and discipline, between the individual and society, between the conscious and the unconscious, and so forth. They are problems not to be wished away in a spurious harmony that denies conflict, nor to be solved by forcing all to conform to one or other of the opposing sides. They are problems that are to be engaged by a much richer understanding of rationality and practical wisdom than that proffered by a narrow, technical notion of reason. This loss of a deeper rationality and the dominance of a misconception of the role and place of technological and instrumental reason, Weizenbaum has argued, pose an imminent threat to the human future.

It is in his own field of computer science that Weizenbaum sees this misunderstanding in one of its most extreme and dangerous manifestations. Computer science, he has pointed out, originally began as a human-centered science with the intent that computers under human control would serve human purposes. What went wrong, he has said, was that attempts to capture some aspects of the human in the machine produced a conception of a machinelike human. It was as though one aspect of the human mind, the computer aspect, were externalized and embodied in a machine that was then taken as the model for the entire human mind, which is then viewed as itself only a computer—and, at that, an inferior computer in comparison with an increasingly sophisticated, silicon-based computer technology. This reduction of the human mind to the machine, Weizenbaum has noted, had long been immanent in Western thinking, but the computer gave it a concrete embodiment that to many people has become utterly convincing.

The results of this misconception, Weizenbaum holds, have pushed human concerns more and more to the periphery of our social policies and our views of the world. It has, for example, become increasingly axiomatic in the Western university that every aspect of human life and thought is computable, not only in principle but in fact. Those dimensions of the human being and those human problems not amenable to computer solutions are regarded simply as unimportant or non-existent. There has even been a growing tendency among those involved in the artificial intelligence movement, he has said, to speak contemptuously of the human being, to describe the human brain as merely a "meat machine," and to view human intelligence as deserving to be replaced by what is seen as the more effective, silicon-based intelligence of the computer. At the same time, Weizenbaum notes, we entrust increasingly crucial decisions to computers that we understand and control less and less, and whose capacity for error—as recent reports of mistaken nuclear alerts and banking system errors attest—have acquired truly life-threatening proportions. The task before us, maintains Weizenbaum, is once again to pay heed to the human meanings of the uses to which the information-processing capacities of the computer are put, and to reclaim that more embracing rationality that can make this possible. Humans, he has said, can care and choose; computers can decide but not choose, and they do not care; nor can they have hope.

A second example of the inability of technical reason to safeguard the fully human can be seen in the life dilemmas posed increasingly by the advance of the life sciences. The powers of biology and medicine to intervene in birth, life, and death have been spectacular and many people have benefited as a result. Many of the most advanced biological and medical techniques, however, have posed excruciating problems of ethics, human meaning, and social policy that in their seriousness ·and complexity seem almost to defy solution. Medicine and science, claiming to be morally neutral, have largely left it to others to deal with the problems. The voices of religious and of other moral authorities have often been uncertain, when not strident, and, in any event, not universally recognized. The recent rash of interest in biomedical ethics and in organizing ethics courses in college and professional schools is witness to the desperate desire to find some clear guidelines for coming to grips with the human problems arising from science, particularly the life sciences.

Many of the problems are long familiar, but no nearer, it seems, to being answered. To what lengths do we go in keeping old or injured people alive, if it means a vegetative kind of existence? What are the limits on the uses of behavior control through drugs, electrical stimulation, psychosurgery and psychological conditioning for the mentally ill and criminals? How do we manage contraception and abortion? What restraints, if any, are to be put on artificial insemination by donor and on *in vitro* fertilization? What are the long-term effects on family life and personal relationships of such practices? Other questions are becoming equally acute. It has been estimated, for example, that more than twenty thousand people who have lost their kidneys and would otherwise be dead are alive today because of renal dialysis. The astronomical costs of such medical care, however, appear to be reaching the point that decisions must be made as to who shall be treated and who permitted to die. How are such decisions to be made? By whom? On what grounds? Techniques for identifying defective genes either in the unborn fetus or in parent carriers have added impetus to calls for large-scale eugenics programs. Is the detection of a genetically defective fetus always to be followed by so-called selective abortion as a matter of course, as many now seem to assume or even to demand? What is the full range of considerations that must be taken into account? Some have even gone beyond what has come to be called *negative eugenics*—the elimination or reduction of harmful genes through family planning and abortion—to demand state-directed programs of *positive eugenics* that would seek the "improvement" of the human genetic contribution through selected breeding, the establishment of sperm banks, and strict constraints on individual freedom. What is the definition of the "desirable human being" in such thinking? Who again is to decide? What is the conception of individual rights and the meaning of individual lives that would govern—or be suppressed—in such programs?

Finally, the advent of genetic engineering has introduced problems of an even higher order of urgency. The techniques of transferring cell nuclei, splicing genes, and using recombinant DNA technology not only promise new approaches to the treatment of disease, such as diabetes, sickle-cell anemia, and hemophilia, they also mobilize technical capacities to reorder the very conditions and nature of existing life, human and otherwise. Is there wisdom among us sufficient to permit such an undertaking? At the most fundamental level, J. Robert Nelson has warned, the chances are high that genetic techniques will be used to cause human evolution "to veer away from the norm of truly human quality instead of moving closer to it." He writes:

> Without significant moral improvement of the human race . . . the possible good of employing genetic knowledge only for physical health remains a limited value. This improvement, if it comes, will be signaled by a reversal of most peoples' lack of concern for the well-being of future generations. We despoil the earth, kill thousands of excellent young men as well as other civilians in warfare, and allow thousands of millions more to starve to death or die prematurely for causes which could be obviated. We provide our children with a heritage of ever more devastating weapons of destruction, and with social and political weapons which carry the seeds of still greater destructiveness. In view of this culpable disregard for the welfare of coming generations, is there any reason to have confidence that we will exercise a reasonable and charitable "genetic duty" toward the improvement of the whole race?[60]

And supposing that we have paid due heed to the human propensities for good and evil, do we really understand the infinite complexities of nature well enough to warrant this invasion of her innermost processes? As the genetic engineers increasingly show signs of wanting to turn themselves also into industrial engineers by teaming up directly with drug and other business interests, such questions cannot indefinitely be avoided without becoming moot.

Simply identifying and discussing the ethical problems involved are, however, not enough. Important as an indispensable starting point though that may be, something essential is lacking in such discussion and deliberation. An academic and after-the-fact quality attaches to much of the discussion. Indeed, a familiar pattern of action and reaction has begun to repeat itself: First, a new medical or biological breakthrough is announced and heralded with great enthusiasm for its promised benefits; then, after a time, apprehensions about the new technology start to set in as unsuspected ambiguities reveal themselves, unintended side effects multiply, and possibilities for misuse and abuse appear; it is then that deliberation of the ethical issues is taken up, in the organizing of new courses, in learned journals, in the holding of conferences, and eventually (often in simplistic and distorted form) in the media and popular press. As important and essential as the discussion is, it is not adequate for the real tasks required.

For one thing, identifying and deliberating on the issues do not in themselves generate the active moral impulses of the kind called for by Nelson in the quote above that are required actually to change the situation. As long as we are constrained by a conception of reason that consigns to the irrational those deep sources of understanding grounded in insight, discriminating emotional perception, and informed engagement of the will, we remain cut off from the possibilities of inner transformation and self-mastery. Ironically, much ethical discourse is tied to the narrowest kind of logical, calculative reasoning, hence its oft-noted convoluted and abstruse character and incapacity to move to a fuller, participatory, and active knowing.

There is yet more to the problem. It has been noted that there seems always to be something after the fact about our ethical discussions of scientific and technological issues. The ethical discussion always seems to be trying to catch up with interventions already devised and undertaken in the laboratory. Scarcely is one set of issues recognized than another breakthrough is announced and another set of problems emerges more baffling and threatening than any previous. The ethical discourse lags behind. It finds no toehold in reality, for that reality has already been defined, determined, and, in a fundamental sense, created in the laboratory.

According to the dominant view, the advance of knowledge proceeds in total isolation from human values and meaning. Suggestions that an understanding of the distinctly human must figure in a full understanding of nature and might even inform scientific imagination and conceptualization are staunchly resisted as threats to the freedom of intellectual inquiry and impediments to the advance of knowledge. In the most important beginning deliberations and actions in the laboratory, therefore, the human factor is omitted. It can then only be added on, almost as an afterthought, following, say, the fait accompli of a new pro-creation technology, and in such circumstances must of necessity be limited in its effect. And, when once they make their appearance, human values can then only be asserted and fought over, not dealt with as sources and guides of reasonable inquiry, for their essential rationality has already been denied. Thus, the dualism between physical science and human meaning remains intact and reinforced.

When, furthermore, the images of man drawn from the mechanistic dimensions of science are blown into philosophical world views and are permitted to dominate all thinking, the recovery of the fully human becomes well-nigh impossible. Many popular writings on ethology, for example, portray the human being as little more than a naked ape or a conditioned duck. Some behaviorists hold that man is nothing but a machine, and that all inner, subjective experience is an illusion. Much so-called sociobiology explains human striving for meaning and value, as in altruistic concern, as an evolutionarily determined, elaborate survival strategy of the species directed by the nucleotides in a DNA string. While each of these perspectives reveals aspects of life valuable for human understanding, their extrapolation into total, all-inclusive world views results in the virtual disappearance of the human person. And it is worth noting that each of these views lends itself to those intent on schemes of stringent social planning and control in which individual freedom and rights are viewed as threats to social order and as obstacles to be overcome.

Thus, in analyzing modern biology and ethics, the philoso-

pher Hans Jonas has spoken of the disappearance of any understanding of the human being that might guide the new genetic
technology, or prevent the possibility of its being used to modify
out of all recognition the body and mind of man and of nature
herself. "This has become a theoretical possibility," Jonas writes,
"with the advent of molecular biology and its understanding of
genetic programming; and it has been rendered morally possible
by the metaphysical neutralizing of man. . . . Since the same
evolutionary doctrine of which genetics is a cornerstone has
deprived us of a valid image of man, the actual techniques, when
they are ready, may find us strangely unready for their responsible use."[61] To counter the "metaphysical neutralizing of man"—
the total extrusion of the significance of human persons from
our knowledge of reality—we need a conception of knowledge
and of knowing that firmly embraces and has an essential place
for the fully human.

Notes

1. Alfred North Whitehead, *Science and the Modern World* (New York:
Macmillan Company, 1925), pp. 57-82.

2. Ernst Lehrs, *Man or Matter* (New York: Harper & Brothers, 1950).

3. Whitehead, *Science and the Modern World*, p. 80.

4. James W. Botkin, Mahdi Elmandjra, and Miscea Malitza, *No Limits to Learning, Bridging the Human Gap; A Report to the Club of Rome*
(Oxford: Pergamon Press, 1979), p. 3.

5. Paul R. Zilsel, *Bulletin of the Atomic Scientists* (April 1969), p. 28;
quoted in John Davy, "Science and Human Rights," *The Golden Blade*
(annual) (1968), 25.

6. Frederick Ferré, *Shaping the Future: Resources for the Post-Modern
World* (New York: Harper & Row, 1976), p. 12.

7. Huston Smith has demonstrated the hold of scientistic assumptions within nearly every field of scholarship. Huston Smith, *Beyond
the Post-Modern Mind* (New York: Crossroad, 1982).

8. David Bohm, *Wholeness and the Implicate Order* (London: Routledge
& Kegan Paul, 1980), pp. 14-15.

9. Shirley Sugerman, "A Conversation with Owen Barfield," in *Evolution of Consciousness, Studies in Polarity*, ed. Shirley Sugerman (Middletown, Conn.: Wesleyan University Press, 1976), p. 26.

10. Smith, *Beyond the Post-Modern Mind*.

11. Owen Barfield, "Language, Evolution of Consciousness, and the

48   Insight-Imagination

Recovery of Human Meaning," *Teachers College Record*, vol. 82, no. 3 (Spring 1981), 428.

12. Lewis Mumford, "The Pentagon of Power," *Horizon*, 12 (1970), 10.

13. Barfield, "Language, Evolution of Consciousnes, and the Recovery of Human Meaning," p. 428.

14. Ibid., p. 430.

15. The noted biochemist Erwin Chargaff has spoken of what he has called " 'the paradox of biochemistry,' namely, that biochemistry is helpless before life, having to kill the organism before investigating it." He adds: "Biochemistry is, in fact, much more successful in practicing the second part of its composite name than in following the prefix." Erwin Chargaff, *Voices in the Labyrinth: Nature, Man, and Science* (New York: Seabury Press, 1977), p. 89. See also Liebe F. Cavalieri, *The Double-Edged Helix: Science in the Real World* (New York: Columbia University Press, 1981).

16. Ferré, *Shaping the Future*, p. 33.

17. Michael Polanyi and Harry Prosch, *Meaning* (Chicago: University of Chicago Press, 1975), p. 178.

18. Ibid., p. 145.

19. Bohm, *Wholeness and the Implicate Order*, p. 15.

20. Ibid.

21. Erwin Chargaff, *Heraclitean Fire: Sketches from a Life before Nature* (New York: Rockefeller University Press, 1978), pp. 55-56.

22. Many, if not all, positivists would concur in this description of reason and knowledge. Many would agree that there may well be underlying objective ontological structures in reality, but would maintain that because these can never be described in empirical or logical terms they can never be known; they can only be believed in. These positivists would maintain that there exist, side by side, the realm of knowledge based on the primacy of sense experience and the realm of belief that pertains to all else beyond the strictly empirical. Belief may, indeed, from this point of view, refer to that which is ultimately of most importance in life, but it can never be spoken of as knowledge. To want to extend knowledge to include the non-empirical is, from this point of view, a mark of the unsophisticated and philosophically untutored mind.

Two considerations, however, point to the inadequacy of this neat division between knowledge and belief. First, as we have noted, even our most ordinary conscious experience, including sense experience, itself presupposes other dimensions of non-sensory experience. Secondly, reason in its narrow sense as providing knowledge only of the sensory rests, therefore, on experiences that the positivists have assigned to the realm of belief. Either all knowledge of every kind, including the sensory, is determined and guided by ultimate beliefs, but beliefs that have cognitive value because they do lead to genuine understanding of the world, in which case, however, a more adequate conception of both belief and rationality is demanded than provided by the positivist view. Or technical reason does not provide knowledge of reality but only of how that mysterious, inaccessible reality can be manipulated and used, and which in the long run is not, therefore, subject to rational guidance and control, since these also have been consigned by the positivist to the realm of belief and opinion. If this latter view were adhered to consistently, it would at least make impossible the claim that a science based on technical reason can provide a picture (a world view) of true reality, and it might stimulate some salutary second thoughts about placing too much confidence in the ultimately beneficial outcome of technology.

23. Philip H. Phenix, "'Teilhard and the Uses of Reason," *Forum for Correspondence and Contact*, vol. 11, no. 4 (March 1981), 37-39.

24. Ibid., p. 38.

25. Ibid.

26. Ibid., p. 39.

27. Quoted in, for example, Arianna Stassinopoulos, *After Reason* (New York: Stein and Day, 1978), p. 137.

28. Charles De Koninck, *The Hollow Universe* (London: Oxford University Press, 1960), p. 75.

29. Ibid., p. 60.

30. David Ehrenfeld, *The Arrogance of Humanism* (New York: Oxford University Press, 1978), p. 219.

31. Werner Heisenberg, *Across the Frontiers* (New York: Harper & Row, 1974), pp. 211-12.

32. C. S. Lewis, *The Abolition of Man* (New York: Macmillan Publishing Company, 1947), p. 24.

33. See Polanyi and Prosch, *Meaning*, pp. 104-5.

34. Jacques Ellul, *The Technological System* (New York: Continuum, 1980).

35. Langdon Winner, *Autonomous Technology* (Cambridge, Mass.: MIT Press, 1977), p. 8.

36. Ferré, *Shaping the Future*, p. 4.

37. Science and technology are not the same, although popular writing often confuses the two. Science has its technologies—its procedures and instrumentations—and these intermingle so that, while modern science and technology can be distinguished, they can never be entirely separated. Strictly speaking, technology can never become true science;

science, however, if it abrogates its primary commitment to seek knowledge, can be reduced to technology. Science as technology is interested not in the nature of the world, but only in ways to manage and manipulate it. It is important to maintain the distinction between science and technology.

38. Ferré, *Shaping the Future*, pp. 41-42.

39. Ellul, *The Technological System*, p. 176.

40. Ferré, *Shaping the Future*, p. 42.

41. Ibid., See also Garrett Hardin, "Ecology and the Death of Providence," *Zygon*, vol. 15 (March 1980), 57-68.

42. Chargaff, *Voices in the Labyrinth*, p. 44.

43. Winner, *Autonomous Technology*, p. 73.

44. Ann Crittenden, "Soil Erosion Threatens U.S. Farms' Output," *The New York Times* (October 26, 1980).

45. Quoted in Robert Hanley, "Spread of Pollution Feared in Wells Around New York," *The New York Times* (April 6, 1981).

46. See Amory and Hunter Lovins, "The Surprises Are Coming," *Christianity and Crisis* (March 16, 1981), 51, 62-63.

47. Chargaff, *Heraclitean Fire*, pp. 189-91; See also Jonathan King, "New Genetic Technologies: Prospects and Hazards," *Technology Review* (February 1980), 57-65.

48. Ehrenfeld, *The Arrogance of Humanism*, p. 191.

49. Heisenberg, *Across the Frontiers*, p. 225.

50. Wendell Berry, *A Continuous Harmony: Essays Cultural and Agricultural* (New York: Harcourt Brace Jovanovich, A Harvest Book, 1975), p. 148. Italics the author's.

51. Heisenberg, *Across the Frontiers*, p. 225.

52. Robert N. Bellah, "Cultural Vision and the Human Future," *Teachers College Record*, vol. 82, no. 3 (Spring 1981), 497-506; See also Hubert L. Dreyfus, "Knowledge and Human Values: A Genealogy of Nihilism," *Teachers College Record*, vol. 82, no. 3 (Spring 1981), 507-22.

53. Quoted in Winner, *Autonomous Technology*, p. 103.

54. Maurice Nicoll, *Living Time and the Integration of Life* (London: Watkins, 1952), p. 204.

Sooner or later, cultural groups become aware of their identity and begin to oppose the leveling encroachment of the nation state and multinational businesses. As a consequence, we find increasing manifestations of what might be called the "fourth world phenomenon"— the appearance worldwide of cultural groups and entities that do not wish to be swallowed and absorbed by the already industrialized world or the developing "third world" in which they find themselves: the restive "national peoples" of Soviet Russia; the Scots, the Welsh, the

Breton, the Basque, the Algerian, the Irish, the Corsican, the Flemish, the Quebec, the Amer-Indian, the Amish, and other cultural groups of industrial Europe and America; the Kurds of Iran and Iraq, the tribal cultures of Africa, the Montagnards of Vietnam, and others. By the time the self-consciousness of the fourth world groups has been aroused, however, they have usually fatally compromised themselves. On the one hand, they are themselves beguiled by technology, wanting it for themselves, particularly its military forms, not realizing that the technological imperatives are ultimately more threatening to their cultural integrity than the more immediate imperialism of the nation state. On the other hand, the resistance of the cultural minorities often becomes as rigid, as unresponsive to human need and fraility, and, finally, as terroristic and totalitarian as their oppressors (and oppress in turn other cultural minorities in their midst, as seen, for example, in the suppression of the Kurds and Bahais by the Iranian Shiites)—and no longer remain attractive models for true community building.

55. See Richard J. Barnet, *The Lean Years: Politics in the Age of Scarcity* (New York: Simon and Schuster, 1980), esp. Chapter 8, "Scarce Resources and the New International Military Order"; and Richard A. Falk, *A World Order Perspective on Authoritarian Tendencies*, World Order Models Project, Working Paper Number Ten (New York Institute for World Order, 1980).

56. Barnet, *The Lean Years*, p. 98.

57. Lewis, *The Abolition of Man*, pp. 70-71.

58. Jonathan King, "Scientists in Society," *Anticipation*, no. 25 (December 1980), 64.

59. Joseph Weizenbaum, "Limits in the Use of Computer Technology, Need for a Man-Centered Science," in *Toward a Man-Centered Medical Science*, vol. 1, ed. Karl E. Shaefer, et al. (Mt. Kisco, N.Y.: Futura Publishing Company, 1977), pp. 83-97; See also Joseph Weizenbaum, *Computer Power and Human Reason: From Judgment to Calculation* (San Francisco: W. H. Freeman and Company, 1976).

60. J. Robert Nelson, *Science and Our Troubled Conscience* (Philadelphia: Fortress Press, 1980), p. 111.

61. Hans Jonas, "Toward a Philosophy of Technology," *The Hastings Center Report*, 9, no. 1 (February 1979), 41.

2

Toward the Recovery of Wholeness: The Radical Humanities and Traditional Wisdom _____

New Perspectives

By now important questions may well be stirring in the reader's mind. We have touched upon them, but from this point on, they must receive more and more attention. First, what about the contributions of leading thinkers in every field of endeavor that have begun to challenge the assumptions of a narrow scientistic and technolatrous world view? These have been alluded to, but have still to be taken adequately into account. And, second, what about the achievements, the accomplishments, and the strengths of the modern world? The point has been made that modern modes of thought have advantages that are not to be denied, but how an adequate critique of modern consciousness is possible that does not reject it *in toto* has not yet been considered. Finally, how is the split between knowledge, on the one hand, and values and meaning, on the other, to be overcome? The modern divorce of knowledge and values and many of its consequent ill-effects have been depicted, but the actual possibilities for bringing about their reconciliation remain to be explored.

These are central questions, and the discussion from here on—in this and subsequent chapters—will be concerned with them in one form or another. They are difficult questions. They demand a search not for final answers, which would be suspect from the start (and rightly so), but rather for new directions, new ways of thinking, new premises. They are also positive questions, for they call for moving beyond necessary criticism to seeking possibilities of constructive understanding and action. And, while we will be returning to them again and again, a few preliminary remarks at this point regarding each may be helpful.

Let us look at the first two questions briefly, with an eye toward identifying the major problems or issues that each poses. The first question has to do with the new perspectives that seem to be emerging in many different areas—in science, the humanities, and the arts—demanding a much more comprehensive and meaningful view of the world and of the human being than a narrow conception of reason and of knowing have made possible. In science, for example, a curious irony exists. The positivistic attitude remains strong, and extreme reductionistic and mechanistic modes of thinking and models of reality prevail. For nearly a century, however, there has been developing in the highest reaches of science, particularly in physics but in other fields as well, and among the most outstanding scientific thinkers, an understanding of physical reality that calls into question many of the fundamental assumptions of a mechanistic world view. The phenomena, the data, revealed by contemporary scientific thought and experiment increasingly do not seem to fit, and, in fact, they often burst, the interpretative framework provided by eighteenth- and nineteenth-century scientific assumptions. And yet it is precisely these earlier assumptions in their positivistic form that continue to find widespread, uncritical acceptance when scientists and laymen alike attempt to think about the world and the human being according to "scientific principles." It is as though the images of reality that pervade our culture and education today continue to be drawn from the science of yesterday.

Within the humanities the situation is similar, though perhaps even more confused. There the inroads of positivism have been particularly destructive, since positivism demands that the human be explained by the non-human, a contradiction in terms for the genuinely humanistic perspective. There have always been those humanists, probably the majority, who have steadfastly resisted the encroachment and allures of scientism. Even these humanists, however, have often been content merely to be witness to the importance of human values without asking how they are grounded in knowledge of the world. The result has been a good deal of what might be called humanistic preaching, which, like all piety and preaching severed from cognition, becomes increasingly ineffectual. Nevertheless, in many fields—philosophy, philology, psychology, history, the arts, and religion—there has been a minority of leading thinkers whose main concern has been to lay a foundation in thinking and knowledge for human values and meaning.

From the highest levels of science and the humanities—if not from the second highest, which tends often to be most closely tied to the established orthodoxies—there is, then, emerging a twofold task: It is crucial that the fundamental new insights and possibilities for understanding the fullness of our life experience be attended to, explored, and their implications followed out. Moreover, if genuine wholeness in thinking and experience is to be attained, it is also crucial that the points of integration, if they exist among the various fields of knowledge, be identified and strengthened. On both counts the deepest issues of education are involved.

The second question with which we began asks how it might be possible to do full justice to the achievements of present-day consciousness, while at the same time becoming effectively aware of its limitations and dangers. There is a potential for creative human life, as well as destructive capacities, associated uniquely with the modern world that cannot be gainsaid. Specifically, there has been the emergence of a heightened self-consciousness and sense of personal identity. This sense of a highly individuated self, sharply defined, set off from others and detached from nature, seems to have been particularly characteristic of modern Western culture during the past three or four hundred years, although in this century it is becoming an increasingly common experience among the rest of mankind. Many thinkers, adducing mounting evidence from anthropology, psychology, comparative religion, philosophy, and especially philology, speak of the evolution of human consciousness through time.[1]

The concept of an evolution of consciousness suggests something much more radical than merely that human explanations of the world and of human beings' place in the world have changed from period to period. It suggests, rather, that the actual quality of experience of self, of the world, and of human possibilities has changed. The human being's own experience of the self, of the "I" and its relationship with the surrounding world, appears from much evidence to be fundamentally different from that of earlier times. Individuation has brought with it capacities for creative action also hitherto unavailable. With individuation, for example, has come the possibility, if not always the reality, of genuine freedom. And as an expression and instrument of this freedom there has emerged technological reason in all its power. Each of these—individuation, the potential for freedom, and the power of reason—are real achievements in the human being's evolutionary development and carry potential for further achievement yet unrealized.

Yet, each, if separated from its grounding in a larger context of meaning and purpose, becomes, as only a moment's reflection demonstrates, aberrant and destructive. A sharpened sense of self, closed from meaningful communal participation, tends ineluctably toward a kind of atomistic individualism that pits all against all and, at one and the same time, makes each vulnerable to overwhelming collective pressures. Freedom, without responsibility and direction, slides into license and anarchy. And, a narrow reason cut off from a larger, more encompassing rationality, runs, as we have seen, into the nihilistic and deadly. The task is to maintain the achievements of the modern world while, at the same time, recovering the sources of meaning that prevent their becoming aberrant and destructive. Thus, the task becomes clearer—there can be no solutions that would relieve us of grappling with the opportunities and dangers of the present. Demands for a return to a pre-scientific, pre-technological age, even when they alert us to important dimensions of life missing in the modern world, are ill-suited to the real task at hand. How we undertake this task, however, at what crucial points we must concentrate our attention and efforts, remains to be considered.

With these preliminary reflections in mind we can begin to look more directly at some of the sources for thinking about the problem of achieving an integral connection between human values and meaning, on the one hand, and knowledge, on the other. We will consider, first, what I will call the *radical humanities*, and with them look at some of the related claims of a growing, resurgent interest in older religious and philosophical traditions. Then, against that background, we will examine more closely in the next chapter some of those aspects of modern science itself that point beyond the confines of a closed mechanistic world view.

The Radical Humanities

There has been recently a growing interest in the humanities. Despite this, something quixotic continues to cling to those who attempt to affirm the humanities as essential to education and the human future. It is frequently only when the epithet "elitist" makes its appearance that the defender of the humanities has at least the satisfaction of knowing that he is being taken seriously, and is not being simply regarded as a "mere aesthete," an "intellectual softball player," "nice but not sharp." A standing temptation exists, therefore, to make an argument for the humanities on the grounds that they really are, *mirabile dictu*, useful: It is discovered—and rediscovered—that they nourish the flexibility that prevents being locked into dead-end vocational specialization, that they provide the perspective, breadth, and capacities for self-expression and direction said to be dear to the truly imaginative corporate employer or market research director. However, to resort to this notion of a deeper, or higher, utilitarianism—even though common sense as well as experience suggest that it may indeed be true—is, at bottom, to abandon the humanities in themselves, and to give the case for them away. Can the case be made? Is it possible to speak of a renewal of the humanities?

Unfortunately, the humanities face even weightier problems beyond those posed by the crasser pragmatism and utilitarianism of our culture. One of the most serious difficulties confronting the humanities—and humanists—has been the realization brought home with unavoidable force in our century that an immersion in culture does not itself nourish humane conduct. We now know, as George Steiner put it several years ago,

> that the libraries, museums, theatres, universities, research centers, in and through which the transmission of the humanities and of the sciences takes place, can prosper next to the concentration camps. . . . We know also . . . that obvious qualities of literate response, of aesthetic feeling, can coexist with barbaric, politically sadistic behavior in the same individual. Men such as Hans Frank who administered the "final solution" in eastern Europe were avid connoisseurs and, in some instances, performers of Bach and Mozart. We know of personnel in the bureaucracy of the torturers and of the ovens who cultivated a knowledge of Goethe, a love of Rilke.[2]

And John Lukacs has written:

> The performance of the intelligentsia during the last fifty years has been generally marked by cowardice, opportunism, dishonesty, and irresponsibility, far more than by intellectual courage, self-dedication, rectitude, and responsibility: honorable exceptions have been few. Of course intellectual occupation is seldom conducive to exceptional bravery: the clerks and the theologians of the Middle Ages, too, were wanting in the latter. The difference in the twentieth century was that now people had been taught to expect much from intellectuals who then deceived them.[3]

There is, no doubt, some hyperbole in this, and the issues involved are very complicated. Nevertheless, it remains the case that, while both science and the humanities have been implicated in the moral and cultural compromises and defeats of our time, we still are particularly shocked by the failure of the humanists. The "betrayal of humanity by humanists" remains especially offensive and jarring. Residually, then, at least, the humanities still seem to possess the principles for their own self-judgment and indispensable resources for cultural criticism and renewal. If, however, they are to live up to their potential for providing meaningful guidance and a powerful calling to account, the humanities must be conceived much more radically than is usually the case. What might be the defining characteristics of the radical humanities?

The Quintessential Human Values and the Irreducible Human Problems

The central concern of the humanities, Huston Smith has written, is to serve "as custodians of the human image." "One way or another," he writes, "in cycles and epicycles, they circle the question of who we take ourselves to be—what it means to be a human being, to live a human life."[4] A radical understanding of the humanities insists at the minimum that the quintessential human qualities—freedom, love, creativeness, the value of persons, and the love of truth—be placed firmly at the center of all efforts to define, to educate, and to plan for the human being. This requires a sense of vital priorities and an ability to discriminate between that which is of most worth and that which is also necessary but not sufficient. In education, for example, it would require an awareness that the spread of information (the trivia of which has become a major psychic and environmental pollutant) is not the same as growth in knowledge. And it would require an awareness, above all, that quantitative and discursive knowledge is itself not the same as understanding, that knowledge that does not serve the attempt to understand is itself destructive.

It is here that we can begin to get a grip on the old question of the relation between the natural sciences and the humanities. Recently an eminent university president voiced his concern with the need for the public to understand science. "We have yet to solve the problem," he said, "of scientific literacy for the nonscientist. . . . Twenty-one years have passed since C. P. Snow suggested that the humanist who cannot describe the Second Law of Thermodynamics is as illiterate as the scientist who has not read Shakespeare. We should get on with it."[5] The difficulty here is knowing exactly what is meant by "scientific literacy for the nonscientist," or, for that matter, for the scientist.

If scientific literacy involves, as the university president indicated at one point, the ability "to know what it means to think
scientifically" and "to appreciate the differences in our lives that
such knowledge makes," that is unexceptionable and crucial to
humanistic concerns. It is good to know what science is revealing
and how the scientists go about it, and it is important to know
what will be done with this knowledge, and who will control
it. It is essential to public discourse and policy that informed
non-scientists have a say in the uses of scientific knowledge. It
is also good and important to know the limitations of science
and scientific thinking. It is important to know that often technological solutions themselves create more technological problems, to know that quantitative ways of thinking applied to
qualitative questions wreak havoc; it is important to know that
there is no way of disposing of proliferating nuclear wastes; it
is important to know what the explosion of a twenty-megaton
bomb would do to the northeastern seaboard. In all of this, we
do need more scientific literacy.

If scientific literacy, however, suggests an equivalence in value,
without discrimination, among all kinds of knowledge, then it
represents a loss of vital priorities. Many years ago in an essay
titled "The Greatest Resource—Education," E. F. Schumacher
directly addressed the position asserted by Lord Snow. In an-
swering the question, "What is education?" Schumacher wrote,
"It is the transmission of ideas which enable man to choose
between one thing and another, or, to quote Ortega '. . . to live
a life which is something above meaningless tragedy or inward
disgrace.' " From this perspective, he argued, Shakespeare and
the Second Law of Thermodynamics are in no way of equal
value. "What matters," Schumacher wrote,

> is the tool-box of ideas with which, through which, we experience
> and interpret the world. The Second Law of Thermodynamics is
> nothing more than a working hypothesis suitable for various types
> of scientific research. On the other hand—a work by Shakespeare:
> teeming with the most vital ideas about the *inner* development
> of man, showing the whole grandeur and misery of human ex-
> istence. How can these two things be equivalent? What do I miss,
> as a human being, if I have never heard of the Second Law of

Thermodynamics? The answer is: Nothing. And what do I miss by not knowing Shakespeare? Unless I get my understanding from another source, I simply miss my life. Shall we tell our children that one thing is as good as another—here a bit of knowledge of physics and there a bit of knowledge of literature?[6]

But there is yet another meaning to the term *scientific literacy*. It can also mean being able to distinguish between science and scientism, being able to read the difference between the working hypotheses and assumptions of a limited quantitative science and the quasi-scientific, all-embracing world views that have been built out of them. In this sense also, the more scientific literacy we have, for scientists and non-scientists alike, the better. What must be avoided from the standpoint of the radical humanities is any concept of scientific and technical literacy, which, in J. Robert Nelson's phrase, "is affirmed, supported, and advanced by those who still cannot recognize the superiority of human values over mathematical and mechanical forms."[7] Such a lack of vital priorities can only lead to further dehumanization.

Love of Words

The radical humanities seek to foster respect for language and a love of words. For many years writers from George Orwell to our own contemporary, Wendell Berry, have pointed to the connection between the degradation of the human being and the degeneration of language—not that one causes the other, but that the two go hand in hand. Recently, Berry has described the intimate relation between the disintegration of language and the disintegration of community and the disintegration of persons, which he calls "the two epidemic illnesses of our time." "My impression," he writes, "is that we have seen, for perhaps a hundred and fifty years, a gradual increase in language that is either meaningless or destructive of meaning. And I believe that this increasing unreliability of language parallels the increasing disintegration, over the same period, of persons and communities."[8] The capacity of words to serve as bearers of meaning is coupled with the health and meaningfulness of the personal, communal, and cosmic realities from which words spring.

In a world stripped of qualities, words, too, are emptied of their substance. They are no longer capable of bearing witness to that which constitutes the innermost character of personal experience, the ultimate reality of things, and standards for beauty and responsible conduct. Language is sucked into and comes to perpetuate the dualism of an alien objective world void of meaning and an enclosed subjective world void of reality. The literary arts come to represent only the expression of personal emotion and are valued at most as providing, for those who need it, a periodic escape into fantasy from the rigors of the real world, one way to retreat momentarily from the demands of work to the refreshment of play. The trivialization of poetry is the personal equivalent of the entertainment banalization of the communal festival, once *the* meaning-event. In a *disqualified universe* the only objective meaning accorded to words is in their use as functional signs for achieving some specified pragmatic purpose. But this is an objectivity that makes no claim to be guided by the search for truth, or interest in it; it is an objectivity that has explicitly repudiated the possibility of any aesthetic, ethical, and most of all, metaphysical reference. It is a parody of what objectivity was once thought to stand for.

This is a view of language that lends itself to a totally technological approach to life. Ideas and the words that bear on them are valued only for their ability, for their efficiency in getting things done, for moving things—mountains, molecules, men. Ideas themselves are conceived as little more than, to use George Kelly's phrase, "conceptual particles"; and words are regarded as tags for these pieces of the machinery, to be pushed and pulled about, manipulated and discarded, as needs may be. That this view conceals a deep and radical anti-intellectualism in any traditional sense of that term is evident. An older notion that ideas and words are something to be lived with, savored, to steep oneself in, to sink into in the expectation that they will unfold riches that are of intrinsic worth, is considered quaint, *useless*. That words themselves, together with their obvious functional ability, might also participate in meanings that are themselves creative is dismissed as the romantic musing of a prescientific mind.

The willingness to discard words at will and to create new

ones on the spot is symptomatic of the evaporation of any sense of meaningful place, context, and commitment. Jacques Ellul has long called attention to the propensity today to fashion bizarre new words and "hermetic jargons," inaccessible to any but the initiates, the experts in the respective fields. The vogue for inventing and employing bureaucratic acronyms as nouns seems, perhaps, to represent the latest extreme in an attitude that can scarcely veil its contempt for both language and persons. Such acronyms are the very husks of meaning. Such monstrosities as "optimalizing decisions," "parameterizing possibilities," "finalizing approaches," and so on, could be easily dismissed as the products of a failed education and a lack of culture were not a more sinister element discernible.[9] Many years ago George Orwell demonstrated that irresponsibility toward words is a mark of irresponsibility toward persons, the sign of a totalitarian mentality ready to dismantle and refashion language with each twist in policy. "There is an indispensable connection," writes Wendell Berry, "between language and truth, and therefore between language and deeds . . . ," and the breaking of one loosens the other.[10]

A purely functional language is not a language for the forming of community, for the guidance of responsible conduct, or for the apprehension of mystery and vision. It is not a language for education or public discussion. It is a language for manipulation and control—for public relations and indoctrination; a language for operators for whom accountability lies only in doing well the job assigned, not in asking what the job is for. A purely functional language is for functionaries—or for those managers higher up, for whom all accountability is a nuisance.

Even at its most basic—and this is what the proponents of that unfortunate misnomer "back to the basics" all miss—education depends for its life blood on a reverence for language and a love of words. It is fashionable today, for example, to berate the young for not being able to read and write (and their early teachers for not doing anything about it). The question is seldom raised, however, whether our spreading illiteracy may not be in part at least the harvest of an academic culture that for a century has shown little joy in the contemplation of words and respect for their integrity. Is it too much of an exaggeration to say that our dominant academic culture is one in which, with some exceptions, poetry and narrative are regarded as at best pleasant luxuries for those who like that sort of thing, in which high rank is conferred on the worst of jargons, in which whole schools of thought give official sanction to the view that words are only utilitarian and instrumental signs, labels (the notion of living symbols having long disappeared) to be replaced whenever possible by more exact and functional notations? If the custodians of culture treat words simply as labels bereft of deep meaning and ecstatic potency, what is the surprise that the citizens abandon such language to seek their meanings and delights elsewhere?

A respect for language would also help to restore a concern for the interconnections of human experience. In a humane education, specialization would be pursued within an awareness of this larger matrix of meaning. Frequently, the humanities are represented as being concerned primarily with breadth and general knowledge in opposition to specialization. This is a misconception. The humanities are not opposed to specialization, for craftsmanship, competence, and discipline are essential to the humanities. The radical humanities do insist, however, that without an overarching concern for wholeness, specialization becomes fragmentation.

Once the vision of a prior and primary unity drops out of sight, each discipline and its practitioners seek their own hegemony, insulate themselves with their hermetic jargons, develop an awesome, intimidating, and procrustean power, and justify all their activities and their requests for funding in the doing as part of the search for knowledge. The individual and the public are parcelled out, dissected, and disappear as recognizable entities. The unpleasant results for the individual have been nicely described by the biochemist Erwin Chargaff, who writes:

> From birth to tomb we are the objects of research. The smallest fetus will not escape having its horrorscope cast from his chromosomes by cyto-geneticists. When he grows up, despite the efforts of education experts, and receives his Social Security number, he becomes the object of statisticians, sociologists, political scientists, census takers, economists, and the like. In the later

course of his life he will get into the hands of the biomedical profession; and when he finally reaches the other end, his agony will be studied by thanatologists. Ethicists will have deplored his morals, analysts will take apart his soul. Gurus, prophets, trend-setters, and politicians will have misled and confused him. He is the universal grist, and he will figure in innumerable papers, books, questionnaires, and study reports.[11]

And this usually with only feeble complaints, for who wants to be accused of obstructing progress and the discovery of knowledge? The community suffers similar fragmentation and destruction. What appears, therefore, from one level as merely a dry question of curriculum—"What is to be the role of the humanities?"—is seen from another to be of utmost importance for the individual and society as well, with implications for politics, economics, and culture.

If a respect for living language is a first step toward the recovery of wholeness, it is also an essential safeguard against that false wholeness which is really a kind of monolithic uniformity. A living and life-giving wholeness is not sameness through and through, but rather comprises a rich diversity in unity. Many observers have noted the powerful pressures in modern society toward cultural and intellectual uniformity. The global spread, for example, of economic and military technology threatens to homogenize all cultural and institutional life. This is the outward manifestation of a fragmented thinking that paradoxically also strives to reconstitute the world in a unity of its own making, a unity derived from the total integration of countless standardized components. As with milk, the homogenization of culture is the end product of the process of fragmentation. Every sphere of life becomes vulnerable to standardization. Nothing is left untouched; everything is, as it were, covered: spatially, by the spread of an increasingly artificial and fabricated environment, and its wastes; temporally, psychologically, and ethically, by the universal extension to everything of technique and its values and organizational infrastructures.

Language and education themselves become increasingly standardized under the guise of being made universal and democratic. From the ideal of literacy for the creation of independent citizens and the expression of cultural creativity, universal literacy, transmogrified, becomes a means to make more rapid the adoption of technology and the adaptation of individuals to it. Universal literacy comes more and more to consist in the propagation among the populace of "basic skills" and "competencies" suited for little more than the rudimentary reading and reckoning needed for consumption—of both material goods and instructions. For the elite, universal literacy increasingly means, as Manfred Stanley has shown, the development and dissemination of a universal *lingua franca* consisting of a quantitative language system of mathematics and techno-logic.[12] In both cases, cultural and individual differences are suppressed as potentially disruptive and subversive. And the qualitatively significant world of story-telling and poetry, of cultural myth, song, and saga, of religious hope and vision is eliminated.

Words are the conveyors and custodians of quality. A disregard for their integrity and fine nuance is a sure sign that the attenuation of the human capacity for the discernment of quality is well under way.

The masquerade of homogeneity as wholeness is surprisingly successful. Victor C. Ferkiss, for example, has argued that the ideal technological society of the future will be based on self-derived values embodying three fundamental principles: (1) man's continuity with nature; (2) the interconnectedness of all phenomena in the process of becoming; and (3) the immanent this-worldly nature of reality.[13] WIth the possible exception of the last, these have at least a surface similarity to the notion of wholeness. "Man's continuity with nature" and the "interconnectedness of all phenomena in the process of becoming" could both, on their face and without further examination, appeal to ecologists of every stripe; and, even the "immanent this-worldly nature of reality," could, though probably not quite as readily, commend itself as compatible with the Judeo-Christian vision of this world as the arena of divine activity, of the immanence in space and time of transcendent reality. But this is a deceptive and purely formal similarity made possible only because qualitative language is being used to describe a purely quantitative world view and set of values. Even here language is being misappropriated and abused, and once this is recognized then the ultimately reductive and standardized vision for human society that is being proffered becomes apparent. Because of this surface and formal similarity, great confusion comes from speaking of quantitative totality in the language of qualitative wholeness. This dream of universal coherence, however, is itself an illusion. Creeping uniformity and universal standardization do not produce complete world unity, even of a flattened and leveled out sort. Whether presented as nightmares or dreams of future earthly paradise, those science-fiction descriptions of all mankind someday functioning smoothly within a totally integrated and cybernetically coordinated megamachine, seem on reflection to be fantasies indeed. Things are too complex ever to be brought under such final control, but the relentless, unrelieved attempt to do so can probably be counted on to cause ever more casualties, chaos, and emptiness in the human heart. Thus, Ellul writes: "This society, this human being, while not becoming technological objects, robots, and so forth, now receive their unity from the totalizing technology. But the latter cannot provide any meaning; this is its great lacuna. The reconstituted totality is devoid of significance."[14] Moreover, conflict erupts with greater frequency and more violence than ever. With the global society, for example, has also come for the first time the power to destroy the earth—universalization with a vengeance, and the proliferation as never before of multitudinous conflicts that might occasion our doing so. In the end, then, the pressures toward homogenization seem to provide more fragmentation. And the exclusive dominance of narrow reason moves ever closer to grand irrationality. Long ago, Jonathan Swift described the "academy of projectors" where schemes were hatched and pressed for the total, universal organization of man and nature:

> In these colleges, the professors contrive new rules and methods of agriculture and building, and new instruments and tools for all trades and manufacturers, whereby, as they undertake, one man shall do the work of ten; a palace may be built in a week, of materials so durable as to last forever without repairing. All the fruits of the earth shall come to maturity, at whatever season we think fit to chuse, and encrease an hundred fold more than they do at present; with innumerable other happy proposals. The

only inconvenience is, that none of these projects are yet brought to perfection; and, in the meantime, the whole country lies miserably waste.[15]

The Recovery of Imagination

A radical understanding of the humanities would place the highest value, as the humanities at their best always have, on clear, discursive, logical intellect. After all, mathematics and logic have been firmly embedded in those liberal arts that have traditionally been regarded as constituting the heart of the humanities. It is this very concern for the importance of clear thinking, however, that would lead a radical understanding of the humanities to insist on the recognition that rationality extends far beyond the boundaries of the calculating intellect. To deny the further recesses of rationality is not only to forfeit access to all that partakes of wonder, feeling, dream, and myth—the domain of our richest experience of life and meaning—but with them to eliminate the source of all creative intellect whatsoever. Do we not realize, Ellul asks, "that dreaming is no less important, basic, and decisive for man than reason, or rather, that reason ceases to exist if there is no dreaming, no lighthearted imagination, no myth and poetry?"[16]

This is not a call to a return to dark instincts, pure spontaneity, and blind passion. That would be a kind of pure obscurantism and rampant emotionalism that beclouds minds and leaves individuals vulnerable to demagogues and mindless enthusiasms of every sort. As it stands, however, Ellul's statement could be taken to call for little more than a vague feeling-tone of piety and playfulness in order to keep the reasoning intellect supple and open in its movement. Something much more important than this, however, is at stake. What is actually being affirmed is the prior and primary importance of the imagination as the foundation of all thinking that is alive, creative, and rational.

While much attention will later be devoted to the Imagination, a few preliminary comments may be warranted here. The current use of the term *imagination* associates it almost entirely with the "imaginary," with that which is fictional and illusory. Even in this trivialized sense, there is often a recognition of the importance of the imagination in knowing, if in no other role than that of providing what are called "useful fictions"—fictions because they are considered unreal fantasies, useful nonetheless because they provide explanatory options that logical reason can sometimes make use of. The full understanding of the quality and status of Imagination can only be regained, however, when the Imagination is recognized as that *fundamental* capacity for Insight that is the source of all cognition and of all new meaning and knowledge. The Imagination is that capacity for the grasp of reality which, in Phenix's phrase, constitutes "the faithful uses of reason." Imagination is that participation of the whole person—in logical thinking, feeling, and willing—in the act of cognition. The Imagination places the human being in a context of intelligibility that spans the cleavage between subject and object, a context of meaning that includes both.

The Traditional Wisdom

The radical humanities take seriously the traditional wisdom of mankind. They seek to avoid that temporal provincialism which holds that only the modern age counts and has the right opinion. C. S. Lewis dubbed this condescending attitude toward earlier times and other cultures, "chronological snobbery," namely, "the uncritical acceptance of the intellectual climate of the age and the assumption that whatever has gone out of date is on that account discredited."[17] This temporal and cultural complacency, in truth a kind of deep-seated parochialism, has been highly developed in the modern West. "Not long ago," Robert N. Bellah has observed, "it was common to rank the cultures of the world in terms of how closely they resembled our own. Modern Western Culture was seen as the standard of rationality and progress toward which all other cultures are or ought to be approaching"[18]—and, here, other cultures would include earlier periods in Western history, as well as the so-called primitive peoples of non-Western culture. As Bellah and others have noted, however, growing doubts and disillusions about the modern world and its problems have in recent years challenged this attitude. Nevertheless, it persists in various forms.

A cultural and temporal provincialism lies behind the still widely unquestioned willingness to promote the sacrifice of any traditional views and values, whatever their acknowledged contributions to the preservation of human dignity, that impede technological and economic development. It is seen more subtly in that conceit of modern doubt which assays the claim of traditional wisdom with false humility—"we can never really know"—and thus elevates its own uncertainty and inner doubt to exalted status. And, perhaps, temporal-cultural provincialism is most highly refined in that indiscriminate taking up of non-Western and non-modern traditions—"turning East" seems to be the most prevalent form—in order to solve present difficulties without at the same time requiring any real change of modern, Western premises and goals. This is the attitude that approaches other cultures and times for techniques—forms of meditation, therapy, social dynamics, and so forth—that can be separated from their own cultural and social origins and used for satisfying better the untransformed desires spawned by modern civilization. It is a kind of cultural strip mining. A good deal, though not all, of the so-called New Age consciousness involves such a technologizing of the ancient wisdom, a taking over of processes without context, of techniques without content, and succeeds in decking out the Modern Western Mind Set in what is thought to be more appealing garb, but does not challenge or alter it in any fundamental way. This takes the other culture even less seriously than does outright rejection.

If the claims of the traditional wisdom are to be taken seriously, the attempt must be made to answer at least two questions: (1) What central premises and assumptions are at stake? and (2) What actual changes do these premises mandate in ways of life, cultural goals, and social arrangements? To these, perhaps two further questions should be added: To what extent is the traditional wisdom desirable for the modern world and in what form? What obstacles and difficulties stand in the way of its effectual realization in the modern world?

Despite multifarious life forms, values, and symbolic-institutional patterns, the traditional cultures of mankind have shared certain central assumptions about the nature and meaning of the world and of human existence. Having spent much of his life studying closely the individuality and diversity of the world's cultural traditions, the philosopher and historian of religion Huston Smith has also concluded that what emerges in an overview of their outlooks is "a remarkable unity underlying the surface variety."[19] A more complete discussion than space permits here would have to explore in greater detail not only the diversity, but also the full range of development and expression within what Smith calls the "human unanimity." Here we can look only briefly and in the most general way at some of the most fundamental convictions common to the traditions and at some of the central questions they pose to the modern world.

The Priority of Mind

Tradition has always presented the world of the senses as grounded in a "higher," suprasensible order of Reality. This higher order is at once a transcendent, infinite Mystery and the inexhaustible, immanent source of all meaning and existence. It is the ground from which the world of space and time derives and to which it bears witness. It has been experienced variously as an immediate, pervasive, at times overpowering, numinosity, as a world of intricate qualitative relationships and ordered harmony, as an all-encompassing matrix of meaning, value, and creativity. And it has been called by diverse names, each with its own strengths, each with its own limitations: the realm of the gods, the spiritual world, the divine Wisdom, the ground of Being, and multitudinous others. Among the religious philosophies of the traditions it has been grasped as the domain of intelligent being and consciousness, of Mind. The fundamental conviction of traditional wisdom is that Mind is the primary ground of reality.

The traditional outlook is a total inversion of the whole modern schema of things. In the place of extreme reductionist modes of explanation, tradition insists that the lower can finally only be understood by means of the higher, the simpler by the more complex, and not the other way around. In Huston Smith's terms, tradition maintains that the inferior—matter—cannot on principle provide an adequate explanation for the superior— mind. In the view of tradition life cannot be understood, as it is in the dominant modern outlook, as a product of inanimate matter. In traditional wisdom, Mind, not matter, is the primary ground of reality, and life itself is an attribute of mind, of consciousness, which remains prior and primary. In contrast, the dominant modern view sees mind not only as having gradually and inexplicably emerged from once-lifeless matter, but to be at most the product of individual brains to which it is confined. In this view there is no place for the possibility that the mind of the individual participates in and is an expression of a larger, more encompassing intelligibility. Thus, for the dominant modern view the mind of the individual remains enclosed within itself, separated and alienated from the nature from which it supposedly came. In the more extreme, and by no means uncommon forms of reductionism, mind is, in fact, considered to be only the name used to designate those functions of the brain that cannot yet be described in electrochemical terms. In this regard, it is interesting to note that even those extreme determinists who would deny the existence of mind in any degree always appear to make an exception in their own particular case; they always seem, as the neurophysiologist John C. Eccles has commented, to be talking about someone else, not themselves. For tradition, mind does not exist in nature; nature exists in mind. Mind contains the nature it perceives and creates, a nature that is not a lifeless mechanism, but a living matrix.

The awareness within tradition of an extended and higher reality situates the human being not at the apex, but within a larger hierarchy of being and perfection. The human being occupies a unique place in the world. The human subsumes within himself all of the natural world, the essential characteristics of the mineral, the plant, the animal, and, yet, at the same time, is open within himself to those levels of reality transcending the visible world of time and space. As one capable of intuiting meaning, the human being is a moral being, for meaning, to be discerned, imposes the necessity and capacity to discriminate, to choose the higher over the lower, to hold and to be held accountable. This is the central human quality; this is what makes the human being human. Apart from this, man is but a higher animal, the most clever, perhaps, of them all; but when he denies his true humanity, man does not return to the level of the animal, which has its own inherent integrity, but sinks to that of the sub-natural. Man has consciousness, as do the animals, but in the human being consciousness becomes aware of itself and capable of grasping and of being grasped by that intelligibility that informs the world and calls it forth. The human being is capable of knowing within himself Being in the world, and thus enjoys an integrality with nature of which a mechanistic naturalism has not the dimmest presentiment. For this reason, tradition speaks of the human being as the microcosm within the macrocosm, the point wherein is contained and reflected the whole.

In a remarkable essay written from the standpoint of the traditional wisdom, Gai Eaton speaks of "Man as viceroy."[20] The central position of the human being within the world confers upon him certain privileges, but it also demands of him, as of no other creature, responsibilities. Man carries, in Eaton's terms, "vice-regal responsibilities" for other persons and for the whole of nature. The notion that the human being need care about none but his own kind, or only those of his own kind who are members of his own family or group, is foreign to the traditional view of man. It is particularly with respect to the human beings' responsibilities toward nature and other creatures that the sharp contrast between the traditional view of man and that of the modern world becomes most apparent.

Precisely because of his unique position, man is held especially accountable by tradition as a steward and guardian of the earth and of other living beings. It is only as man has lost a sense of his own meaning that he has begun to arrogate to himself absolute rights over all that is non-human. It would be abhorrent to traditional man to treat minerals, oceans, land, and animals all as of no more worth than to be exploited for human survival and treated indifferently as void of feeling and life. Traditional man could only view with deepest repugnance the unrestrained readiness to experiment on animals to satisfy every whim of human need and curiosity, or to employ farming techniques that view animals solely as "units of production," to be treated accordingly.

The traditional reverence for the earth and its web of life was, perhaps, exemplified no more vividly than by the red Indians of North America. With them it is clear that concern for the earth and its creatures is not sentimental or ignorant of the harshness of nature and its many cruelties. The Indians lived a hard life and knew daily the necessity to kill. But to the Indians the killing of animals was accompanied by an awareness of debt and gratitude to fellow creatures and by a sense of responsibility to repay nature for the lives taken. It was also undertaken out of an appropriate dread, expressed in the elaborate rituals of purification that made possible the assumption of responsibility for the killing of animals, a dread born of the awareness, as Eaton writes, that abuse of the animal creation "must lead to our own destruction and that whatever we do to them will, by a simple process of cause-and-effect, have to be done to us in one way or another."[21]

In 1856 Chief Seathl of the Suwamish tribe of Indians (who lived in what today is the state of Washington) replied to a "request" from the president of the United States that he "sell" his tribal lands to the government. In a long and moving letter Chief Seathl said at one point:

> If I decide to accept, I will make one condition. The white man must treat the beasts of this land as his brothers. What is man without beasts? If all of the beasts were gone, men would die from great loneliness of the spirit, for whatever happens to the beasts also happens to man.
>
> One thing we know which the white man may one day discover: Our God is the same God. You may think that you own Him as you wish to own our land. But you cannot. He is the God of men. And His compassion is equal for the red man and the white. This earth is precious to Him. And to harm the earth is to heap contempt on its Creator. The whites, too, shall pass— perhaps sooner than other tribes. Continue to contaminate your bed and you will one night suffocate in your own waste. When the buffaloes are all slaughtered, the wild horses all tamed, the sacred corner of the forest heavy with the scent of men, and the view of the ripe hills blotted by talking wives, where is the thicket? Where is the eagle? And what is it to say goodbye to the shift and the hunt? The end of living and the beginning of dying.[22]

In the work of Alexander Solzhenitsyn, a contemporary who also invokes the traditional wisdom, there appear, but only rarely, incidents, seemingly irrelevant at first notice, that on reflection nevertheless leave no doubt that for the author wanton cruelty to animals and insensitivity to nature are not unrelated to the Gulag mentality and the dehumanization of man himself. Chief Seathl would have understood.

Central to tradition is the importance of the virtue of restraint. For tradition, not everything that is possible is permissible. Werner Heisenberg, whose respect for tradition is immense, has spoken of the need to reclaim a sense of restraint if technology, for example, is to serve "the real interests of human society." "We should . . . no longer do everything," he writes, "that we are technically able to do." And he adds that "immediate collaboration among universities, industry, and officialdom to solve this central problem of restraining technology is certainly a most urgent task . . . in short, technology must be subordinated to real human needs."[23] And, yet, the calls for restraint from increasing numbers of such outstanding persons as Heisenberg himself continue to evoke little actual acceptance. The notion of restraint, it is frequently said, is a wholly negative attitude that represents a failure of nerve and an anti-intellectual impediment to the progress of knowledge and is inimical to the scientific spirit. The objection bears a closer look.

Part of the problem, as Catherine Roberts, a microbiologist writing on the problems of "The Scientific Conscience," has pointed out, is that the English word *restraint* is a rather limited, and in its modern connotation indeed negative, translation of a much broader concept, which in Greek is designated by the word *sophrosyne.* A variety of meanings are included in the Greek word, and Dr. Roberts lists some of them as including: "a sane mind, practical wisdom, clear vision, right-judgment, self-restraint, moderation and temperance, as well as humility, humanity, mercy, and modesty."[24] And to these might be added what Wendell Berry has called an attitude of "forebearance and care," along with a sense of propriety, correct proportion, proper scale, and beauty. Clearly, there is little that smacks of any of these—least of all "forebearance and care," proportion, humility, and beauty—in the incessant drive to try out any and every conceivable research possibility, and in the pell-mell scramble for funding that threatens to become the distinguishing mark of the modern university. It is obvious that restraint in its comprehensive, traditional meaning is anything but anti-intellectual.

Instead, it is an affirmation of a deep wisdom from which can come a thinking that is truly alive and life giving.

There can be no truly creative human responsibility, writes Heisenberg further, apart from what he calls "the spiritual realm, the central spiritual order of things" to which the great religious traditions bear witness. From the spiritual realm come the guiding ideals that both govern ethical conduct and lay a foundation for ultimate trust and hope. "These ideals," writes Heisenberg, "do not spring from inspection of the immediately visible world but from the region of structures lying behind it, which Plato spoke of as the world of Ideas, and concerning which we are told in the Bible, 'God is a spirit.' "[25] Here Heisenberg speaks as does tradition of a realm of mind and spirit in which the material world of the senses is grounded. Note, however, that for Heisenberg, as again for tradition, our ordinary knowledge provides no more than a partial and imperfect reflection of the realm of mind and spirit. While he implies that this deeper reality is touched upon, though only tangentially, in some philosophy, it is not finally accessible to empirical observation and our ordinary ways of thinking.

Ordinary thinking, which is limited to the immediately visible world of experience and to abstractions drawn from it, can never furnish those "guiding ideals" which are the source of genuine moral freedom and creativity because, infinite in scope and ever beyond the reach of total realization, they remain always new and alive. Ordinary thinking can produce ethical systems that provide norms or standards of conduct, but these norms are drawn from observed behavior of some experienced human community, or from the ideas of how some within the community would like for people to behave. Such norms are themselves abstractions removed from the actual experience of concrete human beings. They can, to be sure, command wide agreement as "common social values," and may even inspire respect for law and order or stir whole nations to patriotic fervor. But they remain rigid standards of behavior, and are essentially abstract, static, and coercive. And they are forever subject to being overthrown by champions of other norms and standards. Apart from the living sources of knowledge, we are, in fact, always vulnerable to the coercive power of all our abstract ideas. The experience of the twentieth century is testimony to the tendency of political, philosophical, and scientific abstractions of all kinds, immensely useful within their own domain, to lose touch with concrete experience and real human needs and to become totalitarian ideologies that are used to rationalize any act of violence against man and nature. Traditional wisdom claims to have had access—through its seers, its prophets, its revelatory events and scriptures—to a higher order of reality that can put our abstractions in perspective and keep them connected with living experience.

The pressing question, however, is whether the traditional wisdom itself is either accessible or understandable in the modern world.

The Problems of Tradition

The major problem in any attempt to recover the traditional wisdom is to be encountered in the phenomenon alluded to earlier as the "evolution of consciousness." Do individuals in modern and traditional cultures experience the world in the same way? Or has human consciousness changed over time so that the experience of another order of reality, which the traditions take for granted, has become largely inaccessible, and nearly always incomprehensible to modern man?

There is evidence to suggest that this latter is indeed the case. Within the earliest traditional cultures, the so-called primordial or tribal-shamanic cultures, there seems to have been an almost immediate awareness of an all-pervading numinous presence to such an extent, in fact, that the modern distinction between the sacred and the profane would have made little sense, since everything in the world was experienced as ultimately meaningful, and as immersed in and emanating from the sacred. This was a form of consciousness which gave a sense of direct participation in the meaning-filled life of the world.

With the rise of the great religious cultures—such as those of the classical Hindu and the related Confucian and Buddhist cultures, and of the classical Mediterranean, Christian, and Islamic cultures—there already seems to have been a fading of this immediate sense of the numinous, with the consequent emergence of a sharpened distinction between the sacred and the profane, the natural and the supernatural. Nevertheless, the sense of participation in a higher order of reality and meaning remained strong and found expression in extensive ritual orders and social rhythms, disciplines of spiritual formation, literary and artistic forms, crafts, and complex social and political arrangements. During the last three or four centuries, however, this participatory awareness of a meaningful world has dimmed almost to the point of extinction. At the same time, the fading of a sense of communal and cosmic participation seems to have been accompanied by an intensified sense of individual selfhood, and by an experience of the self's relation to the world very different from that of earlier periods of human history. Rather than the sense of a self indwelling and sustained by a living and meaningful world in which the boundaries between self and world, self and other, are not sharp but flow and merge into one another, the modern experience has been increasingly that of a self separated sharply from other selves, and detached from nature, standing as self-enclosed subject over against nature as object. No longer is nature participated in and experienced directly, but rather she is analyzed, broken down, and brought under technical control. As Owen Barfield and Charles Davy have argued, the emerging experience of a sharply formed individual consciousness seems to go hand in hand with the onlooker consciousness and objective methods of modern science.[26]

If there be some truth to this notion of an evolution of consciousness, or if at only the very least, modern persons of the scientific age experience self and world quite differently from their predecessors, how is the traditional teaching to be recovered? Will it not require for its very possibility some far-reaching change of consciousness? What might this mean, and would it be desirable? The first answer to these questions is that there are various ways to approach tradition, and that some commend themselves as more feasible than others, some more desirable—and some that are indeed possible are to be avoided at all costs. One test of the adequacy of the various approaches to tradition that must be kept in the forefront is whether they recognize and provide safeguards for the achievements of modern consciousness.

The reader will recall that throughout this discussion we have taken pains not to reject science and technology as such, even while submitting their misuse and abuse to sharp criticism. By the same token, we have affirmed the development of a heightened sense of selfhood and the powers of reason, and of their combined potential for the enhancement of human freedom. The integrity and freedom of the self and the significance of reason are possible only when they are connected with larger dimensions—the community, mankind, history, the transcendent. Severed from these, the isolated individual and a narrow reason threaten to become, as they are today becoming, utterly destructive. One way to these larger dimensions is offered by the radical humanities which themselves point to the cosmic dimensions of significance reflected in the great religious and philosophic traditions. The question to be addressed, however, is whether a deep connection can be established between modern consciousness and tradition without one overwhelming the other, either by way of erosion or inundation.

A first type of approach to traditional teachings is the way of belief. There are hard and soft versions of belief. The hard version maintains that the teachings of the tradition are to be believed literally and in every instance, and that they pre-empt in every way knowledge derived from any other source, whether from ordinary thinking and empirical observations or from other traditions. For the hard version of belief, the claims of tradition and, usually, the claims of one particular tradition, are asserted to the exclusion of all else. All claims to knowledge are sifted and judged according to their conformity with the ruling articles of belief, and the individual, the community, social leaders, and the exercise of human reason are all to be brought into total compliance with these. This approach is currently widespread in the world, and can be seen in the resurgence on every hand of forms of what might be called *atavistic fundamentalism*, from the Ayatollah's theocracy in Iran to the Moral Majority in the United States. Confronted with the fundamentalist mentality, the temptation of the liberal-minded, right-thinking modern person to indulge in a bit of "chronological snobbery" has never been stronger nor seemingly better justified. But, however justified, such an attitude does not conduce to a better understanding of either the motives or the issues involved.

The spread of atavistic fundamentalism—the turning of past teachings of great complexity and delicate nuance concerning the spirit into literal statements about the world—represents in this literalism, curiously enough, a real concession to modernity. Such fundamentalism seems to arise among those who accept the dominant modern view that all real knowledge must consist only of propositional statements of fact about the empirical world, and who at the same time have an intimation that matters of ultimate importance are contained in the traditional teaching and are in imminent danger of being lost forever. For them the only alternative seems to be to convert the symbol-filled efforts of the tradition to convey an experience of another world of Reality also into propositional statements about an empirical world. Thus does literalism kill the spirit. In a misconstrued effort to maintain a connection with that mysterious source of meaning and significance, Mystery is destroyed and made banal and pedestrian. When the fear of what is in danger of being lost combines with anger at those who threaten its loss, a literalistic fundamentalism of belief will generate and justify all manner of oppression.

But before condemning fundamentalism out of hand, it might be well to ask what threat of genuine loss, if any, has inspired such fears. Why, for example, are forms of fundamentalism particularly resurgent in traditional cultures undergoing modernization and development? Are genuine cultural values endangered, and is there any alternative other than the Hobson's choice between a fundamentalistic literalism, which is really only an illusion of the preservation of those values, and a scientistic and technicist literalism, which is, indeed, their sacrifice?

The refusal to recognize Mystery, and the ensuing atrophy of the capacity to do so, has made the modern world particularly susceptible to the claims of irrational belief. Not a little of the current world conflict appears fired and sustained by competing forms of fundamentalism: traditional teachings hardened and drained of their wisdom, abstract political ideas raised to totalitarian ideologies, scientific abstractions become all-embracing scientific world views—all forms of fundamentalism, literalistic belief systems demanding unquestioning submission.

By contrast a soft version of belief makes room for knowledge, but does so by adopting a kind of "Two-Realm Theory of Truth."

In this approach, there is the realm of knowledge provided by positivistic science. And, alongside it, but in a separate compartment, is the realm of meaning and value, which is the domain of belief based on feeling or on a vague sense of a larger meaning and significance behind everything. Poetry and art, the religious traditions, and mystical experiences or reports of these are regarded as providing added confirmation and support for the affirmation of meaning, but these are not thought to have anything to do with knowledge. This view is familiar as yet another instance of the modern dualism between subject and object, ideas and things, knowledge and values, and suffers all the problems of this dualism.

At its strongest, the two-realm theory can call attention to other important dimensions of experience besides the quantitative, and sometimes succeeds in fostering a general attitude of respect for human values and ideals in the face of an overweening positivism. But such an attitude that has no integral connection with, no rooting in, our knowledge of reality is difficult to sustain. Relegated to the gaps and along the fringes of knowledge, meaning will constantly recede as the boundaries are extended and the gaps filled in until it eventually evaporates, appeals to tradition, to mystical feeling, and to a general sense of a need for meaning notwithstanding.

The second approach to tradition is best described, perhaps, as eclectic-exploitative. This is the approach that seeks to take from other cultures whatever ideas and practices seem suited to correct deficiencies thought to exist in one's own culture. Today Oriental religious philosophies and practices seem particularly appealing to young Westerners for such purposes. This is an approach that easily becomes exploitative because it absorbs elements from other cultures on an almost entirely utilitarian basis, without permitting the outlook of the other to challenge or alter one's own fundamental premises and assumptions. It is eclectic in that it chooses indiscriminately with little or no consideration of the total social-religious context within which specific cultural practices and views acquire their own integral meaning. There occurs in this approach no real synthesis, and no real transformation of consciousness.

When the traditional religious cultures are made use of in this way, the result is frequently the reinforcing and sanctioning of some of the worst aspects of the borrowing culture, and, simultaneously, the distortion of the tradition. Eastern meditative practices, for example, require for their full meaning the total religious-social setting of their original culture. Wrenched loose from it and introduced into an alien context, they take on totally different functions and meanings from those originally intended. The Buddhist scholar, Lama Govinda, has described, for instance, the distortions that occur in Zen Buddhism when its practices, and even ideas, are adopted without regard for the total living tradition of complex metaphysical assumptions, social institutions, and life-styles of their original context. Then, he writes, Zen tends to "become an excuse to live as one always did, only giving different labels to the same actions: waywardness will be made into spontaneity, weakness into the principle of nonviolence, laziness into the ideal of nonaction, lack of logic into spiritual profundity, and emotionality into inspiration."[27]

Likewise, there exist certain surface or formal similarities to modern modes of thought in traditional emphases that can be used to lend support and confirmation to the modern Western mind set. The traditional emphasis on the importance of common purpose and communal values, for example, when transposed directly into modern industrial civilization can foster, not the formation of actual communities rooted in time and place, but rather social collectivism and bureaucratic standardization. The Eastern notion of "no self," which in the living tradition is bound up with intense awareness of vast hierarchies of conscious reality extending beyond the immediately empirical, is ripped from context and appealed to as support for behaviorist theories of determinism and denials of selfhood. The universal affirmation in the traditions of man's oneness with nature provides confirmation for naturalistic conceptions of ecology and the doctrine that man is nothing but a higher animal, the total inversion of the vice-regal position accorded to man by tradition. The traditions' methods for personal transformation often are made to blend nicely in a therapeutic culture with a privatized morality and attempts at attitude adjustment that permit the coming to terms with the system without actually having to question it. In this approach the tradition is misused to bolster a mind set that is its very opposite.

The third approach is that of the "ark of salvation." This represents a serious attempt to adopt the total world view and life-style of the tradition, but to do so by abandoning the contemporary world to its own devices, refusing either to engage in the solution of its problems or to recognize within it any ground for hope. The argument usually advanced by those who take this position is that our situation today is, indeed, *in extremis*, that modern civilization is doomed and that the only hope for the future lies in the formation now of enough disciplined counter-cultural communities for some to weather the coming disaster and in the aftermath to have the resources to rebuild civilization anew and on a different foundation. By definition this requires a communal effort for the creation of a protected and undisturbed arena within which the new life-style can be pursued without adulteration. If this total separation is not completely successful, and the pressures in the industrial world against it would appear almost insurmountable, compromises become necessary. These compromises usually demand a falling back on some version or other of the Two-Realm Theory of Truth: a line is drawn between those areas in which the new life-style can be vigorously adhered to, and those in which it is necessary to traffic with the outside world. In such a situation all the problems of the Two-Realm Theory begin to make their appearance.

Even if this approach were fully successful, its desirability is open to serious question. For it to remain intact and in successful operating condition, the ark of salvation requires of all its members stringent communal controls and the curtailing, within well-defined limits, of all individuality and expressions of freedom. There are those who maintain that precisely this is required to counter and correct the modern aberration of an isolated, atomistic individualism. But what does it avail the counter-cultural community, if it succeeds mainly in reinforcing and focusing more intensely the very collectivist forces in modern society that it seeks to escape? And what gain, if its outcome is, ironically, one more controlled experiment in behavioral conditioning?

The main difficulty with the ark of salvation is its tendency to undervalue, if not to reject outright, the potential within modern consciousness itself, for all its aberrations, to strike fresh connections with those dimensions of mind and meaning that have always been the central concern of traditional wisdom. Again and again in the contemporary world examples of effective resistance to tyranny—*vide* the dissidents in every oppressive society—and of the creation of life-giving communal forms come not from those whose individuality has been quashed or never formed, but from those in whom it is most highly developed. Paradoxically, it seems that only the individual who is possessed of a keen sense of authentic selfhood is today capable of freely transcending a narrow personal perspective for the sake of others or, in more traditional terms, of overcoming that self/other divide that has so fractured and fragmented our experience. Paradoxically, the exercise of personal freedom has become the opening in our world for the influx of universal, spiritual values. It is here then, perhaps, that the clue is to be found for another approach, a fourth way, to the recovery of meaning and quality at the heart of things, which the living tradition, not the dead form of tradition, has been concerned to maintain.

Modern consciousness, the "onlooker consciousness" in Barfield's terms, with its individuated sense of self standing detached from the world, at once the possibility of fragmentation and of heightened freedom—this consciousness is not an attitude or outlook that can be changed at will. It is more a form or structure of experience, which, whether we like it or not, is our given; it is our point of departure for whatever undertakings we venture upon. We cannot go around it or get behind it. It is this that many approaches to tradition forget: that those today who take up the traditional teachings do so with a sense of the self and world that is not shared by those with whom the teachings originated. We can, to be sure, seek to dissolve or undo our modern structure of consciousness, but to do so is not to return to a purer state, but to fall back to a lower, more chaotic state. We can continue our way without change, but with a growing awareness that this leads us farther and farther into meaninglessness and fragmentation. Or we can seek a transformation of our ways of knowing as a first step in a transformation of consciousness that, while safeguarding the possibilities for individual freedom and the achievements of modern reason, will recover for them a life-giving wholeness.

It is in the domain of knowledge and cognition that an integral connection with tradition suited to the needs and condition of the present is to be wrought. It is here, for example, that common ground between the radical humanities and traditional concerns begins to appear. Both speak of a kind of knowing that is more than a mere getting and having of information and a doing of something to someone or some object on the basis of that information. Both speak of a knowing that goes beyond accumulation and manipulation to a knowing that is participation and being. Traditional wisdom is redolent of a knowing that comes not from a detached looking on, but from an immediate participation in the known, a kind of indwelling in the surrounding reality of nature and the cosmos, and a knowing which is expressed through myth, symbol, and image. Traditional cultures are full of symbols that serve to sum up and convey the experience of living in a universe in which everything visible is an expression and invocation of the larger reality from which it comes. Modern culture has nearly lost this sense of the living symbol. The classical notion of the symbol as that which participates in the reality it represents has become nearly incomprehensible. The living symbol as a multi-dimensioned and inexhaustible source of new meaning and discovery has been increasingly replaced with the literalistic conception of symbol as mere "sign," something that arbitrarily stands for something else as a label pasted on from without, not as an integral embodiment of it. Hence, the phrase, "just a symbol." We have even tended to impute our own literalism to those whose primary language was symbolic, supposing that their myths and images were only the pre-scientific gropings of a childlike mind.[28] Against this, Nicolas Berdyaev has written, "Every significant myth is connected with reality . . . ,"[29] but it is a reality which must be grasped symbolically.

In its full sense the symbol is an opening to a world of meaning that is exhausted neither by the empirical world of the senses nor the abstract world of the intellect. The symbol reveals the qualitative dimensions of the world in which the human mind participates. To describe this world Henry Corbin has coined the Latin phrase *mundus imaginalis*—the imaginal world, the Imagination.[30] The Imagination is not, therefore, the fictive, the unreal, the imaginary in the conventional sense: it is, on the contrary, the most real of worlds. In traditional terms, Imagination is the world of mind and spirit. Knowledge that has its source in this world is not subject to personal whim, wishful thinking, or daydreams. It is a knowledge, writes Kathleen Raine, poet and scholar of the understanding of Imagination in the Western Platonic tradition, which is "no less exact, no less extensive, structured, and objective than the laws of nature," it is "knowledge of man's inner world." And because this inner world, when contact with its innermost recesses is made, turns out to open into a world of universal meaning, the Imagination has concrete implications for all of life. Having lost our roots in the Imagination, Dr. Raine argues, our age is hard put to recognize the differences between the significant and the meaningless, and even has lost an understanding of the pathological. "Our age," she writes, "can gape at the great works of the past—megalithic circles, the pyramids, the Parthenon, Chartres, the Alhambra, or comparable works of poetry, music, or painting. But with our vast technical skill we ourselves do not possess the knowledge to create such works; for that knowledge was a spiritual knowledge."[31] The Imagination is the bridge between individual consciousness and a world of living meaning.

It is here that the radical humanities in their concern for the integrity of language and the traditional wisdom find common ground, for words in their primary nature are symbolic. The devaluation and degeneration of the symbolic has also been accompanied by an increasing disintegration of words. Increasingly, the meaning contained in words is regarded not as having a reality and integrity of its own, but as something arbitrary and determined solely by the function of words for particular, utilitarian purposes: by their place in the sentence or larger linguistic system or by their effectiveness as mere signs or pointers for moving other things around. Rather than being recognized as a constant source—perhaps the only remaining source—of new meaning in our world, the symbolic richness of words is denigrated in philosophy as a cause of unwanted confusion, an obstacle to unambiguous technical proficiency, and as something to be eliminated (through "analysis and clarification"). "Language," writes Jacques Ellul, "is losing its mystery, its magic, its incomprehensibility. It no longer expresses dreams. Or rather, by being technologically deciphered, language becomes a way of bringing dreams, inspirations, aspirations, and ecstasies into the technological environment."[32] In other words, as language disintegrates, as it becomes solely the carrier of single meanings assigned to it by its utilitarian functions, it loses its essential character. It serves less and less as a symbolic disclosure of meaning that is manifold and real in itself. Recall Owen Barfield's observation that the disintegration of the richness of language is part and parcel of the tendency to think that there really is no such thing as quality as an objective as well as subjective reality.

One crucial way to recover the reality of qualities and meaning, Barfield suggests, is by attending to the actual meanings and changing meanings of words. This he calls the "contemplative study of words" as distinguished from the usual scholarly analysis of language which focuses not so much on the meanings as on the grammar, syntax, and structure of the utilitarian function of language. Important for certain purposes, when it becomes the sole approach to the understanding of language, linguistic analysis tends more and more, as Ellul remarks, "to reduce human language to a certain number of structures, functions, and mechanisms giving us the impression that we now understand this strange and mysterious phenomenon better than before."[33] But in the process language is stripped of its inner essence as the revealer of the qualitatively new and real.

Barfield does not propose a contemplative approach in place of linguistic analysis but as the latter's necessary foundation and complement. The phrase "the contemplative study of words" suggests an orientation of open, active receptiveness to the new meanings and new possibilities in our situation that language in its richness alone can disclose. Without this we are shut in upon ourselves. The contemplative study of words can show us that "the words I speak have meanings that I did not originate," that words can reveal a larger reality beyond the merely quantitative, that words, in short, are to qualities what numbers are to quantities. It can reveal to us anew that the integrity of language is intimately bound up with the integrity and possibility of a truly human existence. Erwin Chargaff gives expression to the contemplative orientation of language when he writes, "I suffer from logophilia: I love little words and have a deep pity for them when they are mistreated. I consider them one of the greatest wonders of the world, these thought-creators, these crystalline tears and peals. They are the last witnesses of the Creation, the only tokens of a humanity that is disappearing fast."[34]

The recovery of the symbolic nature of words would make us aware that, as Barfield writes, "it is in the very nature of words that they use the material to name the immaterial, the phenomenal to name the noumenal—and indeed the numinous." We could begin to grasp once more why respect for language and respect for the human being and for nature are all inseparably interwoven. We could begin, as Barfield says, "to dispel the almost universal assumption that thinking is a function of the physical brain."[35] Human beings, writes William Barrett, "could begin to talk because they were already within language. Meanings are first and foremost not in the mind [merely as a self-enclosed entity], but in the world, in the linkings and interconnections of things we find there."[36] The recovery of language in this sense would make it possible to see qualities and meaning as rooted objectively in that immaterial reality to which words in their fullest can provide access. It would permit a recovery of the creative reality of the Imagination.

Here, in the Imagination, modern consciousness, the radical humanities, and traditional wisdom have a common meeting ground, and the possibility for engagement with one another that can be integral and mutually enlivening. Is it possible that similar ground also exists within modern science?

Notes

1. See the bibliographic essay for works dealing with the evolution of consciousness.

2. George Steiner, *In Bluebeard's Castle: Some Notes toward the Redefinition of Culture* (New Haven, Conn.: Yale University Press, 1971), pp. 77-78.

3. John Lukacs, *The Passing of the Modern Age* (New York: Harper & Row, 1970), pp. 117-18.

4. Huston Smith, "Flakes of Fire, Handfuls of Light: The Humanities as Uncontrolled Experiment," *Teachers College Record*, vol. 82, no. 2 (Winter 1980), 191.

5. Michael I. Sovern, "Inaugural Address," mimeographed (New York: Columbia University, September 28, 1980), p. 7.

6. E. F. Schumacher, *Small Is Beautiful: Economics as if People Mattered* (New York: Harper Torchbooks, 1973), pp. 79-80.

7. J. Robert Nelson, *Science and Our Troubled Conscience* (Philadelphia: Fortress Press, 1980), p. 21.

8. Wendell Berry, "Standing by Words," *The Hudson Review* (Winter 1980-1981), 489.

9. These are examples that Ellul gives, and I have let them stand not because they are extreme, but because they are so typical as to be commonplace in the "professional" literature. The professional education literature is an especially rich source of debased language. Jacques Ellul, *The Technological System* (New York: Continuum, 1980), pp. 49-50.

10. Berry, "Standing by Words," p. 494.

11. Erwin Chargaff, "Knowledge without Wisdom," *Harpers* (May 1980), 48.

12. Manfred Stanley, *The Technological Conscience, Survival and Dignity in an Age of Expertise* (Chicago: University of Chicago Press, 1978), p. 205.

13. I have here used Nelson's formulation of Ferkiss's principles. See Nelson, *Science and Our Troubled Conscience*, pp. 23-24; and Victor C. Ferkiss, *Technological Man* (New York: New American Library, 1969).

14. Ellul, *The Technological System*, p. 204.

15. Jonathan Swift, *Gullivers' Travels* (Everymans Library, 1961), p. 189.

16. Jacques Ellul, *The Betrayal of the West* (New York: Seabury Press, 1978), p. 154.

17. C. S. Lewis, *Surprised by Joy* (New York: Harcourt, Brace, 1955), pp. 207-8.

18. Robert N. Bellah, "Cultural Vision and the Human Future," *Teachers College Record*, vol. 82, no. 3 (Spring 1981), 497.

19. Huston Smith, *Forgotten Truth: The Primordial Tradition* (New York: Harper Colophon Books, 1976), p. ix. See also Huston Smith, *The Religions of Man* (New York: Harper & Row, 1958). See also Jacob Needleman, *Consciousness and Tradition* (New York: Crossroad, 1982).

20. Gai Eaton, *King of the Castle: Choice and Responsibility in the Modern World* (London: Bodley Head, 1977).

21. Ibid., p. 126. See also Frithjof Schuon, *Light on the Ancient Worlds* (London: Perennial Books, 1965), especially Chapter 4, "The Shamanism of the Red Indians."

22. From a letter released by the United States government as part of the bicentenary celebration. Reprinted in *Studies in Comparative Religion* (1977), pp. 187-89. See also Catherine Roberts, *Science, Animals, and Evolution* (Westport, Conn.: Greenwood Press, 1980).

23. Werner Heisenberg, *Across the Frontiers* (New York: Harper & Row, 1974), pp. 203-4.

24. Catherine Roberts, *The Scientific Conscience* (New York: George Braziller, 1967), p. 10.

25. Heisenberg, *Across the Frontiers*, pp. 219-20.

26. Owen Barfield, *Saving the Appearances: A Study in Idolatry* (New York: Harcourt, Brace and World, n.d.); Charles Davy, *Towards a Third Culture* (Edinburgh: Floris Books, 1978; Faber and Faber Ltd., 1961).

27. Lama Anagarika Govinda, *Creative Meditation and Multi-Dimensional Consciousness* (Wheaton, Ill.: The Theosophical Publishing House, 1976), p. 217.

28. See Eaton, *King of the Castle*, p. 166.

29. Nicolas Berdyaev, *The Divine and the Human* (London: Geoffrey Bles, 1949), p. 134.

30. Henry Corbin, "*Mundus Imaginalis* or The Imaginary and the Imaginal," *Spring; An Annual of Archetypal Psychology and Jungian Thought* (1972), 1-19.

31. Kathleen Raine, "Towards a Living Universe," *Teachers College Record*, vol. 82, no. 3 (Spring 1981), 459.

32. Ellul, *The Technological System*, p. 49.

33. Ibid.

34. Erwin Chargaff, *Heraclitean Fire: Sketches of a Life before Nature* (New York: Rockefeller Press, 1978), p. 203.

35. Owen Barfield, "Language, Evolution of Consciousness, and the Recovery of Human Meaning," *Teachers College Record*, vol. 82, no. 3 (Spring 1981), 433.

36. William Barrett, *The Illusion of Technique* (Garden City, N.Y.: Anchor Press, Doubleday, 1978), p. 170.

3
Toward the Recovery of Wholeness: Another Look at Science

Earlier the statement was made that current scientistic world views appear increasingly to be based on a science of yesteryear. Since at least the beginning of the twentieth century, much has happened within science that calls into question the exclusively reductionistic, mechanistic, and objectivistic understanding of reality that nineteenth-century scientific assumptions seemed in so many ways to support. Increasingly in this century, the data generated in scientific inquiry, the interpretive frameworks employed to make sense of the data, and the understanding by scientists of their own methods of inquiry have all become less and less congenial to a world view reared exclusively on a positivistic foundation.

Those at the highest levels of scientific inquiry—those few most responsible for the major insights and reformulations of modern scientific understanding—have often been the most articulate in pointing out the untenability of most of the premises from which positivism has derived its support. It does seem to be the case, however, that at nearly every other level, among both scientists and laymen, reductionistic, mechanistic modes of thinking remain strong and even continue to extend their sway. Nevertheless, deep cracks have begun to appear in the underpinnings of the dominant scientistic world view, as its support within modern science itself has begun at crucial points to slip away. In many of its central developments, both in the interpretation of its findings and in its understanding of its own methods of inquiry, modern science and a positivistic scientism appear increasingly incompatible.

Intimations of a Holistic View of Reality

The Ethical Foundations of Science

A contradiction, sometimes noted, more often overlooked, has long characterized discussion of the relationship between science and technology and ethics. On the one hand, it has been maintained that science and technology are morally neutral, and that when and if moral issues do arise, it is society, not science, that is responsible for dealing with them. On the other hand, it has been customary, and often among those who simultaneously make the first claim, to extoll the moral qualities demanded of the scientists: a devotion to truth, impeccable honesty, respect for the evidence, and so forth. Obviously the two claims are incompatible, and many thoughtful scientists such as Jacob Bronowski and Michael Polanyi have long argued that not only is the value neutrality of science an illusion, but that the pursuit of science is, in Polanyi's terms, an "intensely personal act" that demands deep moral commitment.[1]

Both Polanyi and Bronowski have spelled out the ethical foundations on which science as an inquiry into reality must rest. Without a devotion to truth, science would not be possible (though this does not hold true in the same way of technology, or of science understood as technological). And with devotion to truth, other moral qualities and commitments are also demanded. Without fidelity to others, a commitment to tell the truth, and the willingness to trust the word of others, the building of a scientific community, within which the sharing of information and the weighing and evaluation of experiment and interpretation and mutual criticism can take place, would be impossible.[2] Without a sense of personal responsibility and integrity scientific objectivity would be impossible. Objectivity in this sense involves neither the false detachment of the onlooker attitude toward a world thought to have no integral relations to the knower, nor the illusion of value-free inquiry. Rather it requires a deep interest—a personal involvement—in the subject at hand, and a desire to know and to communicate as clearly and comprehensively as possible what in one's best lights can be known of that subject. True scientific objectivity thus stems from an intensive sense of personal responsibility, a moral commitment, that requires and makes possible a vigilance against the intrusion of wishful thinking, narrow perspectives, false interpretations, and personal interests that would merely use the subject at hand without respect for its integrity. Further, it follows that science is possible only where the highest premium is placed on individual freedom and responsibility, and on the right of individual dissent. The values that make science possible have wide-reaching social implications.

Many spokesmen for science, like John Dewey, who long ago rejected the notion of a value-free science, have frequently written in such a way as to imply that science has a monopoly on such value commitments as devotion to truth, freedom of inquiry, personal responsibility, and objectivity. But, obviously, this is an inflated claim. Science has no monopoly on these; indeed, difficult as they may be to realize fully, they are, from one perspective, very "modest" virtues, in that we would expect them of any decent person. At the same time they are momentously important, and without them science would not even be possible. "If these values did not exist," writes Bronowski, "then the society of scientists would have to invent them to make the practice of science possible. In societies where these values did not exist, science has had to create them."[3]

The full significance of this, however, has not always been made clear. Even if it embraces no more than an investigation of the quantitative dimensions of the physical universe, scientific inquiry is grounded for its possibility in a qualitative, value-laden, ideal foundation. The ethical foundation of science is prior and primary to the pursuit of science. The irony of the scientistic world view of a meaningless universe of quantitative objects denies the foundations on which the possibility of scientific inquiry rests. Herein lies the tragedy of many scientists today who have been concerned about the many problems that threaten the earth: there is no grounding in the dominant scientistic world view for their own commitments as scientists or for their own highest ideals as to how science ought to be used.

Here, perhaps, what appears at first glance to be an anomaly can be seen on further consideration to be something of crucial significance. Among some of the clearest and most effective voices being raised in defense of the responsible uses of science, and against the destructive course on which mankind is set, are those of a small but growing number of scientists. It is the natural scientists, such as the late Rachel Carson, Barry Commoner, the late E. F. Schumacher, and Amory and Hunter Lovins, who have made us most aware of the urgency of our environmental and ecological crisis, and who have pointed the way to a meaningful response. It is the small group of physicians and nuclear physicists of the Committee for a Sane Nuclear Policy (SANE) and of Physicians for Social Responsibility who are reminding us most vividly, at a moment when politicians and the military are talking about "winnable nuclear war," that such war would make the continued existence of human beings, and probably of all life on earth, impossible. It is a few biologists, George Wald, Jonathan King, Erwin Chargaff, Robert Sinsheimer, and a handful of others who alone, against our most prestigious universities and even the Supreme Court, continue to call our attention to the unresolved issues in genetic engineering. It is a small number of physicians, such as Henry Beecher, Bernhard N. Nathanson, Robert Mendlesohn, and others, who despite opposition from their own profession, have been most active in raising the ethical issues of medical experimentation, human values in medical practice, and the problems generated by professional entrenchment and obduracy. Humanists have long criticized physicalist and mechanistic philosophies, but for the most part they have held back from following through the implications of their criticisms for actual scientific research. They have been content mainly to counter the naive literalism of a narrow scientism with an ineffectual, subjective idealism of the humanities. What a small number of scientists may be beginning to make real is the bearing of their own ethical commitments in science on the uses and expressions of science.[4]

In the preface to his *Science and Human Values*, Bronowski remarks that were he to write the book again he would give more attention to those values which he says, "are not generated by the practice of science—the values of tenderness, of kindliness, of human intimacy and love."[5] It is not clear from the brevity of his comment how closely Bronowski considers these other values also to be integrally related to science. A moment's reflection, however, makes apparent how important such values are to the human uses of science, and that their absence is a guarantee of an inhuman use, or misuse, of science. Perhaps it is this that the ethical critics within science are beginning to realize. And, perhaps, they are pointing still further to an affirmation that the values of love, compassion, and tenderness also have—just as we have seen personal interest, integrity, and fidelity to have—cognitive power. If respect for the other, for that or the one to be known, is essential to true knowledge, even on the purely quantitative level, do not love, compassion, and fidelity have the possibility of making us receptive to further revelations of the other in the dimension of quality? In any event, it suffices at this point merely to underscore that the priority of qualitative, personal commitments as the foundation and possibility of all science directly contradicts the assertions of a narrow, positivistic, mechanistic naturalism. In the primacy of the ethical foundations of all science, it becomes clear that moral development is essential to a complete scientific education (if not—and we leave this open—to technological training). On this, the radical humanists, the traditional wisdom, and science share a common concern and point of departure.

Participatory Knowing

The twentieth-century revolution in physics posed a fundamental challenge to two axiomatic conceptions of science: the mechanistic, particulate conception of matter and the notion of an objective scientific observer uninvolved in the nature he was describing. The significance of this revolution has yet to be digested, and its implications are matters of contention. Furthermore, the older habits of thinking remain strong and mixed in with the newer scientific conceptions and models of reality. For both reasons great caution is needed in exploring the implications of the new science.

By the middle of the 1920s it had become apparent to leading scientists that the older conception of reality—the dominant conception from the fifteenth through the nineteenth century—was no longer adequate. The notion of reality composed of separately existent and irreducible bits of matter, "ultimate particles," moving about in empty space, related to one another in mechanistic fashion, and serving as the fundamental building blocks of the universe, had given way to a world of hidden forces, surging energies, and infinitely complex relationships of interaction and interdependence. A world of dynamic energies and interrelationships had come to replace the static, mechanistic world. Actually, as Werner Heisenberg has observed, as scientists began to grapple with the phenomena of electricity early in the nineteenth century, they had already found themselves plunged into a hidden world of dynamic, powerful energies for which mechanistic, building-block conceptions were proving less and less useful. The discovery of the undulatory, wavelike aspects of matter, and the necessity to think of electrons as paradoxically both particles and waves, and even in the case of other microentities as being like waves, particles, and forces, fully undercut the old imagery and models. Even space and time, with the conception of a unified space-time continuum, began to lose their absolute, unchanging character.

In place of a fixed, stable, and relatively simple world of matter, there emerged, in David Bohm's phrase, "the infinite qualitative variety of nature," a nature which, Bohm comments, seems to have in it "an infinity of different kinds of things, . . . an unlimited variety of . . . properties, qualities, entities, systems, levels, etc., to which apply correspondingly new kinds of laws of nature."[6] The history of physics in the twentieth century has been that of a search for an adequate understanding of this new world, as well as the gaining of increased capacity to unleash its forces, even when full understanding has been lacking.

Both Einstein's theory of relativity and quantum theory, Bohm has argued, challenge the mechanistic order and imply that the entire universe is not primarily a composite of ultimate particles, but rather an "unbroken whole." The particular elements are themselves abstractions, often very useful and powerful abstractions, from an "undivided wholeness," that is itself their ground and the prerequisite for their understanding. Relativity theory, Bohm points out, while demanding a more unified, flowing conception of reality, is still basically compatible with notions of mechanistic causation and interaction. Quantum theory, however, posed a much more direct challenge to the mechanistic order, for it shows that movement is discontinuous, that entities such as electrons have both wavelike, particlelike properties, and that they interact in non-causal, non-local ways that violate "the requirements of separateness and independence of fundamental constituents . . . basic to any mechanistic approach." The awareness of the radicality of the challenge, Bohm notes, has still to be adequately assimilated by physicists, who continue to retain mechanistic conceptions in much of their thinking. Nevertheless, the fundamental change in modern physics has been toward a conception of the world to be conceived primarily in terms of flowing energy patterns, systemic wholeness, and mutual interaction and interdependence.[7]

With this changing conception of reality, and in fact intimately bound up with it, has come a revolution in thinking about the relations between the knower and the known. In sub-atomic physics the conception of an objective world separated fully from the human being as detached observer has disappeared. In the debates of the 1920s as to whether matter was wavelike or particlelike Heisenberg established that we only know the sub-atomic world in connection with our theories about it and the experimental consequences of those theories. Even our own act of observation is an intervention so that the experimental results do not describe nature apart from our involvement with nature. The physicist John Wheeler has described what is involved in these words:

> The quantum principle has demolished the once-held view that the universe sits safely "out there," that we can observe what goes on in it from behind a foot-thick slab of plate glass without

ourselves being involved in what goes on. We have learned that to observe even so miniscule an object as an electron we have to shatter that slab of glass. We have to reach out and insert a measuring device. We can install a device to measure position or insert a device to measure momentum; but the installation of the one prevents the insertion of the other. We ourselves have to decide which it is that we will do. Whichever it is, it has an unpredictable effect on the future of that electron, and to that degree the future of the universe is changed. We changed it. We have to cross out that old word "observer" and replace it by the new word "participator." In some strange sense the quantum principle tells us that we are dealing with a participatory universe.[8]

And Heisenberg himself writes: "Natural science does not simply describe and explain nature; it is a part of the interplay between nature and ourselves; it describes nature as exposed to our way of questioning."[9] At this all important point, the dualisms, set forth philosophically by Descartes in the seventeenth century, between mind and matter, subject and object, the knower and the known, have begun to collapse.

Lest it be thought that this awareness of knowing as participatory has importance only for the world of sub-atomic physics, let it be remembered that there exists almost total agreement among psychologists and philosophers that our recognition of objects and events in the everyday world around us is shaped by our ideas as much as by our sensations. There is not pure perception (not, at least, in our ordinary experience). Our ideas, feelings, bodily states, and concepts all combine with our sensations of sight, touch, and hearing to produce the world of objects we recognize. It has been reported, for example, that persons blind from birth, who have gained their sight in adult life through surgery, have often had great difficulty in making sense of the strange, confusing patches of color and light with which they have suddenly found themselves confronted. Only after a long, laborious effort of developing appropriate mental concepts and associations were they able to achieve a sense of distance and the power to recognize and discriminate among objects that most people acquire in growing up.[10] "On almost every received theory of perception," writes Owen Barfield, "the familiar world—that is, the world which is apprehended, not through instruments and inference but simply—is for the most part dependent upon the percipient."[11] There are, to be sure, as Barfield's statement implies, important differences between the familiar world and the strange world revealed by physics. The one is live, rich, imprecise; the participation is more immediate. The other is abstract, quantitative, removed; the participation is through the theories, the instruments, and the conceptual models of the scientist, though it should never be forgotten, as Polanyi and others have shown, that these also express the values, feelings, outlook, and imagination of the scientist. The differences between the two worlds is important and must be taken into account. But the important point to be stressed here is that the awareness that in science there can be no description of a world separate from and influenced by the observer removed, once and for all, that distinction between personal knowing, on the one hand, and an objective, and by virtue of that, purer scientific way of knowing on the other.

The inability of science to describe an "objective reality" in itself has, however, given rise to two contending interpretations of what science is. One is what has been called the instrumental or operational conception of science. "According to this view," as it is succinctly described by Charles Davy, "a scientific theory is simply a set of concepts which brings a series of observations into rational order and is considered valid (for the time being) if it successfully *predicts*. It can then be presumed to correspond to some order or pattern in nature, but it does not and need not tell us what the pattern is, so to speak, made of. To ask what matter 'is,' is meaningless."[12] All our knowledge is entirely bound up with the products of our own minds, with our theories, instruments, and the experimental situation devised by our minds, and there is no going beyond these. In this view, the mathematical formulations and conceptual models are in themselves purely formal, having no intrinsic meaning other than their own internal coherence and the order they allow us to impose on the data obtained from our instrument readings. Because these formal constructs correspond in some way or other, we know not how, with the powers hidden in nature, they may be extremely useful in releasing and manipulating those powers, but they have no larger significance beyond their practical context. The criterion of truth, in this view, is either the satisfaction of aesthetic elegance, a purely internal criterion, or of prediction and control, a pragmatic and instrumental test of truth; anything else is considered metaphysical and nonsensical.[13]

The instrumental is the dominant conception of science in the world today, and it is, therefore, extremely important to see clearly what it involves. First, while it stresses that there is no knowledge that does not involve the knower actively, it does not disturb the basic dualisms that have characterized modern thought. The only difference is that the dualism is now not between subjective and objective knowledge, but between the unavoidable subjectivity of all human knowing and a world outside that is objective in the sense that it can never be known. The dualism, rather than being overcome, is heightened, and an agnostic, if not totally cynical, attitude toward truth is engendered. The test of truth is prediction and control; the test of truth is power and might.

Second, because, from the instrumental viewpoint, we can have no knowledge of nature in her own right, she can make no claims upon us. We are free to do with her as we can and will (not knowing, of course, what we really do).

Third, the instrumental conception of science dissolves the distinction between science and technology. In fact it reduces science to technology.

Fourth, science as technology makes it possible to retain the primacy of mechanistic, reductionist ways of thinking, while at the same time taking the "revolution in physics," and its extension to other areas, into account. Reductionism and mechanism have, after all, proved themselves the most effective of all approaches for technique and technology, and scientific theory can offer no context for their guidance and restraint because it has itself been divested of all but formal and instrumental significance. Any check upon technical application that a concern for truth in scientific theory might have exerted has been eliminated. Thus, scientific discoveries and concepts that are thought by some to challenge the mechanistic order are instead hauled into its service.

Finally, it bears repeating, science as technology is particularly susceptible to control by powerful, vested social interests. Science becomes the uncritical servant of those political, economic, and military interests that have reasons to manipulate and control and the means to support those who can show them how. A purely instrumental science also is defenseless against, in fact it invites, the incursion into its ranks of personalities for whom, in Charles Davy's words, "power and adventure and discovery are more important than any visions of beauty, justice and love in human relationships [and, he might well have added, responsibility to the demands of the search for truth]."[14] At the same time, it is to the advantage of those social interests that control technological science to foster the illusion among the public that the thought-models of science, which, for the sophisticated scientist of the instrumental persuasion, serve only as "useful fictions," are indeed objective, literal descriptions of the world. Potential criticism of the uses of science are thereby deflected or defused by public acceptance of the notion that science is a value-free presentation of reality, and that only the ignorant would question it in any way. Scientistic world views thus come more and more to resemble nothing so much as those religious and political thought systems that throughout history have served to justify and bolster the claims of certain interests in society to special privilege and position.

Fortunately, we have been exploring the logical tendencies of only one interpretation of modern science. There is another approach, one which as yet is held in its various versions by only a minority of scientists, but their members are growing, and among them are to be included some of the leading scientific figures of our time. This approach takes as its point of departure, as does the instrumental view, that our knowledge is a participatory knowledge, a knowledge that describes nature not as detached from us, but as, in Heisenberg's word, in "interplay" with us. But it does not draw the cynical agnostic conclusion from this, as does the purely instrumental approach, that we can therefore never know nature or the things as they are in themselves, because it affirms that the essence of the things themselves is their intelligibility. Any genuine knowledge would by definition have to be participatory and a joining together in interplay of the knower and the known. In this view, knowing is the intelligibility of the human mind discovering and entering into the intelligibility of the universe. Our minds can have knowledge of reality because reality is mindlike.

This view denies the ultimate dichotomy or dualism between intelligibility and being or, in more traditional language, between form and being, structure and substance, mind and matter. The unity of the theoretical and empirical, of the concept and percept, in the act of knowing corresponds with the unity of intelligibility and being in reality itself. The dualisms are, in this view, genuinely overcome. The human being stands within a universe that is infinitely intelligible. Because the human mind can open itself to the intelligibility of the universe, genuine knowledge is possible. Because thie intelligibility is infinite and transcends any one particular human perspective, all human knowing must constantly be checked, subjected to criticism, qualified, and revised as other perspectives come into view. There is no warrant in this understanding for claiming that human knowledge is ever final and fixed, encased in forms immune from further development. There is no grounds for dogmatic certainty; but neither is there for any kind of skeptical nihilism or any evasion of responsibility to the demands of truth.

Modern science thus understood has begun to disclose a multileveled universe of structure and meaning. Michael Polanyi in particular has devoted much attention to this aspect of modern science. There is, as Polanyi argues, a hierarchical structure of human knowledge and a related hierarchical structure of reality. Most simply there is a hierarchy of levels embracing the inanimate, the vegetative, the sentient and conscious, and reaching in the human being to the ethical-ideal. Likewise, there exist corresponding levels in the structure of human knowledge embracing physics and chemistry, biology, technology, sociology, and the humanities (and there are hierarchical distinctions to be made within these). What is important in this hierarchy of hierarchies, Polanyi stresses, is the way each level is related to those above and below. Each level is open upward and enters into ever wider and more all-embracing relationships with higher levels and systems of levels. Each level, however, also possesses its own relative autonomy and validity and is not reducible downward; that is, it cannot be fully explained in terms of the theories pertaining to levels below it. Each level imposes restrictions on the level above, but does not completely determine nor provide grounds for fully explaining it. At the same time the lower is open to the higher and is brought under its control.[15]

This realization of the hierarchical interrelationships of knowledge and reality carries with it two momentous consequences, both of which we have touched upon. In the first place, it means that reductionism cannot serve within science itself as the ultimate principle of explanation or method of inquiry. The phenomena studied by history interact with those studied by sociology, but neither can be reduced to the other. The phenomena of culture described by sociology are certainly affected by the biological demands of human beings, but also have their own meaning which can never be explained completely by biology (nor by economics—nor sociology itself since these cultural phenomena manifest levels of meaning not exhausted by the concepts of sociology). The history of sculpture is not the same as the history of the geology or chemistry of marble. The two interact at crucial points, and the sculptor must have some knowledge of the physical properties and behavior of marble, but by no stretch of the imagination can the history of sculpture be rendered in terms of physical science—just as no geologist, unless he or she is also avocationally a sculptor, can ever bring forth an aesthetic form from a marble block. Physics, chemistry, and biology do not provide explanations of human being and human achievement. Or, to take one more example from Polanyi, the organic processes of living creatures depend on the laws of physics and chemistry, but introduce a higher order of complexity that cannot be explained by the principles of the lower level. "The regulative powers of living beings and their mental powers of comprehension . . . ," Polanyi writes, "both embody principles not manifest in the realm of inanimate nature."[16]

As methods of inquiry, however, reductionism and mechanistic modes of explanation also possess their own relative autonomy and validity in this view. They are not abolished, as some critics of science would demand, but they are placed within an awareness of the larger whole which gives to them their direction and purpose.

And this points to the second consequence of the recognition of the multi-leveled structure of reality. Each successive level is wider, richer, more comprehensive and complex, more meaningful, and less tangible than the lower, which the higher nevertheless to some extent reorders and controls. It seems inescapable that in a very important sense the intangible and the unmanifest are more real than the tangible and manifest. "All meaning," writes Polanyi, "lies in higher levels of reality that are not reducible to the laws by which the ultimate particulars of the universe are controlled. . . . What is most tangible has the least meaning and it is perverse to identify the tangible with the real. For to regard a meaningless substratum as the ultimate reality of all things must lead to the conclusion that all things are meaningless. And we can avoid this conclusion only if we acknowledge instead that the deepest reality is possessed by higher things that are least tangible."[17] In this we approach what we have already seen with respect to the importance of language in which words, the phenomenal, present the meaningful, the intangible. Here the radical humanities and the implications of modern science edge very close together.

Or we can grasp what is at issue from another vantage when we reflect on our own experience as knowing and acting persons. We always know more, Polanyi has endeavored to demonstrate throughout his work, than we can ever say at any moment. The manifest utterance or the visible writing draws upon and brings to expression aspects of a more comprehensive and invisible matrix of meaning which imparts to the words whatever reality and significance they possess.[18] And the choices and acts by which we give shape to our lives represent a striving for that which exists potentially, but that very potentiality possesses the power and reality to bring forth something new. The psychologist David Bakan writes:

> The self-definitional activity of man, in substance and in concept, is his most abiding characteristic beyond any specific definition of him; and both the scientific and the religious enterprises are expressions of this self-definitional activity. *This impulse presupposes that the manifest is but the barest hint of reality, that beyond the manifest there exist the major portions of reality, and that the function*

of the impulse is to reach out toward the unmanifest. . . . No matter
how far our explorations go, and no matter how much we manage
to uncover, there is always the infinite world of the unmanifest.[19]

If, in our earlier terms, knowledge of the universe is possible to
the human mind because the universe itself is mindlike, that in
the universe which is most mindlike is also the most real.

There is a third consequence of the participatory understanding, but one that has yet to be grasped and developed in its full
implications. This is the recognition that the human being is the
clue to an adequate knowledge of the other orders of existence.
The human being is that part of the world that we know most
intimately, and it is a delusion to think that we can know something beyond us better than we know ourselves. Moreover, and
just as important, the totality of the human being includes all
the other dimensions of nature and is, therefore, our principal
source of a full understanding of nature.

The lower levels of existence not only cannot provide a complete explanation of the higher, which are irreducible to the
lower, but are themselves included within the higher, subject
to the control of the higher, and finally to be understood fully
only in the light of the higher. The higher is richer, more complex, and more inclusive than the lower. Vegatative life reveals
dimensions of reality not contained in inanimate matter; and
sentient, conscious animals manifest capacities and qualities
lacking in the plant world. The human being contains all the
others, along with the uniquely human quality of conscious existence capable of reflecting upon itself and knowing both itself
and all else that it contains. "Just as the plant," writes Alan
Howard, "though one with the mineral substance out of which
it grew, became something entirely different by virtue of the life
in it; and just as the animal, though it is also living mineral
substance from the same source as the plant, became something
different by virtue of sentience; so man, though he too is a living,
sentient, physical being like the animal, is different from all
animals by virtue of what is human in him. It is this that makes
man MAN, not his animal origin."[20] And it is this that also makes
MAN the regulative principle and source for our knowledge of
the world. "The living world," writes Walter J. Ong, "and more

specifically the human world, is ultimately the measure of the mechanical, and not vice-versa."[21] Within the human being is unfolded the richest potentialities of all the domains of nature, which are themselves taken up and transformed by the distinctively human. Any understanding of nature that does not make the human being and human experience central is to that extent deficient.

It is from this perspective that the biochemist Charles Birch speaks of the necessity for science to take seriously the human meaning of the universe. "A universe that produces humans," says Birch,

> cannot be known apart from this fact. It is a *humiverse* [emphasis added]. We only begin to know what it is by what it becomes. We do not start with electrons and atoms and build a universe. We start with humanity and interpret the rest in terms of this starting point. In the same way we know more about an oak tree by studying the tree and how it has become a tree from an acorn, than we can learn by confining our studies to the acorn.[22]

Birch's concept of a humiverse suggests an opening wedge within science for a recognition of the cognitive significance of the traditional vision of man as viceroy, as well as for the incorporation of the moral dimensions of his viceregal responsibility.

It also suggests the need for a reappraisal of orthodox evolutionary theory. As it now stands the neo-Darwinian theory of evolutionary change represents the ultimate extension of reductionist, mechanistic thinking. According to it, all life originates in inanimate matter, develops into the single cell, and through the agencies of chance variation, natural selection, and survival of the fittest, evolves into more complicated living organisms that eventually become ever more complex, differentiate, and develop into plants, animals, and finally man himself. All of the infinite variety of life, as well as the macro-phenomena of life itself and of conscious and self-conscious life, are accounted for as the outgrowth of chance combinations among the micro-elements of the cell, which in turn are explained according to the physical and chemical laws of inanimate matter. This is reductionism with a vengeance. The higher orders of existence are simply collapsed into the lower. Such a theory has no way of talking about mind or life other than by the question-begging assertion that these represent greater complexity in organization and structure of the underlying physicochemical units.

Increasingly, many scientists who recognize the distinctiveness of life and of consciousness and the inability to explain them in terms of lower-level theories speak of genuine "emergence" to affirm the irreducibility of the higher, but refrain from specifying further whether emergence means the inexplicable appearance of something utterly new or the manifestation in new forms of something present from the beginning. In effect, they hedge, and inconsistently hold to a strict dualism between mind and matter. To the extent that they give equal weight to both, this represents an advance over previous mechanistic reductionism, but it is also logically problematic. And in the end it seems to do little to deter scientists in their actual experimental theory and practice, as well as the philosophers who build upon them, from treating all the phenomena of macro-evolution and of conscious experience as ultimately still the outcome of material micro-constituents. In effect, talk of emergence provides a kind of escape hatch that seems to make it possible to talk about new phenomena without changing one's basic theories and assumptions.

We can leave aside for the moment the problems posed to the neo-Darwinian theory of evolution by the paleontological evidence (or lack of it), except to note in passing the comment of Professor W. R. Thompson, FRS, director of the Commonwealth Institute of Biological Control, Ottawa, in his critical introduction to the Everyman edition of the *Origin of Species*. "There is a great divergence," writes Thompson, "among biologists about the causes and processes of evolution which arises out of the lack of adequate evidence and this should be made known to the non-scientific world."[23] The issue of main concern here, however, is that Darwinian theory on its own grounds has no alternative but to regard life in terms of mechanism, and consciousness, qualitative experience, and meaning as epiphenomena of lower-level orders of existence. It has no way of recognizing and accounting for the uniqueness and richness of the human being and of human experience.[24]

Polanyi remarks on this state of affairs: "It is the height of intellectual perversion to renounce, in the name of scientific objectivity, our position as the highest form of life on earth, and our own advent by a process of evolution as the most important problem of evolution."[25] In discussing evolution, Polanyi himself does not always appear to be consistent and at times uses language that still seems to assume the emergence of consciousness from a once mindless and dead universe. Nevertheless, Polanyi also seems always aware of the dilemma facing the view that mind emerges from matter, and suggests that if we must persist in language of this kind, our conception of matter itself must undergo radical transformation. "A belief in the gradual emergence of man from an inanimate universe reveals to us," he writes, "that the dead matter of our origins was fraught with meaning far beyond all that we are presently able to see in it. To set aside an achievement as full of meaning as this—as if an emergence of this sort could happen any day by mere accident—is to block the normal sources of inquisitive thought."[26] We not only confront here an unresolved contradiction in the premises of materialism, Polanyi seems to be saying, but to allow it to stand as unimportant or to ignore it as unamenable to the accepted modes of explanation, is an act of anti-intellectualism which would suppress the central conundrum of the modern world view.

The contradiction at the heart of evolutionary reductionism is that it cannot deal with the main affirmation of the participatory view of knowledge, which in attenuated form even instrumental science accepts; namely, that the starting point of all knowing is in the experience of human consciousness from which all else flows. The possibility that this is indeed a humiverse, that the inmost processes of nature are oriented toward the centrality of the human being, is a question that presses from within science itself, and is not to be avoided by science. In his 1973 lecture at Princeton commemorating the five-hundredth anniversary of the birth of Copernicus, a lecture titled "The Universe as Home for Man," the physicist J. A. Wheeler said, "No longer is it possible to throw the question out as meaningless, though it is stranger than science has ever met before."[27]

To take seriously that this is a humiverse suggests further the possibility of a transformation of science itself, a transformation deeper and more far-reaching than any we have considered so far. Human experience becomes the clue to an adequate conception of the whole scientific enterprise. J. A. Wheeler writes:

> No theory of physics that deals only with physics will ever explain physics. I believe that as we go on trying to understand the universe, we are at the same time trying to understand man. . . . Only as we recognize that tie will we be able to make headway into some of the most difficult issues that confront us. . . . Man, the start of the analysis, man the end of the analysis—because the physical world is in some deep sense tied to human beings.[28]

The discovery of the centrality of living mind in all our knowing as a constituent of the universe must surely mean that an adequate scientific rendering of the universe must take living mind into account. If the claim of science to explore the world in its actuality is to be sustained, scientific method must be governed by the full reality of conscious experience.

And when we give it our attention, our experience of the familiar world as conscious human beings presents us with a reality that is redolent with meaningful and qualitative, as well as quantitative, relationships and levels of existence. If the human being is to be the clue to science and to the world of nature, then this requires a method of inquiry adequate to the qualitative richness of conscious experience. At present our science is concerned exclusively with the quantitative; and its methods, among which mathematics has proved the most fruitful, are entirely those appropriate for uncovering and dealing with the quantitative aspects of reality. The great achievement of science, in fact, lies in the care with which it has developed and honed its methods to such a degree of power and precision that no quantitative elements within its range of inquiry can remain hidden for long. And yet remove the qualitative dimension, and conscious experience becomes increasingly abstract and without substance.

The conclusion appears unavoidable: an exclusive quantitative account of the world is incomplete; it is an abstraction drawn from the whole. As such it has its own relative autonomy and validity and can be extremely useful, but by itself is incapable of supplying either the full picture or even the significance of the quantitative elements in the picture. When it is forgotten that the quantitative has but a relative autonomy, that it is a limiting case abstracted from the whole, and is instead extrapolated to an all-encompassing description of total reality, then we begin to witness the rise of those scientistic world views of a lifeless, mechanical universe. Is it possible to develop a new kind of science that would include within its methods an awareness of both the qualitative and the quantitative?

Most scientists today would probably answer no, but out of the understandable fear that such a change would destroy the precision and power that science has attained. Certainly nothing within present-day science embraces the qualitative in its methods even though, as we have seen, quantitative science as such presupposes, as a human enterprise, its starting point in conscious mind and in the value commitments that make all inquiry possible. Objections to the contrary notwithstanding, the possibility of a qualitative science is worth pursuing further, if at this point only speculatively. But it is crucially important to be clear about which is being suggested.

Huston Smith discusses Theodore Roszak's call for a change in scientific thought that would see science dominated by a "rhapsodic intellect" which "would subordinate much research to those contemplated encounters with nature that deepen, but do not increase knowledge." In response Smith quotes approvingly the rejoinder to Roszak by the physicist, Steven Weinberg: "My answer is that science cannot change in this way without destroying itself, because however much human values are involved in the scientific process or are affected by the results of scientific research, there is an essential element in science that is cold, objective, and nonhuman."[29] What is being explored here, however, is precisely not Roszak's rhapsodic intellect which cannot yield knowledge. In adopting this version of the Two-Realm Theory, Roszak betrays his own acceptance of the positivistic conception of all knowledge as quantitative, scientific knowledge, which Weinberg is quite right in describing as cold, objective, and non-human. But this latter is knowledge of a limited kind and of a limited domain; it is, to repeat, a limiting case of the whole with its own restricted autonomy which it exercises in dealing with the physicochemical laws of dead matter. Science, however, also presumes to treat of living matter, but has not a living, qualitative method for doing so and is, consequently, always thrown back upon the necessity of leaving out consciousness and of reducing life to the inanimate. On its own terms science, as it now stands, is not equipped to offer an adequate account of the very physical nature, with its infinite variety of life and sentient beings, which this science claims as its proper domain. In order to do so science would have to supplement—not supplant—its mathematical and quantitative methods with equally well-developed methods of qualitative inquiry. The participatory view of science and the centrality of the human being in the universe suggest that such a transformation of science is possible and necessary.

Charles Birch, the biologist, points to the transformation required in our ways of knowing by the central experience of consciousness. "Human experience," he writes,

> is a high level exemplification of reality in general. There the subjective world of feeling is real for us. But that world extends beyond the human when we see everything through this window, be it cats or elephants or electrons. . . . What emerges in the human we weave back again into the total process. The world then becomes more life-like than matter-like. It is not as tame as our sluggish, convention-ridden imaginations imply. Mind is no longer just in a corner of nature. It is part of nature.[30]

During the latter part of the nineteenth and the early years of this century, the philosopher William James explored a similar conviction that in the workings of our own minds we do apprehend or grasp relationships and qualities that are genuinely given and present in reality. Already in his early work in psychology James gave expression to this conviction with which he continued to wrestle throughout his life. "If we survey the field of history," he wrote, "and ask what feature all great periods of revival, of expansion of the human mind, display in common, we shall find, I think, simply this: that each and every one of them have said to the human being, 'The inmost nature of the reality is congenial to *powers* which you possess.' "[31] Birch is even more specific in describing the importance of attending to the workings of our mind and conscious experience as the basis for transforming our knowledge of nature. "To bring the human being into the picture," Birch writes, "is to bring in mind and consciousness and purposes, sensations of red and blue, bitter and sweet, suffering and joy, good and bad. Because exclusive mechanism cannot deal with these human qualities, its framework is incomplete."[32]

As others have done, Birch is building largely on the work of Alfred North Whitehead and his concern to provide a satisfactory alternative to exclusively mechanistic interpretations of nature. An adequate view, Whitehead insisted, must make a central place for the objective reality of quality. Like Whitehead and his other followers, Birch does not carry through the full implications of this insistence for our ways of knowing, though he does indicate in a general way the directions these might take. By and large, however, he, like his fellow Whiteheadians, stays within a philosophy of science, an interpretation of reality, one that, indeed, offers a challenge to positivism, but one that stops short of developing what this philosophical perspective might entail for actual scientific research methods and strategies. In that it fails to sketch out the consequences of the philosophic view for actual ways of knowing that bear directly on research protocols and methods, this position remains still a version, a more sophisticated and adequate version to be sure, of the Two-Realm Theory. To that extent it continues to leave science itself intact as an exclusively quantitative affair. A purely quantitative science is a limited abstraction from the whole, one component of a potentially much more comprehensive cognitive enterprise.

Nevertheless, Birch does help to identify two points of departure for a genuinely radical transformation in our ways of knowing. One he touches on directly in speaking of the imagination. A participatory, human-centered conception of knowing recognizes, as most leading philosophers of science have come to stress in one way or another, the crucial role of the imagination in science. A transformation of knowledge can require nothing less than a renewal of the imagination, an enlivened, not a "convention-ridden," imagination. The second point, implied but not pursued by Birch, is that the transcending of the detached, onlooker consciousness demanded by a fully participatory conception of knowledge means that a qualitative knowing must entail corresponding changes in the knower. For how is it possible to recognize qualities in reality without in some way developing the capacity to recognize and bring those qualities to birth in oneself? In the absence of an enlivened imagination springing from self-transformation, however, the participatory fact of all our knowing unfortunately lends itself to a thorough-going instrumentalism. A convention-ridden imagination, though it may certainly be brilliantly clever, cannot open itself to the actual phenomena of nature themselves, but instead can only impose on them its own abstract thought-forms—conceptual frameworks and models—for which the only criteria are prediction and control. Thus, simply discovering that all our knowing is always an interplay with nature is but an essential first step toward a way of knowing that yields understanding, as well as manipulation, but a step that by itself is not enough.

New Vistas

Other scientific areas besides physics have begun to change as older nineteenth-century assumptions have more and more been called into question. Developments in every field proceed at a pace impossible to keep up with, and present an overall picture of a confusing, if not always confused, combination of old and new. The instrumental view with its emphasis on reductionistic modes of analysis remains strong, and particularly in biology, with the rise of genetic engineering, seems to have been given new impetus. The irony in this has been underscored, for example, by the observation of David Bohm that "modern molecular biologists generally believe that the whole of life and mind can ultimately be understood in more or less mechanical terms, through some kind of extension of the work that has been done on the structure and function of DNA molecules. A similar trend has already begun to dominate in psychology. Thus we arrive at the very odd result that in the study of life and mind, which are just the fields in which formative cause acting in undivided and unbroken flowing movement is most evident to experience and observation, there is now the strongest belief in the fragmentary atomistic approach to reality."[33] At the same time, a minority of outstanding biologists has begun to stress the necessity of developing ways of thinking that can do justice to the complexity of living organisms in their interrelatedness, their unfolding over time, their interactions with the environment, their manifestation of form, and so forth. At the forefront of this effort have been such persons as Ludwig von Bertalanffy and Paul A. Weiss, who have developed and applied systems theory to the study of biology.[34]

The crux of the systems concept in biology is that living entities must be regarded as dynamic, organized systems. The parts that go into the makeup of the whole are not independent elements, but are dynamically interconnected and integrated by continuous networks of hierarchically ordered patterns of interaction. Nature itself is such a system of hierarchically ordered systems. The congruence of systems theory with the view, expressed particularly by Polanyi, of the multi-leveled structure of reality is apparent, and in it the major task of biology is to gain an understanding of the laws that govern living systems. From this perspective living entities, whether molecules, cells, organs, or plants and animals, cannot be adequately understood as assemblages of elementary units operating in physical, linear cause-and-effect fashion. They can only be understood in the light of the laws that govern them as dynamic, integrated, total systems. This does not mean the rejection of reductionism; on this, Weiss, for instance, is adamant and maintains that analysis and synthesis, parts and whole, are polarities that must be held together. The whole is prior, however, and reductionistic analysis is a useful, but limited method of inquiry. Weiss writes: "No matter how precise our knowledge of the composition and behavior of a given part, viewed separately, may be (e.g., gene, neurotransmitter, mitochondrion, cell, heart, etc.), unless we also *know* the interactive rules of order of their coordinated functions as organized wholes, the sum of all that partial insight does not add up to total understanding."[35] Breaking life down into smaller and smaller parts will never lead to the reconstruction, in concept or in fact, of the living whole; it can only produce disintegration or machinelike parodies of the original. Within the biological system, the activities and development of the parts are determined by the higher level processes and patterns of the entire system.

The recognition that almost all systems are open systems—they meet, interact, and communicate with one another in a continuous exchange of energy and information—has also provided an alternative perspective to the older outlook of classical physics of the entire universe as a static closed system of closed systems. The open-system concept makes it possible to deal with change and interchange, both within and among systems, and is being widely applied to ecological concerns, social systems, communication, cybernetics, linguistics, and beyond. The concept seems to have received important substantiation from the work of Ilya Prigogine and others in thermodynamics. Prigogine has shown that even at the level of physical-chemical interaction there are systems in which new structures of order (called *dissipative structures*) spontaneously arise in situations of great instability that according to the classical formulation of thermodynamics would have been expected to disintegrate with an increasing loss of energy.[36] The upshot of Prigogine's work seems to be to demonstrate that even at the lowest levels it is possible for a system at its boundaries to become open to coordination with a higher level of organization. It therefore becomes possible, without contravening the thermodynamic laws of entropy at the level of inanimate matter, to see that it is possible for new and more complex forms and structures of order to arise from lower states of organization. Prigogine and others have not hesitated to apply this discovery to personal and social transformation.

In reflecting on the significance of systems theory for a transformation in our conception of knowledge, and particularly with respect to the relation between scientific knowing and human values, caution should be the order of the day. Certainly the attempt to think organismically, the main concern of systems theory in biology, is a more adequate way of dealing with life and its processes than merely reducing them to the concepts of physics and chemistry. And systems theory has greatly stimulated, and aided, the attempt to think ecologically. The systems concept itself, however, is a mix of quantitative and qualitative notions that are never clearly disentangled. Biological systems theorists not infrequently resort to patently quantitative and even mechanistic metaphors, magnetic fields, for example, in trying to describe the patterns of causal interaction in systems. Further, systems models remain, as Charles Davy and others have observed, conceptual-thought forms which may lead to higher degrees of predictive knowledge and control, but do not provide a deeper experience and apprehension of living nature.[37] Systems theory has not transcended a pervasive instrumentalism.

Furthermore, the extrapolation of systems theory to personal and social realms may be very useful in alerting us to unsuspected complexities, interrelationships, and interactive possibilities and may even make possible great accuracy in predicting the outcome of social policies and events. When applied across the board to human affairs, however, without making a central place for human intentionality, systems theory tends to become a yet more subtle form of mechanistic determinism, and adds conceptual support to methods of technological social control. As an explanatory framework, systems theory by itself becomes simply ahistorical and will tend to becloud rather than to enhance our understanding of human affairs and their inner significances. Moreover, it must be said that the uncritical enthusiasm that has greeted Prigogine's theories as supplying the key to evolution and personal and social change smacks more of a resurgence than an overcoming of scientism. Prigogine's discovery of dissipative structures appears to show that even at the lowest level—the boundary between life and the lifeless—openness and transformation to a higher state occurs. The transformation, however, is from the higher down—or not, if the higher is lacking. To suggest as some have that Prigogine's work should encourage us to expect from personal and social turbulence and perturbation (his word) a jump to a higher state of being and order is ahistorical and blatantly scientistic.[38] The human being as the governing element is left out of the picture. After all, it would probably be much safer and more accurate to predict the outcome of most turbulent human behavior strictly according to the unrefined second law of thermodynamics—increasing disorder and spreading entropy. If the human being is unable to actualize in himself higher energies, the transformation does not occur, predictions from quantitative systems theory to the contrary notwithstanding.

Systems theory has opened new possibilities for understanding in science, and is to be welcomed, but not uncritically.

Perhaps also significant of important developments in biology has been the readiness of a few scientists to take a new look at the orthodox neo-Darwinian theory of evolutionary change. The dominant version of evolutionary theory (at least in America) holds that natural selection working gradually over long periods of time on small genetic variations in individual species accounts for both microevolution (variations within a species) and macroevolution (the appearance of new species and orders). It is assumed that evolution is the result of a gradual accumulation of changes in the individual traits of organisms that have the greatest utility for survival—that is, that have optimum adaptation to the environment.

Critics of the theory—not of evolution itself, but of the neo-Darwinian explanation of how evolution occurs—have long maintained that while it can account for some, perhaps most microevolutionary, change, it cannot account for all of the variety and complexity displayed by nature, and is particularly weak in explaining macroevolution. We have not space here to go into all the pros and cons of a long, sometimes vituperative argument. What is not widely known is that the issues have by no means been disposed of, and many are receiving fresh attention and are being hotly contested.[39]

One main issue is the lack of support in the fossil evidence for gradual, step-by-step evolutionary change. "The extreme rarity of transitional forms in the fossil record," writes biologist Stephen Jay Gould, "persists as the trade secret of paleontology." In other words, the missing links really are missing. What the record does show is that most species exhibit no directional change over the length of their existence on earth, except in the direction of greater specialization, which would seem to ill equip them for producing new unspecialized species. Instead, when a new species does appear in the record, it is not by the gradual transformation of its ancestors: "It appears," says Gould, "all at once and 'fully formed.' "[40] These considerations have led Gould, Niles Eldredge, and others to postulate that major species changes are not gradual, but occur in sudden jumps or punctuations. Gould and his colleague, Richard Lewontin, microbiologist at Harvard University, have offered an equally interesting criticism of microevolutionary theory that is compatible with the notion of evolutionary jumps.

At the risk of oversimplifying their elegant argument, two points in it are worth mentioning. One is that the origin of many traits cannot be explained on the grounds of their utility. Their origins, in other words, are non-adaptive, though they may have later become useful for some purpose or other. While this runs directly counter to the basic neo-Darwinian assumption of gradualism, the second point is even more fundamental and far-reaching. This is the authors' argument that, to start with, organisms cannot be broken down, or "decomposed," into separate parts, but must be treated as "integrated wholes" with total ground plans that govern and place constraints on any change that may occur in individual parts. Some important development, therefore, must take place "in integrated packages, and cannot be pulled apart piece by piece in evolution."[41]

All of these criticisms are developed with great care and caution, and with the authors' explicit statement that they still regard natural selection as the main evolutionary process. They certainly do not entertain philosophical assumptions that seek to go beyond some kind of physical cause and-effect mechanism for understanding evolution. But they do demonstrate a new openness that in itself suggests that those biologists and other scientists who have taken up the larger philosophical issues and criticized neo-Darwinian explanations on more fundamental grounds—persons such as Polanyi, Marjorie Grene, Walter Heitler, Sir Alister Hardy, W. H. Thorpe, Charles Birch, and others—may not be offering views as implausible and far-fetched as the orthodox, and nearly all of our textbooks, would maintain.[42]

Another field of considerable activity in recent years is that of brain research. The dominant view among neuroscientists is that the experience of consciousness is ultimately to be fully accounted for as a derivative of brain function. Two leading exceptions have been the world-famous neurologist and brain surgeon, the late Wilder Penfield, and Sir John C. Eccles, neurophysiologist and recipient of the Noble Prize for medicine.[43] Both have maintained on the basis of their own medical experience and laboratory research that mind and brain are not identical and that it is a mistake to suppose that the brain does everything and that our conscious experiences are simply a reflection of brain activities. Both are among the ablest in describing the immense complexity and power of the brain itself. Eccles has illustrated the brain's incredible potential, for example, by contrasting the myriad musical compositions possible on the piano with its mere eighty-eight keys with the virtually infinite pattern-generating capacity of the brain's two to three million modules (about four thousand cells per module).[44] Nevertheless, they are convinced that mind and brain are distinct with, in the awake state, intense interaction across the frontier between them. Both Eccles and Penfield are willing to use the current metaphor to speak of the brain as computer—an infinitely complex computer—but with the difference from many who so speak that the self has then to be regarded as the programmer. The computer without its programmer has neither responsibility nor purpose. Moreover, as Eccles especially has stressed, meaning is basic to our self-existence, but meaning is in the mind, the programmer, not in the computer which can only deliver information.

From this point of view, the infinite complexity of the brain is exactly what is required for mental activity to manifest itself in a direct and focused way in the physical world. This would mean, of course, that in their intense interaction brain states would affect mightily the quality, state, and capacity of the mental manifestation. But it would not mean that the uniqueness of personal selfhood would be identical with the brain, nor that the contents of consciousness, mind, qualities, or meaning can be reduced to cerebral physicochemical events. Through the study of genetics, neuroembryology, neurophysiology, and developmental psychology, one could conceivably establish all the brain correlates of mental activity, but would nevertheless still be forced into an entirely different realm of mental activity to determine the meaning, truth, and falsity of any idea, perception, or statement, including first of all any interpretational statement about the significance of one's neurophysiological research.

Within science itself perhaps the most intriguing and far-reaching suggestions for a transformation of our thinking is to be found in the work of the theoretical physicist David Bohm. A protégé of Einstein's, Bohm has been recognized as one of the most creative and unconventional of contemporary physicists. In 1952, Bohm published two classic and highly controversial papers criticizing the usual interpretations of quantum physics, for which Bohm has also written one of the standard textbooks, and a few years later, in his book *Causality and Chance in Modern Physics*, he went further to present his criticism of our ordinary notions of causality, mechanical determinism, indeterminism, and natural law. Now, in his most recent book, *Wholeness and the Implicate Order*, Bohm has set forth nothing less than an alternative to the way we normally think of reality, a view of the world that he argues is demanded by relativity and quantum theory, but one that comprehends much more than these.[45] Bohm proposes that the world of our experience is a projection of an all-embracing, immense, multi-dimensional order of reality. He calls this the implicate order. All that we experience of the sensible world—space, time, matter, life, and thought—is "enfolded," or contained as implicate, within this more fundamental order. The entire space-time world and its logical relationships make up the explicate order, which is a partial unfolding (a making explicit), and a special case or sub-totality of that which is enfolded in the implicate whole.

Many of the most critical problems in our present situation arise, Bohm argues, because we approach the world with a thinking that is fragmentary and fragmenting. We mistakenly take our own thoughts, categories, theoretical constructs, and models as true pictures of reality and view the world in terms of them when they at best provide only partial and provisional insights abstracted from the whole. We approach the world then with a fragmented thinking, and the world responds in kind, giving fractured, bits-and-pieces answers to our questions and probings. And, as we have tried to show, this "breakdown of the world," extends into every dimension of our lives. "Wholeness," Bohm insists, "is what is real, and fragmentation is the response" of that whole to our limited, fragmentary way of knowing.[46] Thus, Bohm begins also with a participatory view of knowing. Our knowing and our experience are not separated; they are fully bound up in one another. They implicate one another. Limited ways of knowing produce limited experience. What is required is a transformation of our ways of knowing so that the primacy of the whole is recognized and wholeness can be restored to experience. What we need, Bohm says, is a new form of insight which he calls *Undivided Wholeness in Flowing Movement*.[47] This is itself, he cautions, an insight that ought not to be regarded as final and fixed, for that would be a contradiction in terms.

Bohm's major theoretical work recently has been devoted to showing that modern physics is one of our most powerful witnesses to the reality of the implicate order. Relativity partially, and quantum theory more thoroughly, he thinks, both challenge the mechanistic order and posit the need for another more fundamental reality whose essential order and coherence is quite other than that suggested by classical mechanics. Our naive notion of distinct particles and rigid objects occupying points in absolute space and time dissolve into fields and continua of interpenetrating energies and interaction. Quantum theory particularly leads to radical revision of our standard conceptions of reality. The discontinuous nature of movement, such that a quantum system passes from one discrete state to another without passing through connecting intermediate steps, points to a single structure of deep indivisible links "so that the entire universe has to be thought of as an unbroken whole."[48] The fact that matter behaves sometimes like waves and sometimes like particles depending on the conditions in which it is operating implies more an organic form of relationship than the interaction of parts of a machine. Moreover, the evidence within quantum theory that entities at a distance seem to have an immediate relationship that connects them without any direct contiguity defies our ordinary notions of separateness, independence, and mechanistic causality. Even so-called empty space is revealed as not empty, but full, a *plenum* of infinite, unmanifest energy. The entire sensible world, Bohm says, is, therefore, like a "tiny ripple" on a vast sea of immense energy. All of this from within modern physics, he argues, points to the existence of an order of universal wholeness in flowing movement as the ground of all that we experience.

The entire world in which we find ourselves and are a part, including not only matter, but life and consciousness as well, is an unfolding, or partial manifestation, of this infinitely more comprehensive holomovement, the implicate order. Although partial at any particular moment of experience, the manifest, explicate world nevertheless has its own provisional reality and, as Bohm stresses, its own relative autonomy and validity. Likewise, while they are limited, the theories and logical categories with which we ordinarily attempt to fix and understand the world have their relative validity. Bohm, no more than others of similar outlook that we have seen, has any intention of denying the importance of ordinary modes of perception and logical thinking, including reductionism as a method of inquiry for special purposes. But just as the things which appear to us separate and unconnected in the experience of space and time are interrelated at a deeper level, so, too, our analytical thinking and sequential logic, however necessary and useful, are limited, essentially static, instances of a dynamic, flowing, unifying intelligibility. To forget this is to trap ourselves in habits of thought cut off from the source of new insight and new possibilities of experience.

While in Bohm's view modern physics requires a recognition of the implicate order, he is not trying to establish its reality solely on the basis of the latest evidence from the physicist's laboratory. Rather, he is arguing that all of our experience can only be understood within the context of the implicate order. If I read him correctly, he is even willing to grant that in the flowing interconnectedness revealed in quantum physics we may actually still be dealing with higher, more intangible levels of the explicate, but that the flowing interconnected movement revealed even here, nevertheless, itself becomes intelligible only as a manifestation of the implicate.

Furthermore, all our experience bears witness to the implicate order. In fact, he maintains that in certain of our ordinary experiences we may have a more direct awareness of the implicate than we do of the explicate. Our most immediate experience of the implicate order, he suggests, is that of our own movement in which body, thinking, feeling, and will are all intricately involved in a total, flowing process. If we try to make it explicit by analyzing what is happening, we find ourselves unable to move, or we trip ourselves up. In the interaction of thinking, feeling, and will we experience and unfold the implicate order in our own person. Language as the embodiment of meaning, as the expression in the material of the immaterial, also can provide an immediate experience of the implicate order; but the disintegration of language as a carrier of meaning and the hardening of language in fixed and static categories can also make language a main barrier to the implicate order. Language can disclose but also veil the implicate order. Music, he thinks, may provide the fullest direct experience of the unfolding of the implicate order, for music is movement in which any particular moment acquires its significance as a transformation of what has already been played and as an anticipation of what is yet to come. And all this is sensed immediately in consciousness and physical-emotional response. Without the presence of all together, each implicated in the other, the musical experience disappears. The implicate order, which at one level physics reveals, must then also be seen as a multi-dimensional reality with perhaps infinite degrees of implicate order on order, the entirety being, nevertheless, an unbroken whole.

That life and consciousness, as well as matter, are unfolded from the implicate order underscores the essential unity and flow of all reality. Bohm, therefore, describes the implicate order as a holomovement, or as holonomic. This is not to say that Bohm reduces consciousness and life to the same thing; they are parallel movements within a common ground, in which "all implicate all." Each taken by itself apart from its implication in the other is an abstraction and a special case that we may need to focus on exclusively for certain purposes. As Bohm puts it: "Leaving out life, we get inanimate matter; leaving out consciousness, we get life; leaving out something unspecified, which lies beyond, we get ordinary consciousness, and so on."[49] He does not want to use the terminology we have employed earlier of hierarchies, if this implies a lower and a higher which are separate and do not participate in each other. Each dimension is at once transcendent and immanent. Life cannot be reduced to matter, nor consciousness to life; yet each is implicit in the others, for matter finds its further expression in life, and life in consciousness.[50] Similarly, consciousness is not merely abstract thought but also includes feeling, desire, will, awareness, attention, perception, acts of understanding, and so forth. Hence, a full-bodied thinking will be informed and enlivened by the intelligibility implicit in feeling, desire, will, attention, and so forth. A narrow reason, to use our earlier terminology, is but a partial expression of rationality in its wholeness. And our ordinary consciousness is a limited, relatively independent expression of a more comprehensive living intelligence.[51]

The unavoidable presence of thought at every point in our experience underscores the unity of mind and being. The more complete the implication, the greater the apprehension of unity. So that, Bohm says, "in the infinity" knowing and being converge toward identity. Thus there is opened the possibility of knowing participation in mental energies, or (can the term really be avoided?) strictly spiritual dimensions of the implicate order not accessible to our ordinary states of consciousness and quality of thought. But to have access to these would require the development in us of a commensurate intelligence, a transformation of consciousness.[52] It would require an infusing of our thinking with the higher intelligence of love and compassion which would be at the same time a transformation in our own being. Herein lies the possibility and beginning of genuine Insight-Imagination.

To repeat: It is crucial to understand that Bohm is not deriving the implicate order from physics, although at first glance this may appear to be primarily what he is doing. Rather, he is arguing that the evidence of physics only makes sense in the light of such an order, to which all of experience witnesses. Even if current physics were to change, which Bohm says it inevitably will, this would not require a jettisoning of the implicate order, although it undoubtedly would mean revising our understanding of it in particular instances. Bohm is not, therefore, tying his world view to the latest advances in physics. That would be simply substituting a new, streamlined scientism for an old, outmoded one.[53] From our larger experience, however, he is attempting to move toward a common language by which the insights from many domains—science, philosophy, religion, and the arts—can be shared and genuine dialogue among them be undertaken and pursued.

Summary: Participation and Insight

Throughout we have tried to resist the temptation to derive a world view from the latest research in science. To do so would be, as we have just noted, to concoct a new scientism—one more congenial, perhaps, to our desires to take into account dimensions of experience left out by the old scientism, but a scientism all the same, and one that, no less than the old, would leave our world view at the mercy of some future development in science that might throw it into doubt. To peg our understanding of the meaning of experience on that which we think is permitted by science, whether the so-called old or the new, will always tether that meaning to a necessarily limited knowledge of the world, and ultimately will prevent our being informed and guided by it. And yet to leave our knowledge, and most of all our scientific knowledge, unconnected with our affirmations of meaning and value will sooner or later lead to the fading away of the latter, or drive us back on to some kind of two-realm theory of truth with all its schizophrenic dualism and constant oscillation between sentimentality and cynicism. Where is this connection to be made, and how?

Without further consideration, the still dominant form of modern science can offer little assistance in building this connection. Modern science is concerned almost exclusively with quantity and quantitative relationships, and its main goal and criterion is measurability. It is based on observation of the quantitative elements in sense perception and inferences drawn from that observation. This is also true of those fields, such as sub-atomic physics, where scientists attempt to reach into the realm of imperceptible micro-phenomena by means of guiding ideas and sophisticated measuring devices constructed in accordance with those ideas. Although the sub-atomic physicist has been described by some as attempting to plumb reality by a "non-ordinary mode of perception," which is true enough, the underlying assumption that all knowledge is derived from sense perception of physical reality is maintained by regarding the measuring instruments as subtle refinements and extensions of our ordinary senses (and so we get talk about ultimate particles and so on existing "out there," even though we cannot see them). Or an instrumental view of science is adopted that regards the formulas and experimental apparatus merely as recipes and tools for moving things about and getting results, although they are said to tell us very little about what it all signifies. Probably most common is a combination of both: scientists who, when pressed, concede that their own is an instrumental understanding of science, but who, nevertheless, in their public and popular statements continue to feed the naive realism that conceives of science as dealing with absolute and objective realities independent of any observer. And in every case, the subject matter is rendered in terms of quantitative measurements and quantitative relationships.

In itself a purely quantitative science offers no aid in helping us apprehend qualities, since these are excluded from the start; and it has nothing to contribute in enabling us to deal with qualitative issues and problems. In other words, a purely quantitative science has nothing to contribute to the great central questions of human existence. Plato's statement, for example, that it is better to suffer injustice than to do injustice, cannot be decided one way or the other by anything the physicists and biologists (or sociologists for that matter) have to tell us. To persist in thinking that a purely quantitative science can decide the central human questions can only drag the human being down into a quantitative realm where qualities no longer exist, into a sub-human realm. A purely quantitative science cannot even deal with the qualitative aspects of nature. It deals only with the inanimate, abstracted as purely quantitative; it has been able to deal with life and living processes only according to concepts and approaches derived from its world of the inanimate.

There is more, however, to science than this. Despite all the necessary caveats and cautions about attempting to derive guidance from a quantitative science on issues of human meaning and the qualitative dimensions of life, we still need not retreat to some kind of two-realm theory of truth. In our look at some of the main developments in modern science, three areas in particular have emerged that hold rich promise for a genuine connection between scientific knowing and that of the radical humanities and traditional wisdom. All three are interconnected and imply each other.

A New Openness in Science

Again and again we have seen a growing realization among scientists that theirs is so far not a complete science. It promotes only a partial view of even the world disclosed to the senses, including the inorganic world. At point after point we see scientists, therefore, attempting to develop new concepts and new ways of thinking that can begin to take in the full realities with which they are concerned: a growing realization, for example, that living entities must be understood organismically, that survival and natural selection do not seem to be the whole story of evolution, that brain and mind are not identical, that the mechanistic order of physical reality is strictly limited, and so on. Some of these efforts are mixed, and often seem to involve an attempt to pour new wine into old wineskins, but the openness is genuine and not to be denied. Above all in importance has been the discovery of the multi-dimensional structure of reality in which lower orders with their own relative autonomy are at the same time open to the higher and capable of being determined by the higher. The greater the degree of intelligence and qualitative relationships the more inclusive the reality. Perhaps the most radical proposal of all has been David Bohm's concept of the implicate order. Here the entire sensible world is seen to be a continual manifestation of an infinitely complex and multi-dimensional order of intelligence. In the implicate order, mind and qualities are not derived from or regarded as epiphenomena of the inanimate, but are the ordering principles of the entire holonomic movement from which matter, life, and thought all come to expression.

This new openness in science points to the possibility of a science, including a physics, much richer in qualities than at present and guided by appropriate qualitative methods of inquiry. There seems to be no reason in principle to prevent the development of a qualitative as well as a quantitative science. It is, in fact, an intriguing speculative question to ask where we might be if we had not 400 but 800 years of science behind us, during which, at the midpoint, a second Galileo had arisen to launch us on developing methods appropriate to knowing the qualitative aspects of nature with the same devotion and concentration that the first Galileo started us in the development of quantitative thinking. (Unfortunately, as a result of the first 400, we may not have 400 more years to go.) Because we experience qualities as both subjective and objective, as both in us and in nature, a truly qualitative science would have to begin with the entire human being and include human thinking, feeling, and willing as essential and central to its entire method of knowing. It seems to be something of just this sort that Charles Birch is calling for in his notion of a humiverse.

The Centrality of the Human Being in All Knowing

This is the second area within modern science that opens the possibility of a transformation in our ways of knowing. It has become a fundamental recognition in physics that all knowing is an interplay between the knower and the known, a participation of the subject in the object. Unfortunately, it has been possible, as we have seen, to absorb this recognition without having to follow through to the end all that it implies. By adopting a totally instrumental conception of science, in which the sole criteria are prediction and control (or a purely operational view in which the acceptability of the various available mathematical and conceptual schema is determined by the criteria of formal symmetry and simplicity), the full implications of participation are short-circuited. It has, thereby, even been possible to leave relatively untouched, or to smuggle in tendentiously, as the need arises, the older assumptions of an exclusive reductionism, of an objective reality independent of the observer, and of the derivation of all phenomena, including thought, from strictly material processes and events—despite mounting evidence that the first, reductionism, has a severely limited validity, and that the others, objectivism and materialism, are simply wrong.

Nevertheless, the radical implications of participation remain and are being increasingly recognized. Among other things, the fact of participation means that no scientific observation or interpretation, quantitative or otherwise, is possible apart from a larger matrix of meaning that is prior and primary to all else.

Thought is present at every point in every act and focus of knowing. The physicist, for example, increasingly speaks of matter in terms of the purest thought available to him, mathematics. This does not mean that the mind of the knower creates the known, but that the knower and the known share in an intelligibility that makes both possible. The intelligibility in the mind of the human being discovers the intelligibility in the universe, which transcends and includes both the knower and the particular focus of knowing.

The question of truth that arises is whether our intelligibility is adequate to receive the full compass of intelligibility that stands to be revealed. Or, are we locked into narrow thought patterns and habits that prevent our becoming open to the infinite range and depth of reality? The power of thought cuts two ways, for it may entice us to become satisfied with a limited and limiting participation in the known. Thought, which reveals, if fixed, made static, and turned in upon itself, may also be that which veils, distorts, and deadens. The omnipresence and power of thought manifests itself negatively in the destructiveness of limited, habitual, fixed thought. What, then is the source of newness that keeps thought alive?

Insight

All genuine new knowledge comes by means of a breakthrough into a dimension of intelligibility previously inaccessible. In this breakthrough, old thought patterns and categories dissolve and are reordered at a higher level of intelligibility in which there is something new that was not present before. David Bohm has described this intelligence-breakthrough as Insight. An essential distinction exists between the new knowledge that comes from Insight, and the kind of knowledge that comes from merely rearranging what is already given. Technical and discursive reason, logic, and classification all may be useful in ordering our thoughts, and sometimes even in rearranging them in new patterns and relationships. But they work with the given, and do not bring any new elements into play; in this sense logic and discursive reason are bound to the past and can only repeat, sometimes in a more ordered way, sometimes in a more rigid way, what has already been laid down. Newness in knowing—

new perspectives, new lines of inquiry, a new grasp of the whole, a new level of meaning—comes only in an immediately participative act of Insight or Imagination.

In every kind of science, as in every other field, the source and possibility of all new knowledge is Insight. Unfortunately, as Bohm has pointed out, many scientists continue to miss this. The dominant view among scientists of how advances in scientific knowledge occur is still, he writes, "turned upside down." The process of rearranging known concepts and images in a logical order and in new patterns is still considered by many scientists to be primary, while rational and imaginative insight is regarded as less important. "And so," writes Bohm, "it is not seen that the deep origin of our general lines of thinking is in creative and original acts of insight, the content of which is then further unfolded and developed . . . , ultimately to serve as hints or clues which help to indicate or point to new acts of insight, and thus to complete the cycle of the process of knowledge."[54]

Once the primary importance of Insight becomes clear, it also becomes startlingly evident that this is the point at which genuine connection between human values and meaning and knowledge of every kind, including scientific knowledge, is to be sought. The recognition of the primacy of Insight in all knowing opens up whole new vistas of possibility. We can once more entertain the twofold possibility, of which so many in our time have despaired, of (1) reenlivening and reinstating at the heart of our culture and education all those subjects—religion, art, literature, philosophy—that deal with meaning and value as also capable of providing genuine knowledge of the world, and (2) placing the human being at the center of all our knowing, but the full human being, not that empty husk of itself, which is about all the modern mind set has left us. A renewed appreciation of technical, instrumental reason as the indispensable servant, but not master, of the creative potentialities of the human being becomes possible. The fundamental wholeness that joins scientific Insight, artistic Insight, and moral Insight again comes into view. And education has the possibility of acquiring again what it once had: an excitement about knowing. In these times could anything be more inviting?

Notes

1. Michael Polanyi, *Personal Knowledge, Towards a Post-Critical Philosophy* (Chicago: University of Chicago Press, 1962); idem, *The Tacit Dimension* (Garden City, N.Y.: Doubleday, 1966); idem and Harry Prosch, *Meaning* (Chicago: University of Chicago Press, 1975); and Jacob Bronowski, *Science and Human Values* (New York: Harper & Row, 1956; 2d ed., 1965).

2. For example, see Polanyi, *The Tacit Dimension,* p. 64.

3. Bronowski, *Science and Human Values,* p. 63.

4. Among those who have raised ethical questions from within science, see, for example: Jonathan King, "New Genetic Technologies: Prospects and Hazards," *Technology Review* (February 1980), 57-65; Robert L. Sinsheimer, "The Presumptions of Science," *Daedalus* (Spring 1978), 23-26; Henry Beecher, *Research and the Individual: Human Studies* (Boston: Little, Brown and Co., 1970); Bernard N. Nathanson, *Aborting America* (New York: Doubleday, 1979).

5. Bronowski, *Science and Human Values,* p. 64.

6. David Bohm, *Causality and Chance in Modern Physics* (London: Routledge & Kegan Paul, 1957), pp. 133, 139.

7. David Bohm, *Wholeness and the Implicate Order* (London: Routledge & Kegan Paul, 1980), Chapter 5, "Quantum Theory as an Indication of a New Order in Physics." See also pp. 172-79.

8. John Archibald Wheeler, "The Universe as Home for Man," *American Scientist,* vol. 62 (November-December 1974), 689. See also Bernard d'Espagnat, "The Quantum Theory and Reality," *Scientific American,* vol. 241 (November 1979), 158-81.

9. Werner Heisenberg, *Physics and Philosophy; The Revolution in Modern Science* (New York: Harper & Row), p. 81.

10. E. Lester Smith, ed., *Intelligence Came First* (Wheaton, Ill.: Quest Books, 1975), pp. 11-12.

11. Owen Barfield, *Saving the Appearances: A Study in Idolatry* (New York: Harcourt, Brace & World, n.d.), p. 21. The philosopher of science Errol Harris has written, ". . . perception is always interpretive, not of hard, simple sense given data, but by way of organization imposing schemata upon confused and primitive sentience, in which though differences occur, they are not, except by attention and reflective thinking, explicitly distinguished and organized. Perception, in consequence, proves to be continuous with, and is an inchoate form of, theorizing, an implicit process of hypothesizing, testing and modifying implicit hypotheses which issues in an implicit judgment, that is the immediate percept. Much of this is of course subconscious—or as some writers say—preperceptual; but most of it can be introspected and all

of it has been in impressive measure experimentally demonstrated by psychologists of impeccable scientific reputation. . . . Our perceived world is a sustained judgment or series of judgments on the basis of a conceptual scheme—a system of schematic concepts—which constitute a more or less coherent whole." Errol Harris, "Testament of a Philosophic Dissenter," *The Carlton Miscellany*, vol. 17 (Spring 1979), 57, 58.

12. Charles Davy, *Towards a Third Culture* (London: Faber and Faber, Ltd., 1961; rev. ed., Edinburgh: Floris Books, 1978), p. 91.

13. Philosophical perspectives stemming largely from the thought of the eighteenth-century philosopher Immanuel Kant have lent powerful support to the instrumental conception of science. Kant held that all our perceptions of the world are ordered and interpreted within the given structure of human consciousness. In Kant's view, it is, therefore, impossible to penetrate to knowledge of what things are in themselves for we only know them as they manifest themselves according to the patterns, processes, and structures of the human mind. Rather than understanding the laws of nature, we impose the laws of our own mind on nature, organizing and ordering it in such wise that it becomes useful *to us*. In itself, according to this interpretation, nature remains forever hidden and unknown.

14. Davy, *Towards a Third Culture*, p. 103.

15. See Polanyi, *The Tacit Dimension*, pp. 42-47. Similarly, Errol Harris has written, "The world-picture derived from the sciences . . . is a single hierarchical structure of dynamic wholes, forming an ascending scale of complexifications. But even this description is oversimplified. At every level the whole which predominates over its constituent elements is a dynamic structure, manifesting an active principle of ordering and self-specification. . . . Each critical complexification displays more versatile properties, the atom more than the molecule, the virus and the cell more than inorganic structures. As we go up the scale the organic nature of the wholes is more self-determining, more versatile and more capable of self-maintenance. The holism is throughout the product of activity, the effect of which is integration and unifications. . . . " Harris, "Testament of a Philosophic Dissenter," p. 52.

16. Polanyi, *The Tacit Dimension*, p. 43.

17. Michael Polanyi, *Scientific Thought and Social Reality* (New York: International Universities Press, 1974), pp. 137ff.

18. Polanyi, *The Tacit Dimension*, p. 61.

19. David Bakan, *The Duality of Human Existence* (Skokie, Ill.: Rand McNally, 1966), pp. 5, 9.

20. Alan Howard, "Education and Our *Human* Future," *Teachers College Record*, vol. 81, no. 3 (Spring 1980), 338.

21. Walter J. Ong, *Interfaces of the Word: Studies in the Evolution of Consciousness and Culture* (Ithaca: Cornell University Press, 1977), p. 339.

22. Charles Birch, "Nature, God and Humanity in Ecological Perspective," *Christianity and Crisis* (October 29, 1979), 264.

23. W. R. Thompson, "Introduction," in Charles Darwin, *Origins of Species* (London: Everyman's Library, 1967).

24. The issues at stake here are quite different from those involved in the so-called creationist controversy. See note 39.

25. Polanyi, *The Tacit Dimension*, p. 47.

26. Polanyi and Prosch, *Meaning*, p. 147.

27. Wheeler, "The Universe as Home for Man," p. 688.

28. Quoted by F. Helitzer, "The Princeton Galaxy," *Intellectual Digest* (June 1973), 32.

29. Huston Smith, *Forgotten Truth: The Primordial Tradition* (New York: Harper & Row, 1976), p. 11.

30. Birch, "Nature, God and Humanity," p. 263.

31. William James, *The Principles of Psychology*, vol. 2 (New York: Dover Publications, 1950), p. 314.

32. Birch, "Nature, God and Humanity," p. 261. See the essays, many of them written from a Whiteheadian perspective, in David R. Griffin and John B. Cobb, Jr., eds., *Mind in Nature, Essays on the Interface of Science and Philosophy* (Lanham, Md.: University Press of America, 1977).

33. Bohm, *Wholeness and the Implicate Order*, p. 15.

34. See Paul A. Weiss, *The Science of Life: The Living System—A System for Living* (New York: Futura Publishing, 1973); and Ludwig von Bertalanffy, *A Systems View of Man*, ed. Paul A. LaViolette (Boulder, Colo.: Westview Press, 1981).

35. Paul A. Weiss, "The System of Nature and the Nature of Systems: Empirical Holism and Practical Reductionism Harmonized," in *Toward a Man-Centered Medical Science*, vol. 1, ed. Karl E. Schaefer (Mount Kisco, N.Y.: Futura Publishing, 1977), pp. 49-50.

36. I. Prigogine and G. Nicolis, *Quarterly Review of Biophysics*, 4 (1971). Prigogine's theory is deftly and succinctly discussed by A. R. Peacocke, *Creation and the World of Science*, The Bampton Lectures, 1978 (Oxford: Clarendon Press, 1979), pp. 97-100.

37. Davy, *Towards a Third Culture*, p. 124.

38. For examples of this social application of a physical theory, see Marilyn Ferguson, *The Aquarian Conspiracy: Personal and Social Transformation in the 1980s* (Los Angeles: J. P. Tarcher, 1980), pp. 162-67; and *Tarrytown Letter* (March 1981). As the discussion should make clear, we are, to say the least, skeptical that this can be done without further ado.

39. The contest spoken of here has very little to do with the more notorious, so-called creationist controversy. In the creationist controversy the only two parties admitted to the dispute are the creationists who, in the interests of a literalistic fundamentalism, deny evolution as such, and, against them, the Darwinian and neo-Darwinian evolutionists who, in the interests of an increasingly dogmatic scientism, claim their own as the only valid version of evolutionary theory. In the creationist controversy we have thus been presented with the spectacle of two dogmatisms—a dogmatic theology and a dogmatic scientism—attempting to preempt the field of discussion and to force all who do not agree with them into the camp of their opponents. The tragedy of this controversy is that alternative views—third ways—which do not dispute evolution, but find the neo-Darwinian explanations unconvincing, have been almost totally ignored, and the public misled into thinking that the only available theories are between creationism and versions of Darwinism. That many outstanding philosophers of science and increasing numbers of leading, working biologists challenge neo-Darwinism, without subscribing to the tenets of so-called creationism, has gone almost entirely unnoted. Not a little of the responsibility for this must be attributed to journalists of science, who, with rare exceptions, have allowed themselves to be used unquestioningly as apologists for neo-Darwinism, and in doing so have been colossally remiss as professionals in remaining ignorant of the deeper, real issues and debates within the scientific community. In their mistaken and openly self-congratulatory perception of themselves as champions of modernity, these journalists of science have done neither science nor the public a service. Much the same could be said for many professional educators. For possible alternatives to both creationism and neo-Darwinism, see the following discussion in the text and notes 40-42.

40. Stephen Jay Gould, "Evolution's Erratic Pace," *Natural History*, 86 (1977), 12, 14, 16. See also Niles Eldredge, "Gentleman's Agreement," *The Sciences* (April 1981), pp. 20-23, 31.

41. S. J. Gould and R. C. Lewontin, "The Spandrels of San Marco and the Panglossian Paradigm: A Critique of the Adaptationist Programme," *Proceedings of the Royal Society of London. Series B. Biological Sciences*, 205 (1979), 581-98; quotes are from pages 591 and 594.

42. See, for example, Marjorie Grene, *The Knower and the Known* (London: Faber and Faber, 1966), pp. 185-201; Sir Alister Hardy, *The Living Stream: Evolution and Man* (Cleveland: World Publishing Co., 1968); W. H. Thorpe, *Animal Nature and Human Nature* (London: Methuen, 1974); and Charles Birch, "Nature, God and Humanity." For a more complete review of recent literature questioning the scientific adequacy of neo-Darwinism, see the bibliographic essay.

43. Wilder Penfield, *The Mystery of the Mind* (Princeton, N.J.: Princeton University Press, 1975); and John C. Eccles, *Facing Reality: Philosophical Adventures of a Brain Scientist* (New York: Springer-Verlag, 1970); idem, *The Human Mystery*, Gifford Lectures, 1977-1978 (New York: Springer-Verlag, 1979); idem, *The Human Psyche*, Gifford Lectures, 1978-1979 (New York: Springer International, 1979); and idem, "The Self-Conscious Mind and the Meaning and Mystery of Personal Existence," *Teachers College Record*, vol. 82, no. 3 (Spring 1981), 403-26.

44. Eccles, "The Self-Conscious Mind," pp. 416-17.

45. David Bohm, *Causality and Chance in Modern Physics* (London: Routledge & Kegan Paul, 1957); idem, *Wholeness and the Implicate Order*. See also "The Enfolding-Unfolding Universe, A Conversation with David Bohm," *Revision*, vol. 1 (Summer/Fall 1978), 24-51; and "The Physicist and the Mystic—Is a Dialogue between Them Possible? A Conversation with David Bohm, Conducted by Renee Weber," *Revision*, vol. 4 (Spring 1981), 36-52. See also David Bohm and Renee Weber, "Nature as Creativity," *Revision*, 5 (Fall 1982), 35-40; and Rupert Sheldrake and David Bohm, "Morphogenetic Fields and the Implicate Order," ibid., pp. 41-48.

46. Bohm, *Wholeness and the Implicate Order*, p. 7.

47. Ibid., p. 11.

48. Ibid., pp. 175, 172-89. See also pp. 111-71.

49. Bohm, "The Physicist and the Mystic," p. 24.

50. Ibid., pp. 24-27.

51. In this connection, Bohm explicitly denies the value of natural selection as a sole explanation of evolution. "I would like to propose with respect to evolution," he says, "that natural selection is not the whole story, but rather that evolution is a sign of the creative intelligence of matter exploring different structures which go far beyond what is needed for survival. Although survival in the environment determines which of these will go on and which won't, it cannot be the only factor in evolution. If it were, there would be no reason for the development of human beings with such a complex brain. Indeed, rats are far better at survival than we could ever hope to be. It is thus hard to see survival as the whole explanation. One could say, rather, that evolution results from the creative movement of matter, which is infused with intelligence." Ibid., p. 34.

52. Ibid., p. 35.

53. Some attempts to take into account new perspectives in modern science do not seem to evade entirely this problem of substituting a new scientism for an old. Fritjof Capra raises some questions in this regard in *The Tao of Physics: An Exploration of the Parallels between Modern*

Physics and Eastern Mysticism (Boulder, Colo.: Shambala Publications, 1975). In this book, Capra eloquently describes the new situation in physics which points beyond mechanistic modes of thought: the importance in modern physics of insight; of knowing as participative; of the multi-dimensional nature of reality; of the need to recognize the essential unity of polar opposites; of the dynamic character of reality; of the interconnection of all things and events in the universe; and of the replacement of the notion of solid particles of matter moving in a void by the recognition of interweaving patterns of energy. So far so good, and on this score Capra's account is to be welcomed. But Capra moves farther, finding in the harmonies and patterns being disclosed by modern physics correspondences and parallels with the cosmic harmonies and patterns of the ancient spiritual traditions of the East. Most of Capra's book is devoted to exploring these correspondences which he finds between modern physics and Hindu, Buddhist, and Taoist mysticism; however, in the process, correspondences and parallels, which raise intriguing questions for further enquiry, merge without difficulty into simple identities and equalities. In other words, for Capra the harmonies and patterns dealt with in modern physics as it now exists are seen as identical with the spiritual harmonies of the mystical traditions.

In this a critical jump has been made and a number of serious, unaddressed problems appear. In the first place, rather than pursuing, as Bohm seems to be doing, the further transformations in physics and modern science demanded by the participative mode of knowing scientists are increasingly finding necessary, Capra accepts physics as it now exists and finds confirmation for it in the Eastern traditions. As we have seen, however, physics today still remains almost entirely instrumental and quantitative; the patterns, forces, interactions, and harmonies described and dealt with by modern physics are purely quantitative. The spiritual harmonies of the ancient traditions, on the other hand, are in their very essence primarily qualitative, and cannot be identified out of hand with lower-order quantitative relationships. By making this too-easy identification what seems to happen in Capra's account, in effect, is that the essence of Eastern spirituality is dragged down to a lower level, deprived of its own inner identity, and ends up lending sanction and support to a Western science that goes on its way unchallenged and unchanged. The conclusion appears difficult to avoid that Capra unintentionally repeats an age-old Western approach to other traditions, which we have called the exploitative-eclectic, in which no real encounter between East and West takes place, but in which those formal and superficial similarities in Eastern thought and practice are selectively appropriated to provide legitimation and confirmation for what Western science intends. At no point is this more clear than in the fact that Capra's Western scientist, despite his purported encounter with the East, does not have to undergo any personal transformation in order to pursue his quest for knowledge; whereas, in every spiritual tradition, bar none, the first and fundamental prerequisite for higher knowledge has always been self-purification and self-transformation through long, demanding, unremitting, inner personal discipline.

In the second place, there is a further, related problem in Capra's simple equation of the interconnected patterns and harmonies of modern physics with those of the spiritual traditions. It may very well be that modern physics is stumbling inadvertently into realms of being with which the spiritual traditions have long been conversant. But it does not follow necessarily that this is all for the good and to be greeted as something from which beneficial consequences will flow. Every spiritual tradition has, again without exception, maintained that certain ostensibly higher-order energies are really lower-order and highly destructive, and are to be viewed as *demonic*. It is not at all apparent why Capra should identify, for example, the energy patterns of modern physics with the nirvanic harmonies of Buddhism rather than with the forty thousand hells of the Mahayana doctrine. The latter would seem, on the face of things, to be more descriptive of the chief products of modern physics—and, "by their fruits ye shall know them": atomic bombs and an exceedingly poisonous substance, plutonium, perhaps more aptly named than has been recognized, after the god of death and the underworld. Before embracing uncritically the forces released by modern physics as fundamentally beneficent, the words of Mephisto to Faust might well be recalled:

The little folk ne'er scent the Devil
E'en though he have them by the collar.

A third problem, an intellectual-historical problem, haunts Capra's account throughout because it is never faced. Although there are indeed parallels between modern physics and Eastern spirituality, the brute fact remains that Eastern spirituality never generated anything even remotely resembling modern science. Modern science, and modern physics, are the products of Western culture, and it is nearly accurate to say, of Western European culture. This suggests that the place to start, if we are to understand adequately the origins and implications, and both the dangers and full promise, of modern science, is not with the East, but with the cultural, philosophical, and religious-mystical traditions of the West.

None of these comments is meant to detract from the significance, the usefulness, and the intriguing insights of Capra's work, but simply to raise some questions that require much more attention, if we are to avoid falling back into a new scientism.

For criticisms of Capra's and related views, see Peacocke, *Creation and the World of Science*, pp. 360-63; John Davy, "Man and the Underworld," *The Golden Blade* (annual) (1980), 61-79; and "Reflections on the New-Age Paradigm; An Interview with Ken Wilbur," *Revision*, vol. 4 (Spring 1981), 53-74. The Western origins of modern science are treated in Stanley L. Jaki, *The Road of Science and the Ways of God*, The Gifford Lectures, 1974-1975, 1975-1976 (Chicago: University of Chicago Press, 1978).

54. David Bohm, "Imagination, Fancy, Insight, and Reason in the Process of Thought," in *Evolution of Consciousness, Studies in Polarity*, ed. Shirley Sugerman (Middletown, Conn.: Wesleyan University Press, 1976), pp. 51-68.

4
Insight-Imagination ⸺

Insight

In exploring the significance for our education and culture of the participatory nature of all our knowing, perhaps the best place to begin is with the imagination. In recent years there have been recurrent surges of interest in the importance of the imagination. Some scientists and philosophers of science have begun to emphasize the role of the imagination in science, particularly in the formulation of scientific hypotheses;[1] and spokesmen for the arts have regularly argued for the primacy of the "creative imagination" in their field. In addition, in education, reform movements are periodically mounted in the name of encouraging the development of creative imagination and personal expression. But in many cases the imagination is still confused with the fictive and the "imaginary" in the sense of being basically unreal. As a result, in both science and education, the imagination is pushed into the background, and the main focus remains upon the content of knowledge that the imagination, it is conceded, has produced. And in the arts the conception of the imagination has been so weak that both it and art come to seem dispensable. This splitting of imagination from knowledge is a false separation to start with, and it consigns to second place that which is primary. Any attempt to understand the full significance of the participatory nature of knowing requires an adequate grasp of the imagination, for it is only through the imagination that we have any knowledge whatsoever. In our discussion we will draw upon the work of many, but especially upon that of David Bohm and Owen Barfield, who have done perhaps more than any others in recent years to show the central importance of imagination and insight in all our thinking and knowing.

In a major study of how philosophers since David Hume and Immanuel Kant have thought about the imagination, Mary Warnock speaks of the imagination as "our means of interpreting the world" and "also our means of forming images in the mind."[2] The images make possible our interpretations; for they are *the way* in which we see and interpret the world and objects in the world. The imagination, the image-making power of the mind, therefore, shapes our everyday perception of the world, for there is no perception separated from interpretation. The imagination lifts perceptions from raw, undifferentiated experience and gives them their shape, form, and significance. It is, therefore, the imagination, Warnock says, that enables us to see the world as significant and as representing that which is not immediately present. There is in the imagination "a sense that there is always *more* to experience, and *more in* experience than we can predict." And it is the image-making power that enables us "to present this vision to others, for them to share or reject." The imagination, then, is necessary for perceiving and understanding the world, makes possible human discourse and purposeful activity, is the source for creating and understanding works of art, and is that "by which, as far as we can, we 'see into the life of things.' " And it arises from the emotions as much as from the intellect, from the heart and from the head. The imagination is an unbroken field encompassing the whole human being. And it is that which joins us in knowing-interplay and participation with others and the world. To neglect the imagination, to mis-educate, to abuse it, to narrow and confine it, is to choke the human lifeline at its source.

With a grasp of the centrality of imagination it also becomes possible, and is important, to make some distinctions among the various ways the imagination works, not all of them equally desirable. One way of doing this is to look from the other side at knowledge itself, much as we have at the imagination, paying particular attention to all that is included in knowledge, even, or especially when, it is not ordinarily recognized by us as such, and to ask how the various kinds of knowledge arise and are interrelated.

There is a fundamental distinction, David Bohm has argued, between the new knowledge that comes from deep, energetic Insight, and the kind of knowledge that comes from merely rearranging what is already given.[3] All genuinely new knowledge comes by means of passionate, energy-filled insight that penetrates and pierces through our ordinary ways of thinking. The function of insight is twofold: to remove blocks in our customary and fixed conceptions of things, and to gain new perceptions. When we fail to attend to the central role in knowing of this deep imagination, or insight, we become trapped in the already given. In order to enable us to understand better the primary importance of insight, Bohm says we need to look closely at the different aspects of our knowledge.

There is, first, what Bohm calls *passive, abstract knowledge*. This is the kind that often comes immediately to mind when the word *knowledge* is first mentioned, and it is, unfortunately, the only kind of knowledge that entirely dominates some fairly common conceptions of education. This is the knowledge that is stored up as information in books, computers, tapes, and so forth. It is, he says, "waiting passively" to be used at our convenience. At the same time, he points out, there is *active knowledge*, or what Polanyi calls tacit knowledge. This is the knowledge contained in our nervous system, muscles, and unconscious. It is the kind of knowledge that includes our various skills, such as riding a bicycle, hammering a nail, painting a picture, or, in important aspects, carrying out a scientific experiment. There is always more to this knowledge than we can put into words, indeed, more than we are conscious of. And yet we are always drawing upon it, putting it to use, bringing it to bear in every aspect of our lives. Without this active or tacit knowledge we could not even apply or make sense of abstract information at our disposal.

Bohm also makes the important observation that included in our active knowledge are our beliefs that are based on presuppositions, "a kind of knowledge of which we are not generally aware." Our presuppositions are crucially important. They provide the framework and point of departure for all our understanding and dealing with the world, and they pervade and deeply affect our whole life and way of experiencing everything. Without them we could not function. Unfortunately, however, because they are seldom brought to consciousness, our presuppositions have the tendency to lock us into patterns of thinking and behavior that cut us off from the newness and wholeness of reality. Our presuppositions easily become prejudices that often cause great harm, and always ill-equip us for responding creatively and appropriately to others and the situations in which we find ourselves. It is here that Bohm also wants to include in our knowledge both *correct* and *incorrect knowledge*. Initially this is rather surprising, since many would maintain that incorrect knowledge is not really knowledge at all, but something else—illusion, perhaps. Bohm, however, argues that our knowledge at any moment is always a mixture of the correct and incorrect, and that "until a given item of knowledge is actually found to be incorrect, there is no way to distinguish it from correct knowledge." And it will, therefore, work in us as individuals and societies in the same way as correct knowledge. "Knowledge whether correct or incorrect, contributes in a basic and inseparable way to what the individual or society is." Our knowledge is never complete, and it is often incorrect; it is always in need of new insight.

It is essential, Bohm says, that we realize that the various parts of knowledge are really abstractions from a total living process. "In its actual concrete existence," he writes, "knowledge is an *undivided whole* in *flowing movement*, an ongoing process, an inseparable part of our overall reality." It is often useful and necessary to abstract out the parts and use them and deal with them separately. But when we forget that doing so has only a provisional and temporary validity, and start to regard the parts as absolute and fixed, our troubles begin. We then divide our experience into separate fragments and rigid, watertight compartments. We find ourselves hemmed in by all kinds of unquestioned presuppositions that act as blinders. Our favorite categories and interpretations become mistaken for unchanging truths, and become mental grooves and ruts from which we cannot break out. We begin to take knowledge as something purely objective, value-free, and unconnected with ourselves— as something "abstract to be 'applied' to a separately existent concrete experience." Unfortunately, there is in our knowledge, Bohm says, a tendency for it to acquire the presupposition that at any given time it is absolute truth, and therefore, absolutely necessary. Knowledge as "absolute necessity" then becomes, not enlightenment, but a form of "endarkenment." Our personal lives and our society are filled with such mistaken absolute necessities that really serve as fixed priorities, traps, barriers, and compartments closed off from the new. What is required to cut through fragmentation and compartmentalization is insight.

Insight, Bohm describes as "an act of perception, permeated with intense energy and passion," that penetrates and removes barriers in existing thought and frees the mind to serve in new ways and directions. Insight announces itself as a whole, as a perception that includes "new forms of *imagination* [new images] and new *orders* of reason." Insight is an act of inward perception, "not only in the sense of *looking into* the very essence of the content that is to be known and understood, but also in the sense of looking into the mind that is engaged in the act of knowing." Insight is undivided, "total and immediate," it cannot be captured in thought, and "it affects all the different functions of the mind—physical, emotional, intellectual, and so forth." And, above all, "insight is not restricted to great scientific discoveries or to artistic creations, but rather it is of crucial importance in everything we do, especially in the ordinary affairs of life."

Bohm does point to examples of important thinkers because in them the nature of insight can be most clearly seen. Newton's conception of gravity, Einstein's notion of the constant speed of light, and Helen Keller's sudden grasp of the significance of words all came to them as perceptions, as images, not as hypotheses or conclusions drawn from logical deductions. It has been said of Mozart and Schubert that often their muscial compositions would arrive in their minds all at once, full-blown, and only then have to be laboriously translated into the notations necessary for others to play. To these examples many others could be added—Friedrich August Kekulé's sudden vision of the snake swallowing its own tail that gave him the basis for explaining the structure of the benzene ring, Henri Poincaré's mathematical inspirations, William Hamilton's insight into the Quaternion Theory in mathematics, and others. In each instance, a certain common pattern of discovery seems to be present: first, an intense period of concentrated, passionate interest and work on a problem or task, then a moment of relaxation in which the insight, unbidden and unexpected, appears—as it did to Hamilton crossing the Dublin bridge or to Poincaré stepping onto an omnibus in Coutance with his mind far away from his mathematical work—followed, finally, by a third period, again, of intense concentration, checking, developing, and working out the meaning of the insight.

It would be a mistake to attempt to codify the process as if this would guarantee our attaining insight. What is important here is that always a high level of passionate interest and energetic concentration is required—the old saw that insight comes only to the prepared mind seems confirmed by every account—and that the insight is first given as an immediate whole, a new image or order of reason. To be sure, the full meaning and implications of the initial images have to be worked out through hypotheses, formal logic, mathematics, and the ways of our ordinary thinking, and this may be an arduous process, requiring years; perhaps, in some cases, a lifetime. But these are nevertheless secondary: the insight, the image—not the hypotheses or logic—comes first.

Bohm stresses the importance of clearly distinguishing the deep act of imagination in insight from what he calls *imaginative fancy*. Most of our mental images are based on memory and as they well up in the mind either reflect what is already known or combine and recombine in a kind of associative way. The patterns and new images thus produced may in one sense be new, they have in Bohm's terms a "mechanical kind of novelty," but they consist of what is already given and merely recombine and re-present it in different ways. This process of imaginative fancy may be very useful in preparing the mind for the unsuspected, in unfolding all that is present in memory or the given situation, or in playing out beforehand a proposed plan of action. But is does not itself yield new insight.

And imaginative fancy can also be extremely limiting and stultifying. Because mental images are intimately linked with the entire person, including will, desires, fears, wishes, and so forth, they have a powerful effect on the whole of a person's perceptions and behavior. When such fancy is taken as absolute it becomes a barrier to further knowledge. If the images in imaginative fancy bring to expression particularly powerful memories imbued with fear and anxiety, for example, they can distort all of life. Or, when in literary or scientific thought, certain images are accepted as absolute, perhaps because they have been associated with long periods of successful application and have acquired professional approval and public acceptance, they begin to function as unquestioned presuppositions that also block, rather than facilitate inquiry. This is not to say that whole books, research programs, and entire disciplines may not be dominated by such images and consist largely in the learned spinning-off of associated images and thoughts in imaginative fancy that fills lectures and libraries, is awarded fellowships and funding grants, and is a great cloud of endarkenment. To challenge the sanctity and absoluteness of many publicly and professionally accepted images often means not only having to join what to the respectable appears as the lunatic fringe, in order to get any chance of fresh perspective, but it is also to invite disregard, professional banishment, or worse. Imaginative fancy may be very helpful; it can be harmful; and it does not necessarily usher in new insight.

Similarly, for Bohm, formal logic must be seen as an abstraction from a larger movement of rationality. It is in his view "the intellectual counterpart of the imaginative rearrangement of known images that takes place in imaginative fancy." Formal logic is necessary and essential in providing categories and methods for introducing order and control into life. Formal logic, he points out, is always based on the complete fixing of our categories, assumptions, hyptheses, axioms, and so forth, that are usually regarded as " 'solid ground' for the universe of discourse." This universe of discourse is necessary, but it too is an abstraction, which, if made absolute along with its logical connections, serves to veil the universe of reality. Formal logic is secondary to insight and is never the source of new knowledge. Formal logic and discursive reason not in the service of insight simply lock us all the tighter into our given presuppositions and rigid mental compartments, and stand as obstacles to further perception.

The making absolute of formal logic and of imaginative fancy go hand in hand. The tendency in the modern world to identify the imagination with imaginative fancy is probably the main reason why the imagination is usually thought of in its shallowest form as the imaginary, the unreal, the playful and whimsical, or the phantasmagoric. Every ten years or so there seems to break out among educational reformers a rash of enthusiasm for developing the creative imagination. The creative imagination in this context, however, almost always turns out to be little more than imaginative fancy, and the reforms end up not amounting to very much. In fact, they usually trigger a reaction calling for tighter discipline and a clamping down on unformed spontaneity and personal expression (that are always mistakenly thought to be the essence of creativity when imagination is reduced utterly to fancy). This attenuation of the imagination is the parallel of the narrowing of reason that is characteristic of the modern mind set. Reason, imagination, and insight in the fullest sense are nearly identical—each is a way of bringing out different aspects of an unbroken whole—but when they are narrowed and fixed, as in fancy and logic, they separate and clash. And fancy and logic by themselves, either separately or together, do not lead to insight.

Insight according to Bohm operates in two ways, negatively and positively. Negatively, it removes the blocks and barriers that prevent new perception. This negative task requires a "relentless questioning" of everything that does not make sense in all our given presuppositions, assumptions, and taken-for-granted knowledge. A major concern of education ought to be to create a climate of trust in which radical questioning can take place without fear. Bohm insists, therefore, that the relentless questioning of which he speaks is quite different from that academic skepticism which corrodes everything and leads nowhere. This relentless questioning is undertaken within the context of insight and already embodies a trust in the possibility of gaining new perceptions. The negative is in the context and service of the positive, which is the new perception. A comment by Mary Warnock in her similar descriptions of the operations of imagination points in the same direction. She writes that while the imagination makes the world familiar and meaningful to us, we can also use it "to render our experience unfamiliar and mysterious"—we can scramble and untidy what has become fixed, customary, and conventional, and in so doing open ourselves to vast new dimensions of experience and meaning hitherto blocked from view.[4]

Becoming aware of both the questioning (negative) and the perceiving (positive) aspects of insight may also suggest another way in which insight functions. Perhaps there is some disadvantage in portraying as the chief examples of insight only persons such as, say, Einstein and Kekulé, who are clearly unusual and for whom insight comes as a flash. They do serve to illustrate vividly what is essential in insight—its wholeness and immediacy, its appearance as image and perception, the clarity and energy it requires. But these examples may, although they need not, also obscure the possibility of a more gradual and indirect working of insight. This would come from regarding new images and perceptions as potential insights, in much the same way that one might entertain a hypothesis. If, when treated as hypothesis, the image or perception begins to illuminate experience, connects loose ends, and makes sense of things in new ways, it can begin to function for us as insight or preparation for insight. We do not even have to be convinced by the hypothetical view; in fact, may have at first good reasons for rejecting it, and still be willing to put it to the test by letting it work upon us provisionally.

We might take as an example the conception of evolutionary change suggested by Bohm—and the similar view found at places in Polanyi's work.[5] If I am a convinced neo-Darwinist, I can simply, and most likely will reject Bohm's view; or I can entertain it hypothetically, momentarily holding my objections in abeyance, and allow it to work upon my understanding of the evidence in the possibility that it might indeed be the gateway to new insight. What is required of me is good faith, openness, and a capacity to question old categories and established presuppositions.

Or another analogy might be the experience of contemplating a work of art, say, a painting of high quality. The actual insight that led to the creation of the painting was the artist's, not mine. But, if in standing before the painting and allowing the whole image to work upon me, my sensibilities and perceptions begin to be moved and awareness is aroused that I previously lacked, I begin to share in the artist's insight. Again, the prerequisite is an openness, and a willingness not to shut out the new the moment familiar mental habits, categories, and compartments begin to be shaken. Bohm does not speak explicitly of insight understood as working in this way, but he does seem to suggest it. In fact, he presents the implicate order, for example, as a species of insight too much neglected and one worthy of being contemplated as a source of further insight. His notion of insight itself is presented and developed in the same spirit. The relentless questioning of mental blocks and conventional categories, in other words, may take the positive form of entertaining another's image or insight as potentially one's own. This is neither an uncritical, slavish acceptance of another's point of view, nor a despair at not being graced oneself by sudden enlightenment. It would seem to make sense to speak of "living into Insight."

Essential throughout, however, are attention and energy—an intense awareness of the questions to be asked and a passion for pursuing them. This twofold driving power of insight Bohm is also willing to describe in older, more traditional terms: clarity and passion, mind and heart; but mind and heart concentrated, focused, and fused. Insight itself is this fusion, an "active intelligence" beyond any of the energies that can be defined and grasped by ordinary thought and emotion.[6]

It is in this sense that we have used insight and imagination interchangeably, and will continue to do so, to speak of the active participation of the knowing mind in the known. Both are ways of talking about the source in our knowledge of new meaning and new understanding. The imagination is not only that sense in Mary Warnock's phrase that "there is always *more* to experience, and *more in* what we experience than we can predict" (and control), but it is also the means wherein that *more* to and *more in* can be revealed.[7] Those conceptions of knowing and theories of education that downgrade or have no place for the imagination condemn us to a world of increasing homogeneity, sterility, and staleness. In them, the possibility of newness is lacking.

Owen Barfield has devoted much attention to the imagination as the source of new meaning in language. Like Bohm, he observes that ways of knowing based solely on the methods of logic can never introduce new meaning and new understanding. The fundamental principle of logic is that the meanings of the words it employs hold constant; "logic presupposes, first and foremost," he writes, "that the same word means the same thing in one sentence as it does in another."[8] Logic demands, in other words, that meaning be fixed and unchanging, and the logical use of language can, therefore, "never add any meaning to it." The syllogism, for example, does not lead to new meaning because the conclusion is already implicit in the premises. To avoid misunderstanding, it ought perhaps to be stressed that Barfield here is in no way belittling logic and logical thought. Logic is essential to the whole structure and order of language, and without it, we could not talk. The syllogism, and related logical methods, are necessary for classifying meaning and removing confusion and misunderstanding. But the logical nature of language puts us in a paradoxical situation whenever we want to say something new. We must employ words with fixed, old meanings to convey the new. How is this possible? Barfield remarks that it seems we must "either mean what was meant before or talk nonsense." But a further possibility is that we talk "what is nonsense on the face of it, but in such a way that the recipient may have the new meaning suggested to him."[9]

The possibility of this dual use of language is the essence of metaphor. Metaphor, Barfield says, "involves two different tensions." There is the "tension between two ostensibly incompatible meanings," the old and the new. At the same time there is a tension within ourselves between our capacity "to experience the incompatibles as a mysterious unity" and our being able simultaneously to appreciate that they are incompatible and dual in meaning. He writes: "Without the former [the recognition of unity in the duality] metaphor is nonsense language, but without the latter [the awareness that there really are present two very different meanings] it is not even language."[10] Paul Ricoeur describes metaphor in somewhat similar terms when he writes that "as the metaphorical sense not only abolishes but preserves the literal sense, the metaphorical reference maintains the ordinary vision in tension with the new one it suggests."[11] Barfield elsewhere illustrates the importance of maintaining the tensions in commenting on William Blake's oft-quoted statement that when he looked at the sun, he did not see as did everybody else, "a round thing somewhat like a guinea," but rather "an immeasurable Company of the Heavenly Host crying Holy, Holy, Holy is the Lord God Almighty."[12] Barfield notes Blake's insistence on the need for "double vision," and comments that Blake obviously did not mean that he was incapable of also seeing the sun as something like a guinea. Not to be able to see the first, Barfield says, would be the way of madness, but to see only that, and to be incapable of the second, would be to remain forever stuck at a very low level of meaning at the most.

Metaphorical language is possible because of the power of imagination to perceive the *more to* and *more in* our ordinary experience. Recall Barfield's statement that when words are not merely reduced to labels or logical connections it is their nature to use the material to name the immaterial. In metaphor, the imaginal capacity of the mind is already at work. And it must follow, as Barfield argues, that, if words bear an inner meaning, so too must nature and our experience of nature from which words spring. In the images and perceptions of the imagination, as in the metaphor, the inner meaning of nature begins to become manifest. Knowledge of the new—Insight-Imagination— is a participation in that inner meaning and significance. Knowledge as participation means in Barfield's words that "the mind of man is not, as Coleridge put it, 'a lazy onlooker' on an external world but itself a structural component of the world it contemplates."[13] And here once again is suggested that wholeness and creativity of participation which we are, perhaps, now in position to explore even further.

Wholeness

The Wholeness of Insight-Imagination

We all seem to have some innate sense of relationship to the world and to other persons; yet our habitual ways of thinking often deny this connectedness. Objects are regarded as discrete entities separated from one another, linked only by external relationships of physical cause and effect. And this thinking carries over into a view of other persons as self-enclosed bundles of desires and interests joined only temporarily by common tasks (functions) that are perceived for the time being to provide some mutual satisfactions—but entities ready at any moment, when the tasks are completed or the interests clash, to fall apart once more into their essential loneliness and isolation or, if the interests of each clash too much, to fall upon one another in antagonism and conflict. The recognition of knowing as participation begins to reveal clearly that in this separative vision—with the separating behavior it fosters—we are at the mercy of an abstraction, a partial abstraction drawn from the whole of experience and turned into an absolute.

In attempting to understand better what is involved in the wholeness of imagination, let us begin at what may at first appear a rather unlikely starting point: the notion of the evolution of consciousness, but considered from a somewhat different perspective than earlier.[14] The emerging sense of individual selfhood in the West during the past four hundred years must be taken into account in any adequate conception of wholeness, or any effort to recover wholeness. The emergence of individuality has been closely associated with the rise of science, indeed the two seem to have emerged hand in hand, each reinforcing the other. The modern experience of being a separate individual self, different from other selves and standing outside of nature, capable of looking at nature as an uninvolved observer, seems to be quite different from the experience of earlier ages. In contrast to a modern sense of individuality, humans of earlier periods seem to have felt themselves much more an integral part of their surroundings, immersed in the community, often finding their true identity not in themselves but in the tribe or the group, and embedded in an all-embracing world organism that spoke directly to them in symbol and myth with a reality more ultimate than any conferred by a sense of individual selfhood. In fact consciousness of being a separate, self-contained individual, rather than being immersed and sustained in the communal and the world-whole, would have been experienced as a loss of meaning and reality—a pulling away from the source of things. But the emergence of a sharpened sense of self-identity can be seen as just such a contraction of consciousness from an immersion in the whole to a point of heightened concentration in the individual.

And without this growing sense of being a separate individual standing over against others and nature, it is difficult to see how modern science would have been possible. Only as human beings were able to experience themselves as separate and independent were they able to begin to look at nature with the detachment, objectivity, and clarity that came to be the scientific approach. And as science took root, with its emphasis on precision, the sharpening of critical judgment, the execution of carefully controlled, objective experimentation, it nourished and strengthened the sense of individuality. The repeated, concentrated practice of modern scientific ways of knowing has been for modern man a kind of training or schooling in conscious self-awareness. It may even be conjectured that without the rigorous discipline and repeated practice of the scientific way of knowing, with its demand for detached objectivity—the onlooker approach—human beings would never have been able to emancipate themselves from immersion in the whole. With the onlooker consciousness has come the possibility of individual freedom.

The rise of modern science has been inextricably intertwined with the development of self-directed human reason, the heightening of individuality and the possibility of genuinely free action, uncoerced by communal custom and natural necessity— hence, we can understand well the encomiums on behalf of individual liberty and the hopes for free social beginnings unfettered by the past that accompanied the early rise of science. And yet the gain in individuality, freedom, clarity, and precision has also brought with it severe loss—a loss of significance, a growing experience of isolation from others, a breakdown in communal purposes, and a vision of nature as cold and void of meaning. For all its purported gains it seems that our detached, fragmented approach to the world has gone too far. In our atomistic individualism and mechanistic manipulation of nature we seem to be past the point of diminishing returns, approaching, some would argue, the brink of no return. Herein lie the marks of classical tragedy: a conflict of values all of which are undeniably desirable but mutually exclusive. It does not appear possible to have both the one and the other at the same time. A gain in clarity seems to entail a loss of meaning; a return to the whole seems to require relinquishing the possibility of freedom and self-consciousness. Is it possible to recover wholeness without giving up the possibilities of freedom and individual authenticity? Is it possible to transform our ways of knowing without sacrificing the gains in clear awareness and self-consciousness they have helped make possible?

Still, we are unable to escape the claims of wholeness. Connectedness will not be denied and will reassert itself, if only as an abstract reflection of the full reality. Even the most thoroughgoing reductionism, in social theory as well as in science, attempts to recover some kind of interconnectedness by reassembling the separate parts it takes to be ultimate in a more embracing unity. The unities produced in this way, however, turn out to be abstract and lifeless. Machine models of the universe, while valuable for specific purposes, leave out all that make up the interacting, growing, qualitative richness of living nature. Visions of society composed of agglomerations of atomistic individuals lend themselves to systematic collectivization and the denial of individual rights for the sake of an abstract totality (a totalitarian*ism*). What is initially greeted as a "liberation of the parts" leads to the reassertion of a false wholeness in which intrinsic meaning and essential freedom are both sacrificed.

It is little wonder that increasing attempts are made to counter separative, fragmenting ways of thinking with other approaches stressing cooperation, communication, ecology, interaction, altruism, and systems theories, which emphasize global connections and try to make a firm place for the human being. Repeatedly, however, these counter-views become themselves infected with separative thinking and try to accommodate new perceptions to old perspectives (we will have systems theory, for example, but only in terms of the relations between quantitative units). Or, they are treated as minor refinements necessary for dealing with "special cases" within a basically unaltered reductionism (let us have ecology by all means, but continue to conceive of life itself as essentially nothing more than the complicated assemblages of the bits in a DNA molecule). The recognition of the centrality of imagination in our knowing, however, promises a fundamental change of approach, for the imagination is first and foremost an awareness of the primacy of wholeness and of the relation of the parts to the whole.

The wholeness of the imagination is not one that we deduce or infer by building it up logically out of simpler elements. Rather, it is given in its own immediacy and integrity as the starting point for all that follows. What James Hillman says of the nature of the image in the experience of the individual psyche holds for all the images and concepts of the imagination: "an image is complete just as it presents itself (it can be elaborated and deepened by working on it, but to begin with it is all there; wholeness right in the image)."[15]

"Every imagination," writes John Davy, "is born as a *whole*, as some kind of picture or concept; yet it is also an organic part of all the rest of conscious life, intimately related to our memories and past experience. It has the same relation to our inner life as a part of an organism has to the whole. It can be studied as an independent entity—but if completely separated from its living context, it dies. Both in our consciousness and in living phenomena, organism and the whole are primary, parts and atoms are secondary."[16] Here in this statement of Davy's we can begin to get a firm grasp of what the wholeness of the imagination entails.

We apprehend a great work of art, for example, as a whole. We may marvel at the many and intricate details with which the artist has executed the specific parts of the picture, but they have their meaning and worth only in relation to the whole. We can dissect the picture into classified and separate areas in order to get a better understanding of the role they play in the entire picture, but, if we did not return repeatedly to contemplation of the whole image, the individual areas would have no significance. We can analyze the pigments and material constituents of the painting, but all the detailed information we could possibly amass regarding pigmentation, the number and direction of brush strokes, the tensile strength and surface texture of the canvas, and so forth, could never by themselves provide the vaguest clue to the painting itself. And we would never think of cutting the painting into smaller pieces on the assumption that, if perhaps we could not find a buyer willing to pay the whole price, we could find several buyers willing to take the bargain reductions. The value of the painting is in the whole.

When we contemplate an image presented to our senses by nature, the activity of the imagination is even more complex. Recognizing a plant, for example, a rose, is itself an act of imagination. We never have before us the full being of the plant, but only its partial manifestation at a particular moment. The full plant exists only in time, from the seed and its sprouting, to the growing and leafing shoot, to the budding and blossoming flower, to the final drying up of the plant and the deposit of a new seed. We recognize the blossoming rose before us in the context presented by the imagination, usually unconsciously unless intentionally brought to mind, of the full plant existing in the whole of past, present, and future. The real plant is an intangible, time-being grasped in its reality in the imagination. Furthermore, what is presented to us in the rose is rich with qualities—scent, color, texture, form, and so forth. These are all essential to the rose; the qualities make the rose a rose. To suppose that the essence of the rose lies only in its atomic structure or the material elements drawn from the earth is to leave out the very things that the image of the rose presents to us as essential to its being a rose.

In such a relatively simple sense-experience, the imagination is at work in at least a twofold way: presenting to us the wholeness of the plant as a being in time and the wholeness of the plant in its qualitative relationships and richness. From this wholeness we can then work on the parts with various kinds of conceptual abstractions for special purposes, breeding a disease-resistant plant, for instance. But the abstract concepts, say, of genetic structure that we find useful for the purposes of plant breeding do not give us the essence of the rose as such, and as the sole approach to the knowledge of living organisms are patently deficient.

It also becomes clear that the wholeness of imagination is not monolithic, undifferentiated sameness. It is not simple, bare oneness. The wholeness presented in imagination is more the living unity of a tension of opposites. It is the kind of unity we have seen revealed in metaphor. Both Ricoeur and Barfield have spoken of metaphor as the holding in tension with one another of two incompatible meanings that together reveal a deeper unity of meaning which joins them. In metaphor it is essential that the incompatibles, or polarities, not be overcome one by the other, nor that they be swallowed up and dissolved in sameness, but that they be maintained together in all their strength. And in that tension between them the imagination grasps a larger meaning and deeper connection than appears in either separately. The wholeness of imagination revealed in the tension of polarities is akin to the unity of the human being, which we have seen is manifest in the peculiar nature of the quintessential human problems—problems that cannot be solved by doing away with them but only by living through them in the tension of opposing, equally desirable values. For this reason a living language of metaphorical creativity, not unilinear technical reason, provides both an essential safeguard of the human being, and also a fundamental insight into the living wholeness revealed in and by the imagination.

In the wholeness of imagination we can begin to discern an answer to the question whether it is possible to have both unity and the individual, meaning and clarity, wholeness and freedom. In the unity of opposites grasped by the imagination the parts exist and interact with their own relative integrity, but together express a larger, living wholeness. Through the imagination it becomes possible, in M. C. Richards's phrase, "to experience the whole in every part."[17]

In the imagination, the universal and the individual become windows, one to the other. The freedom of the individual in imagination is the channel for the realization of meaning in wholeness. Jean Paul Sartre has also emphasized the importance of the imagination as the source of freedom in human life. But for Sartre it is this because the products of the imagination in his view are purely fictional and, thus, not subject to natural necessity.[18] In the understanding of the imagination presented here the imagination is the only source of freedom, as it is for Sartre, precisely because it is *not* fictive but because it is actively participative in reality. And were the participating imagination to become more central in our knowing we should begin to be able to move freely back and forth between the whole and the parts, focusing at certain times and for certain purposes, now on the one, now on the many, without breaking the connection that joins them. A far-reaching transformation of knowing, as it is already implied in our ordinary, but still neglected, experiences of the imagination, would be truly in the offing.

We obtain the images and concepts of the imagination by bringing together what we take from sense perception with what we find in our own inner being, in our memories, experience, ideals, attitudes, and our various mental, moral, and physical energies. When we begin to attend fully to the imagination it becomes increasingly clear that the adequacy of our knowing depends both on what we bring from within ourselves together with an openness to all that the other—nature, the other person—stands ready to reveal. Both are apprehended together. What happens within the self as knower has consequences for the world; what happens in the world affects the knower. There is no such thing as a totally detached knowing. We are responsible for the images and concepts we bring to bear in the imagination. We are, in short, responsible for the kind of world we come to know and to create. There can be no adequate, genuine knowledge that does not involve deep changes in the knower. The kind of knowledge, such as purely quantitative knowledge, that requires the least in the way of self-transformation will also be the least penetrating, most superficial kind of knowledge. It will also be the kind of knowledge most subject to misuse and distortion by the unknown, unconscious—and hence irresponsible—projections of an intellectually, imaginatively, and morally untransformed inner self.

We can, to be sure, remain satisfied with less than a fully participative knowing in imagination. However, we do not escape, thereby, the imagination, we simply draw upon it in an attenuated, limited way. We fall back not upon some kind of image-free objective thinking, but rather upon fixed logic and imaginative fancy, both limited to the already given in memory and past experience. Rather than opening to the possibilities of insight-imagination through the developing of the full sources of intelligibility in ourselves and in nature, we begin to allow abstract conceptions cut off from both inner life and outer life to dominate. We begin to project into the phenomena of nature all kinds of abstract concepts that give us some very complex means of prediction and control, but bear almost no relation either to the living, qualitatively rich processes displayed by nature or to the global relations that link human beings to nature and to one another. The power of the imagination is revealed negatively in the hold that the lesser images and concepts thrown up by imaginative fancy can exert upon us, hypnotizing us, as it were, so that it becomes almost impossible to step outside the grooves and compartments of habitual thought. By not opening our powers of cognition in imagination to nature we remain trapped within ourselves, and at the same time impose our abstract and fanciful concepts on nature, imprisoning her. The most important task of education would seem to be the education of the imagination. But for this to take place a much more adequate grasp of imagination and imaginative insight is called for than the current absorption with imaginative fancy makes possible. And this, in turn, requires greater than usual awareness of the involvement of the whole human being in the activity of thinking and knowing.

The Wholeness of the Human Being in Imagination

Thinking as imagination and insight enfolds the whole human being—thought, feeling, willing, valuing. The separation of thinking from willing or of thinking from feeling fragments the person, as it fragments the world presented in thought, and makes genuine insight impossible. The recovery of the wholeness of imagination is also a healing (a making whole) of the human being—and potentially of the world. In imagination and insight the depths of thinking are reestablished. Even a narrow reason and imaginative fancy can come to life and sink roots in a deeper, more comprehensive rationality. The living-thinking of imagination includes feeling and will and embraces subject and object, inner and outer.

Thinking and Feeling

Thinking that is not sustained to some extent by interest (a feeling) cannot serve as a way of knowledge. Unfortunately, the separation frequently made between thinking and feeling often simply blinds reason to the influence upon it of all kinds of interests that have nothing to do with the desire to know. The narrowing of reason, and the cutting of it off from feeling, increases, rather than prevents, the possibilities of its being contaminated by irrationality. Where there is no heartfelt desire for knowledge, thinking becomes impossible, or, more common and more ominous, is drawn into the service of drives and motives desirous not of knowing, but only of using. Thinking as knowing requires from the beginning, therefore, both a heartfelt interest in the other and a respect, a reverence for the other and what the other has to reveal. But interest and reverence are feelings. The deeper we probe the nature of thinking, the thicker and more complex become its connections with feeling. A narrow reason, a truncated thinking cut off from feeling, is unwittingly vulnerable to misuse and misdirection and is deprived of the full powers of rationality.

"Feeling," writes Paul Ricoeur, "is not contrary to thought. It is thought made ours."[19] And thought that is not ours belongs to someone or something else. It is thought that is blocked, trapped, by alien drives, thought that is not open to insight, and that cannot, therefore, lead to knowledge. Here lies what at first glance might appear to be an insoluble double bind. It is clear that the separation of thought from feeling has arisen, in part, from a concern that thought not be hamstrung and led astray by emotions foreign to it. And, it must be acknowledged that such irrational emotions do, indeed, exist. The way forward, however, lies not in narrowing reason and ignoring feeling, but in discovering and strengthening those feelings in which thinking finds its complete expression. Such an approach is quite other than the currently modish and mindless exaltation of feelings as indiscriminately good and healthy, if we but "get them all out." To maintain that feelings are good and thinking is bad (rigid, obsessive, compulsive, anal-retentive, whatever) is but the mirror image and reaction to the notion that thinking is good and the feelings are bad. The task is to find the unity of thinking and feeling in the wholeness of imagination.

It is not merely that our knowing is emotionally conditioned. More important, feeling can be a way of knowing—an organ of perception. The philosopher John Macmurray has argued that the crucial point to understand is the primacy of feeling in cognition. Macmurray writes: "It is not that our feelings have a secondary and subordinate capacity for being rational or irrational. It is that reason is primarily an affair of emotion, and that the rationality of thought is the derivative and secondary one."[20] Macmurray stresses the need to recognize and to speak of "emotional reason" in human beings. It is emotional reason that "is our capacity to apprehend objective values."[21] In other words, feeling is the means by which we perceive values and qualities as objective, as well as subjective, realities. Feeling opens and discovers the world of qualities.

Reverence, for example, we have mentioned as the necessary condition for that authentic knowing in which the integrity of the other is recognized. More than that, however, reverence also becomes the capacity for apprehending essential qualities in the other. Barfield writes that "reverence is not simply a virtue for which we may expect full marks in heaven, or a device for bolstering up the social establishment. It is an organ of perception for a whole range of qualities that are as imperceptible without it as another whole range is imperceptible without an ear for music."[22] One is reminded of Ralph Waldo Emerson's aphorism, "In the uttermost meaning of the words thought is devout, and devotion is thought," with an important difference. Whereas Emerson's words lend themselves to a kind of mysticism of vagueness, there is, as Barfield shows, a precision and penetration in reverence as an organ of perception—as there is in an ear for music (another cognitive feeling)—that is anything but vague or airy-fairy, for it increases in very specific ways the content and depth of our awareness. And the development of such feeling requires the utmost discipline, attentiveness, and sensitivity in the knower.

The feeling perception of all that nature has to reveal calls for a rich life of the senses. When our senses are alive, writes Macmurray, "We see and hear and feel things that we never noticed before, and find ourselves taking delight in their existence."[23] Our analytic intellect may be very bright, but, if our feelings are dull and stupid, we can know only a portion, and probably the least important part, of what nature has to disclose. The range of our senses must be enlivened, if we are to grasp the living reality of nature. And the traffic in this interaction is two-way. "If we are to be full of life and fully alive," says Macmurray, "it is the increase in our capacity to be aware of the world through our senses which has first to be achieved."[24] A narrow reason by itself is poverty stricken; it can know only an empty shell of a world, and can sustain only a starved and cramped personal life. It is important, however, not to mistake the senses as such as the source of our knowledge. The senses are the occasions for feeling perception to come into play; they are the raw materials with which imagination—as the unity of idea, image, and felt reality—goes to work. If we seek to know nature in all her fullness, and do not wish, except for special purposes, to remain satisfied with an abstraction, we need to bring and hold within our imagination all that our feeling perception at work in all our senses has to offer.

Feeling as an organ of perception is, likewise, crucial to our coming to know other persons. We do not logically infer the presence of another from the body in space, with its particular shape and movement, that stands before us. In the other's words, gestures, expressions, the form and aspect of their bearing and presence, we sense in a more immediately feeling way their inner reality. Our capacity to enter into intimate, knowing communion with another also depends mightily on the degree of our sensitivities and our felt inner reality. An attempt to build up a knowledge of the human being that excludes totally the personal qualities present to feeling perception leaves out the one thing most important, the human. A sociology, for example, that does not make a firm place for knowledge of persons, and for personal knowledge, is bereft of emotional reason and to that large extent is irrational.

At one point in his writings, Samuel Taylor Coleridge says that "deep thinking is attainable only by a man of deep feeling."[25] One thing, surely, that he is affirming is that in our knowing the whole person is involved.

Not all feelings serve knowledge, however, and the awareness of this accounts to a degree for the attempts to keep thinking and feeling apart. The more successful this separation, though, the greater the propensity of feelings actually to deteriorate, so that when they do well up they confirm the worst fears of those who would banish them from the rational. And much of the feeling life of modern man and modern society has deteriorated. Many of our feelings consist of little more than indiscriminate conglomerations of fears, fantasies, memories, energy discharges, habitual reactions, and conventional attitudes. Modern culture is aswim in feelings that are unformed, brutish, and maudlin. The emotions need educating as much as does the intellect. To find what this education of the emotions today requires is one of the most urgent and difficult tasks facing us.

The first step must surely be provision for and encouragement of a rich life of feeling and sensitivity. The emotional life can mature only as its growth and unfoldment are nourished, not disdained, not suppressed. A people, for example, for whom beauty is not a first priority, for whom the sensibilities are more and more dulled to the extent that they tolerate ugliness on every hand, in the architecture and sprawl of their cities, in the devastation of their land, in their workmanship, in their language, in the souls of their leaders, in the barrenness of their classrooms, has almost lost the capacity to recognize that the health of society will never be restored through the gross national product, a new election, technological advance, bigger defense spending. The atrophy of feeling perception will have cut them off from communion with the essential qualities of life.

The exercise and increase of our sensitivity to the world means, however, also heightening our sensitivity to suffering. It means not a Pollyannaish trivialization of beauty, but a full-bodied capacity to feel reality, including the terror that is often very much a part of an unsentimental awareness of beauty. Because it in-

creases our vulnerability, the prospect of enlarging and enlivening our sensitivity will not be relished by a society that, in its
pursuit of pleasure, must seek to suppress sensitivity to pain,
avoid the realities of death and suffering, and dampen its ability
to be shocked by the ubiquitous ugliness of modern mass culture. But since the feelings will not be denied, they well up
unbidden to riddle that society with all manner of anxiety and
morbidity.

And the obsession of modern society with a purely utilitarian
education, in which, from the earliest years through professional
training, concern for the life of feeling is excluded or regarded
as non-essential, further incapacitates its citizens for self-re-
newal. It produces a society, in Macmurray's words, "which
amasses power, and with power the means to the good life, but
which has no correspondingly developed capacity for living the
good life for which it has amassed the means."[26] Undoing the
blocks that prevent the growth of sensitivity to the world calls
for establishing an environment of persons and place in which
the life of feeling is valued and encouraged. And this depends
from the beginning on a willingness to become aware in our
culture and education of all that contributes to the blockage.
Recall Bohm's insistence on a relentless questioning of *all that
does not make sense* in our ordinary categories and compartments
of thought as requisite for insight. Should we not understand
this also to mean the relentless questioning of *all that does not
make for sensitivity* in ourselves and our surroundings as the initial
step toward the insight that can come from feeling as an organ
of perception?

If the obvious first need in an education of the emotions is
the recognition that feeling is important, a second is that people
learn to feel for themselves. Paul Roubiczek has described one
of the elements of sentimentality as just that failure of people
to have and to stand by their own feelings.[27] To feel what we
ought to feel or to adopt the conventional attitudes for certain
situations, without attending to our own experience, is sentimentality. This kind of sentimentality cannot lead to insight
because it is conformity to accepted patterns and ways of response. It usually also means conjuring up feelings that are out
of touch with the actual situation and that obscure rather than

illuminate what is really involved. Moreover, those whose feelings have not been enlivened and made their own are prey to others all too eager to supply them with ready-made feelings: commercial advertisers, the sensational press and television, political opportunists, and so forth. The emotions of children and adults starved by a purely utilitarian education will be inclined to feed on every scrap of sensation and sentiment they come across or that is thrown their way. Citizens who have abdicated or never known responsibility for even their ordinary perceptions of the world, which is what having conventional and supplied feelings amounts to in the end, will have great difficulty in taking responsibility for that world. Deep down they will sense it as alien, somehow not theirs at all.

Finally, an education of the emotions will mean learning to discriminate between those feelings that are appropriate to the occasion or situation and those that are not. It means becoming fully attentive to the qualities conveyed by the feelings, not dwelling in the feelings for their own sake (another mark of sentimentality) but being directed by them to the qualities they perceive. This element of attentiveness can turn even habitual emotions into occasions of perception. It can do this by enabling us to become aware of the discrepancy between the qualities displayed by our conditioned and conventional emotions, and those more appropriate to the actual situation that will emerge, if we maintain attentive awareness. Education of the emotions requires discrimination and attentiveness.

Thus, we can also become increasingly aware that it is the very nature of certain feelings, more than others, always to point beyond themselves. Feelings such as love and compassion, for example, exist only in unbroken movement through themselves to the other. Frequently, the names of love and compassion are applied to lesser feelings that indulge and turn in upon themselves, that seek to pull the other into one's own orbit. That, however, is a mistaken identity based on surface similarities. Love and compassion move relentlessly to an apprehension of and engagement with reality, and, therefore, often appear cold and "unfeeling." And they are tough: they endure through changes in mood and circumstance, and tolerate no hiding or drawing back from reality. In love and compassion feeling becomes not only an organ of perception but also an organ of cognition in which experience and knowing are one. It is also here that we can begin to catch a glimpse of the possibility, which all the great wisdom traditions have affirmed, of a knowing free of all sense experience because it moves directly in that qualitative dimension which the senses themselves manifest.

Thinking and Willing

It may also seem strange at first to consider thinking in connection with willing. Do not our ordinary experience and common use of language often suggest just the opposite? We speak of will as unreasoning drive and desire, and refer to it as "blind will." We suggest in vivid bodily imagery that thinking and will are quite different activities when we contrast "using one's head" with "gutting it through." And we have been told by countless therapists and popular psychologists that willpower is rigid, unthinking—willful—in contrast with the flexibility and sensitivity of imagination and feeling. In fact so-called Victorian willpower—"keep a stiff upper lip and grit your teeth"—once considered a prime virtue, has been pretty thoroughly discredited by now as the cause of people's running roughshod over others and at the same time giving themselves ulcers. Consequently, "letting go" has been perceived by philosophers, therapists, and religious spokesmen as the best remedy for willpower, which so often seems to mean "will to power." Unfortunately, "letting go" (or "letting be" in the terminology of the German philosopher Martin Heidegger) turns out to be more complicated than appears on initial inspection. After all, it takes an act of willpower to let go in the first place, and discussions of the process seldom make clear what follows then, whether by one last act of will we "let go" and abolish will (in which case what then if anything is to take its place?) or whether we will to let go and then must continue willing to let go; that is, continue willing to will not to will—it all becomes exceedingly complicated. Moreover, most of us know in ourselves, and other people, how easy it is to let go on one level only to grab hold all the tighter on another. The willfulness of the humble person, the smothering willful aggressiveness of the retiring doormat personality, are by now cliches of the therapeutic consulting room. And how many, at the promptings of their therapists or of their guru, have managed to "let go," to give up their own will, only to find its place taken by the undiluted will of the therapist or guru themselves? Still, for all its achievements, we do sense something destructive and narrow in Victorian will-power, and its tendency to override others against their will and frequently ourselves against our own better judgment.

Much of this confusion, and its attending complications, stems from just such a total division of thinking from willing. While thinking and willing can indeed be separated in some ways, they are in other, more important respects, intimately connected. And not to recognize both the separateness and the connections can only lead to endless confusion. Perhaps some earlier distinctions that we have made can be of help here in sorting out what is at issue. We get two different perspectives on the will (though we need not make the mistake of completely separating them, as if they had no further possible connections) when we consider the will in light of Bohm's conceptions of insight, on the one hand, and imaginative fancy, on the other.

The images and mental concepts of imaginative fancy, it will be remembered, are essentially passive, welling up, usually un-invited, in a replay of the past, or combining in various patterns that may appear novel, but that, nevertheless, add nothing really new.[28] The images and concepts of imaginative fancy are made up of memories, habits, personal biases and predilections, social conventions, and so forth. They can be very useful for they help make memory possible, and by playing with them, allowing them to rearrange and combine themselves in various ways, we can explore many of the unsuspected implications of what we have experienced. In themselves, the images and concepts of imaginative fancy do not involve the will in any essential way.

But, if we begin to take fancy as truth, particularly if we allow its images to be taken literally or to serve as presuppositions for future perceptions and actions, or, if they connect themselves with certain fears and anxieties, they begin, in Bohm's terms, to exert themselves and we seek to realize them as "absolutely necessary." They then attach themselves to the driving force of our will, in a limited and partial but, nonetheless, very powerful way. We begin to seek to establish the images and concepts of fancy against those of others, we fight for them, we grit our teeth, we brook no countervailing opinions. We begin to exercise Victorian willpower in its pejorative sense. It is just this exercise of will as unbridled and basically unseeing desire that Ellul has argued is a primary characteristic and problem of modern technology, which, apart from the restraints of more encompassing perspectives, seeks to oppose itself to, and impose itself on, all else, including human beings and nature.

In the high energy of attention and clarity that in Bohm's view makes insight possible, do we not see an entirely different expression and activity of will? Now will is called into play in all its fullness and energy as the active openness of the whole person to the influx of new meaning and new perception. The driving force and power of will to endure and persevere are all present, but now with a heightened intensity and range of action that it could never have as the mere servant of memory, mental habits, social customs, and anxiety. As an activity of sustained, attentive awareness, will takes its proper place in thinking as a striving toward participation in reality. The marks of will in its fullness are no longer opposition, fixity, coercion, but openness, spontaneity, anticipation, affirmation, and sustained, critical directedness. "Letting go" can even begin to make sense, if it is seen to be not a passive sliding off into flacidity and slackness, but as the discovery of will; not as the abdication and importance of will, but as its real coming to birth.

As the enduring energy of uninhibited clarity and "wakeful anticipation," will is an essential aspect of the imagination. In attentive awareness thinking can also make use of imaginative fancy, without being tied to it, as a source of images and concepts for expressing new insight. Imaginative fancy can now be guided and held open to the inflow of deeper meaning and coherence and to new images and concepts of the imagination to which it as such has no access. In attention and open awareness, will ceases to be Victorian willpower, though even the positive element in this may now be redeemed and enhanced by our no longer being perpetually at the mercy of mental habits and the mental grooves and compartments of convention (including the conventions of unconventional groups—whether of academia, religious bodies, the community of scientists, gay resistance, moral majorities, political liberators, and so on).

But here we also begin to discern yet a further dimension of the activity of willing in thinking. There is a guiding, directing, forming activity in thinking that is not bound to what has already been given and laid down in memory and imaginative fancy. This forming, directing quality bears a similarity to the drive of Victorian will, but, because it is coupled with or, perhaps better put, because it is the completion of awareness, it is not blind and arbitrary. There is in it a tension between openness and involvement from which arises the possibility of creative newness. Coleridge at one point speaks of the debasement of imaginative fancy by "the lethargy of custom," and Barfield, commenting on Coleridge's meaning, writes, "The mind is in thrall to the lethargy of custom when it feeds solely on images which itself has taken no active part in producing."[29] It is this production of new images and the resultant possibility of new insight that thinking permeated and sustained by active directing awareness—thinking as imagination—makes possible.

In his book *Love and Will*, psychotherapist Rollo May draws upon the philosophical term *intentionality* to provide valuable help in understanding the directional, active element in awareness.[30] As a concept, intentionality has an ancient philosophical heritage, but has been particularly developed within modern phenomenology. May skillfully unfolds its rich and varied meanings in illuminating the relation between thinking and willing. Early in this century the European philosopher, Edmund Husserl, the founder of modern phenomenology, used the term *intentionality* to describe the essence of conscious experiences. Consciousness, he said, is never empty, but is always an active consciousness of something; it always has a content from which it cannot be separated and to which it attends. But this attending to some content of consciousness is also never passive, it is always an active, directional, forming attentiveness. The mind is always active in shaping and giving meaning to the contents of consciousness; in short, in attending to the contents of consciousness the mind is always intending them. It is this shaping, directing, meaning-giving activity of the will in mind to which Husserl gave the name *intentionality*. May comments: "The act and experience of consciousness itself is a continuous molding and remolding of our world, self related to objects and objects to self in inseparable ways, self participating in the world as well as observing it, neither pole of self or world being conceivable without the other."[31] The structure and meaning of the contents of consciousness are given always by the formative, directional activity of consciousness, the intentionality of consciousness.

But this is exactly the participative nature of knowing that we have seen some modern scientists beginning to acknowledge. What our exploration is now starting to show is that this knowing involves the whole human being right down to the deepest forces of will. Earlier, we described one aspect of intentionality, without then using the term, when we noted the shaping activity of the mind in our ordinary perceptions of objects. We see objects as we do because we already have ideas and concepts in the mind that give shape to our perceptions. Our thinking the object, for example, a chair, our intending it as a chair, is why we see it as we do, as a chair. We are normally unaware of the involvement of our thinking in seeing ordinary objects and regard them as existing just as we perceive them without any activity on our part. It would be very inconvenient for us, in fact, were this not most of the time a largely unconscious process. We can, however, begin to get some sense of the directional, shaping activity of the mind in perception by looking, for example, at an ambiguous drawing of, say, a stairway, in which we soon discover that with a little practice we can deliberately see the stairs as either going up or down, depending on the way we decide to see them, depending on whether we conceive them going up or down. We then become aware for a moment of our own responsible involvement in shaping what we see. Intentionality works usually below the surface of our ordinary awareness, but we can at certain times bring it to self-conscious and responsible awareness. There are, of course, limits to the activity of intentionality in perception. Something has to be before us, but its shape and meaning lie both within it and within the activity of our own thinking.

For the most part, it is much more difficult to become aware of our intending activity in our normal perception of objects.

For one thing, the objects of our everyday world seldom possess the extreme ambiguity of the special drawing of the illusionary stairs, but, just as important, we see our everyday world in the light of images and concepts supplied by memory and custom that we usually share with everyone else in our society, so there is little occasion for us to become aware that we could or might want to perceive it as different. Our perception of the world around us is already shaped by collective conceptions, assumptions, and images. May relates the intriguing account of the people of the primitive society who were unable to see Captain Cook's ship when it sailed into their harbor because they had no conceptions, symbols, or words for such a sailing vessel. They undoubtedly saw it as something, May notes, a cloud, a mountain, an animal, perhaps, but not as a ship.[32] They could not *perceive* what they were unable to *conceive*. Through our thinking and willing we are actively involved in shaping the world of our experience.

The full dimension of intentionality May endeavors to show by looking at the meanings and origins of the word itself. He points out that the primary meaning, even in the dictionary, for "intend" is *to signify, to mean;* and only then, secondarily, purpose and design. The Latin stem, *intendere,* itself includes the meaning "to stretch." So there is in intentionality, May says, a "stretching toward something," a movement toward meaning. And, he observes further, that at the center of intention is also the word *tend,* "to care for," "to take care of," as well as "to move towards" and "to attend." In other words, he argues, "every meaning has within it a commitment."[33] In the concept of intentionality we begin to see every act of consciousness as a striving for meaning that commits the whole person.

Just as perception is imbued with meaning, so behavior and action are imbued with meaning through our own intentionality. From beginning to end there is a striving for, a drive toward meaning. And so May writes:

> Cognition, or knowing, and conation, or willing, then go together. We could not have one without the other. This is why commitment is so important. If I do not *will* something, I could never *know* it; and if I do not *know* something, I would never have

any content for my willing. In this sense, it can be said directly that man makes his own meaning. Note that I do not say that he *only* makes his meaning, or that it is not dialectically related at every instant to reality; I say that if he is not engaged in making his meaning, he will never know reality.[34]

We know reality by making our own meaning because of the participative nature of knowing that shows itself fully in intentionality. Reality reveals itself in our intentional activity in knowing. Or, to put the same thing somewhat differently, and perhaps more cumbrously, the very meaning, quality, or meaning-imbued activity I cognize in the object is the same meanaing, quality, or meaning-imbued activity by which I do the cognizing. We do not know the other as existing detached from us, apart, and uninvolved with us. We know the other only as we enter into and participate in the meaning and reality we both share. And this intentional striving for meaning, remember, is but another way of speaking of the involvement in knowing of the whole person (which is what at the deepest level we mean by will). It is imagination.

The remarkable corollary of intentionality, the fact of our willing participation in knowing, is that we are responsible for our knowing and for the kind of knowledge we have. It is true that most of our knowing is not yet participative in the full sense. We often "make our meanings," to be sure, but concoct them wholly out of our own desires and impose them on others and on the world. Or in our striving for meaning we draw not upon the new that lies ready to be revealed to us, but upon mental habits and images supplied by imaginative fancy. We are happy to be lulled by the "lethargy of custom," and remain satisfied with conventional wisdom and respectable, accepted ways of looking at things. And there is, in this, participation of a kind, but the resulting experience will be partial and misleading and, finally, destructive. If, for example, we impose only quantitative concepts and mechanical images on the world in our attempt to know her, a quantitative and mechanical world we shall have— and, eventually, thinglike, mechanical selves to go with it. But the one thing we can no longer do is disclaim responsibility for the kind of world we thereby produce by maintaining that we are merely providing knowledge of an objective, detached reality.

If in our knowing we employ only a part of ourselves, or

secondhand images and dead concepts, we are responsible for the fragmented, dull, and dead world they give us. We "make our meanings" in every sense, and are responsible for them, and for what results from them. And this suggests, further, that in our knowing we are, first and foremost, responsible for ourselves. We can only know the world in its fullness to the extent that we bring that fullness to life within ourselves. The notion of the brilliant intellect being able to provide true and adequate knowledge of the world without a commensurate development of character is a myth—a favorite and governing myth of the modern age. It is a myth that has been able to maintain its power only because we have avoided coming to grips with the cognitive dimensions of care and commitment revealed in intentionality.

In speaking of responsibility in knowing, therefore, we are not saying that we must first be good, moral, responsible people, and then bring this responsible outlook and concern to bear in our knowing and in the ways we apply our knowledge. For one thing, what often passes for moral responsibility is little more than the fixities of convention and social habit, the worst examples of the lethargy of custom. What is being pointed to is the need for something much more radical, a renewal of imagination that will break through habitual behavior and attitudes, and for that reason will probably be very unrespectable and at first appearance, quite "irresponsible." More important, the connection between knowing and responsibility as care and commitment, as intentionality, is much more intimate than is implied in the ordinary—usually pedestrian—conception of responsibility. It is not that we bring care and commitment to our knowing; care and commitment are an integral part of our knowing. "In an individual's conscious act," writes May, "will and care go together, are in that sense identical."[35] Similarly, and perhaps in an even more radical vein, Coleridge maintained that consciousness and conscience are intimately connected, that consciousness in its will aspect is conscience.[36]

Both underscore further the cognitive dimensions of will and character. The more highly developed our conscience, the deeper and more intimate will be our consciousness of the world and of others around us. A dim conscience will permit us to slack off and to detach our own consciousness of self from our consciousness of others and of the world around us. But in this detachment the sources that nourish even our consciousness of self are blocked—awareness of other persons, being affirmed as a person by others, participation in meaning that reaches beyond our narrow orbit of existence—and all may eventually be extinguished, along with the self-consciousness they make possible.[37] There is a deep responsibility that is both the condition and exercise of knowing itself.

In intentionality we can begin to see at the deepest level of consciousness the unity of thinking and will. And it is here also that the unity of love and will begins to emerge: in the striving toward meaning and reality that seeks to endure through all changes in mood and circumstance; that seeks participation and involvement with the other, while respecting the reality and integrity of the other; that seeks to remain open in care, attentiveness, and commitment to what the other may reveal. And the name for this unity of thinking, feeling, willing in the whole person is imagination. It is the possibility of a way of knowing that we have only begun to become aware of, but not one that we can much longer afford to ignore.

The Creativity of Insight-Imagination

Consciousness, and the quality of consciousness, affect the world of our experience. As the popular adage goes: Ideas have consequences. But here we must exercise great caution, for some ideas have more consequences, some different consequences than others. Some are powerful and affect the world directly, becoming embodied in institutions, social organizations, technology; others, less powerful directly, often serve only to cloak and veil the world and work their effects in various kinds of illusion, deception, and wishful thinking. But they have consequences, nevertheless. Sometimes the two coalesce, and we get wishful thinking—an unclear welter of unconscious presuppositions, fears, feelings, images, desires—given institutional embodiment with a fearful heightening of the possibilities for confusion and destruction.

An age impressed mainly with the power of the embodiments, institutional, economic, technological, and with little or no eye for consciousness, or convinced of the basic unreality of consciousness, will tend to view consciousness and the forms of consciousness as arising out of the forms of economic production or the political-economic structure of society or its modes of technology. Clear and distinct ideas will be viewed then as rationalizations for the interests imbedded in deeper social-economic-institutional structures, or as political rhetoric designed to gain support for these interests. And there will be a deep truth in this approach, for in an age in which the formative power of consciousness is largely ignored or denied, the only effective way to gain hold of it will be through an analysis of its concrete social embodiments. And in such an age, since the deeper strata and movements of consciousness are studiously avoided, ideas that do emerge with some clarity will often seem disembodied, epiphenomenal, and fit only for rhetorical purposes. Assertions that ideas are important and have consequences will be dismissed as "subjective idealism"—and rightly so to the extent that these assertions themselves also ignore the deeper movements of consciousness. This is why various kinds of Marxist social analyses that focus on the social-economic structures of society for their explanation of human behavior and ideas often manifest a power that so-called liberal, idea-oriented modes of analysis lack.[38]

The tendency to ignore the formative power of consciousness (in both Marxist and liberal views of the world, all of them usually variants of an unmitigated positivism) has meant that the fact that our social institutions not only give rise to ideas, but are themselves the expressions of consciousness, goes mainly unremarked; and, as a result, our institutions, economic arrangements, and technologies go more and more uncontrolled.[39] And, because the formative power of consciousness is denied or relegated to the unimportant, the strengthening of imagination that can alone provide the insight needed for creative participation in reality is sedulously ignored.

At long last, however, this state of affairs promises to change radically with the increasing realization by a growing number of thinkers, in science as well as in many other areas, of the deep participative interaction between the mind and the world. Increasingly, we are being made aware of the fact that the mind is involved in the structuring of the world we experience. The concepts, the ideas, the images, and the impulses at work in the mind form and give shape to the raw materials of sensation, thereby creating the recognizable world we experience. This is ordinarily an unconscious experience, which is to say we are unaware of it while it is going on. Our tendency is to remain oblivious of the mind's intentional involvement in structuring the world, and to view the world of experience, therefore, as existing in and of itself, just as we see it, detached and independent of the mind. Because this structuring process remains ordinarily below the level of conscious awareness, we discover it only afterward, either by thinking very hard about what thinking itself implies, or, as has happened in modern physics, by confronting certain problems that eventually arise from it, first, assuming the independence of the objective world and, then, realizing that this assumption simply does not work after a point and blocks further inquiry. Then the participative nature of knowing begins to emerge ever more insistently and inescapably.

We may also, perhaps, have some direct inkling of this structuring power in artistic creation. "The poet's peculiar genius," for example, writes Jeffrey O'Connell, "and it will vary enormously from poet to poet—consists of the fact that he is able to impose order on the chaos of inarticulate experience as this moves out of the darkness of unconscious impression into the light of conscious control. Both impulses and insights are already organized at a preconscious level and as they emerge into the poet's conscious mind, they attract or else call into being verbal symbols designed to communicate their meaning."[40] For his symbols the poet will draw on his rich storehouse of imaginative fancy, bringing together and recombining the words and images found there in ways, however, that create new images, new metaphors, new symbols capable of expressing and communicating new meaning. Imaginative fancy then becomes an indispensable vehicle for meaning, but it is not the source of new meaning. The artist treads with delicate balance between openness and spontaneity, on the one hand, and conscious control, on the other: too much of the former leads to incoherence, too much of the latter kills inspiration.

In artistic experience we may also have a direct presentiment of the participative quality of intentionality wherein the activity by which we know becomes one with what we know. Using still the example of poetry, Paul Ricoeur writes that poetic feeling "develops an experience of reality in which invention and discovery cease being opposed and where creation and revelation coincide."[41] A similar process seems to belong to scientific insight, particularly in such examples cited by Bohm, in which the scientist after a period of concentrated focus becomes open to the unconscious ordering in the depths of his mind that in the moment of insight gives birth to new meaning and perceptions, which must then be worked out and developed in mathematics, logic, and hypotheses. In the arts and in the sciences the participative nature of knowing seems much the same.

Were we to stop at this point, however, we would not have grasped the full transformation of our ways of knowing and of the world we know that our imaginative participation in reality holds for us. With the recognition of imagination as the involvement of the whole person in knowing comes the possibility of an infinitely heightened consciousness at every level of participation. To begin with, to recognize the centrality of imagination in itself alerts us to our involvement and interaction with the "objects" of knowledge. The importance of images, concepts, presuppositions, values, attitudes, and so forth in giving form to our world comes into the clear. No longer can we remain satisfied with allowing old mental habits and unconscious attitudes to slip unnoticed into our thinking. The responsibility for bringing into consciousness the nature and sources of our imagery and "interests" becomes unavoidable. Moreover, the full range of cognitive perception in all the senses, in feeling and willing, as well as intellect, opens up to us. Rather than falling back in laziness, fear, or habit on the old, the capacity is nourished to bring to birth new images where none existed before, images truly appropriate to exploring the experience at hand. Finally, there is given in imagination the possibility of a direct awareness of those dimensions of quality and meaning inaccessible to sense experience.

In coming to know our own inner being in imagination, we develop the capacity to know the inner being of other persons and of nature. In knowing nature through imaginative participation, our own inner experience is at one with the inside, the inwardness of nature. This is to say that in imaginative participation we come to realize that just as we have an inside, so too does nature have an inside—a qualitative, dynamic, meaning-filled, inner-relatedness. Coleridge, who, as Barfield has shown, probably knew as much about the imagination as any person in the English-speaking world before or since, emphasized the importance of becoming aware of the inwardness of nature and its union with the inwardness of the human mind. "Nature," Coleridge wrote, "the prime genial artist, inexhaustible in diverse powers, is equally inexhaustible in forms. Each exterior is the physiognomy of the being within." Furthermore: "In the objects of nature are presented, as in a mirror, all the possible elements, steps, and processes of intellect antecedent to consciousness, and therefore to the full development of the intelligential act; and man's mind is the very focus of all the rays of intellect which are scattered throughout the images of nature. . . ." Genius, the mind most open to insight, he said, "presupposes a bond between nature in the higher sense and the soul of man." It is the business of genius to acquire "living and life-producing ideas, which shall contain their own evidence, the certainty that they are one with the germinal causes in nature. . . . For of all we see, hear, feel, and touch the substance is and must be in ourselves."[42] Nature and the human mind participate in a common inwardness which is the ground of Insight-Imagination.

That nature has an inside, the behaviorists, for example, the representatives of the logical extreme of a totally mechanistic, outer-oriented positivism, deny—just as they consistently deny an inwardness to the human being. That nature has an inside, modern physics in certain limited respects is beginning to recognize. Interestingly, the inwardness of nature has been partially acknowledged by that small branch of medicine which recognizes the so-called psychosomatic unity of the human being in health and disease, but the physicians have yet to draw the full conclusions from their discovery. Since, as Barfield has argued, the body is really that part of nature with which we have the most direct, intimate, and immediately felt connection, it would seem to follow that if nature at this point is psychosomatic, there is no good reason to suppose that the rest of nature is not also psychosomatic—and we seem to have some sense that this is indeed the case every time we speak of instinct in nature.[43] Among a very small number of biologists, such as Adolf Portmann, who do not confine their studies of life only to the chemical, quantitative properties of cellular matter or to the exclusively cause-and-effect relationships between the development of organic structures and the influence of the environment, both purely outer features of nature, the inwardness of nature is regarded as her most important aspect. For these biologists, the organic forms of animals are outward manifestations of a hidden inner reality, an expression of a world of meaningful inner moods, feelings, and experiences. This does not mean that for them the study of the outer is to be neglected, it is rather that by itself the outer is incomplete and leaves out the most important dimensions of nature. Along with the outward, control-oriented study of nature, it is essential, Portmann writes, that also "by an extraordinary reversal of attitudes, we should turn our minds inward so that we may have a chance of recognizing a far more comprehensive reality behind our experience."[44] It is precisely this holding together in tension of the outer and inner in order that a deeper reality can manifest itself that is the work of imagination.

And the biologist Charles Birch's conception of a humiverse is based on the conviction that our own inner experiences provide the clue to and must serve as the basis of an adequate knowledge of the inwardness of nature. In our inner experience we enter into and participate in the inwardness, the qualitatively rich inside of nature. To strengthen the imagination would be to pull this largely unconscious participation more and more into conscious awareness and, thus, to make possible genuine knowledge of nature in her full reality. To know the inside of nature would entail a different relationship to her than one of alienated manipulation and exploitation, and it would require deep qualitative, personal changes in ourselves as knowers.

In spite of all the evidence, we seem very reluctant even to consider the idea that in our own inner experience we can come to know the inwardness of nature. Why is it so difficult for us? Barfield has pointed out that the major problem is the deeply held assumption—so deeply held that it is taboo to question it—

that consciousness is the product of our physical brain. As long as we suppose that consciousness is caused by the brain, we have no way of entering into participative, knowing relationships with each other or with nature. Our brains are then regarded as objects in space that can only relate "objectively" to the outside of other objects in the universe. From this point of view thoughts are, at most, waves of some sort that reflect the vibrations from objects outside, from other things, and send out signals that contact has been made, the significance of which we then interpret "subjectively." Within this assumption there can be no knowledge of the inner reality of another or of the world. The world thus becomes basically alien, as do other people, all consisting of objects that we encounter, manipulate, or are manipulated by, perhaps even crushed by. It is a fragmented world of unrelieved isolation, threat, and anxiety. In a recent interview, Barfield has said:

> If civilization is to be saved, people must come more and more to realize that our consciousness is not something spatially enclosed in the skin or in the skull or in the brain; that it is not only our inside, but the inside of the world as a whole. That people should not merely be able to propound that as a theory, as some philosophers and others have done, but that it should become more and more their actual experience. . . . That, and also the overcoming of the total obsession there is today, half conscious and half subconscious, with the Darwinian view of evolution— of consciousness or mind having emerged from a material, but entirely unconscious universe. Putting it very shortly, to realize, not simply as a theory but as a conviction of common sense, that in the history of the world matter has emerged from mind and not mind from matter.[45]

Elsewhere, Barfield has written:

> The real world, the *whole* world, does not consist only of the things *of* which we are conscious; it consists also of the consciousness and subconsciousness that are correlative to them. They are the immaterial component of the world. But today the only immaterial element our mental habit acknowledges is our own little spark of self-consciousness. That is why we feel detached, isolated, cut off not only from the world as it really is,

but also from those other little sparks of detached self-consciousness we acknowledge in our fellow human beings.[46]

The nature of insight-imagination, of personal experience, of metaphor and living language, of artistic experience, of intimations from certain consequences of recent science—recall in this connection Bohm's concept of an infinitely, multi-leveled implicate order—of the wisdom of tradition: all suggest ways of beginning to grasp Barfield's meaning and its implications concretely. The priority of mind means that wholeness, participation, and interaction, not fragmentation and isolation, are also primary. It means the existence of a wider context of meaning within which we can check the adequacy of our ordinary thinking, guiding and correcting it, making larger connections within it, and keeping it open to further insight. This higher order of consciousness and meaning, however, is not open to our ordinary thinking and perception, tied as these are to the given, to partial abstractions, to unconscious mental habits, to collective states of mind. Our most pressing task, therefore, is to create within ourselves the requisite organ of cognition, the imagination, that will break through these obstacles and unlock for our thinking the way to its deepest sources.

The growing interest of many scientists, therefore, in the important role of the imagination in their inquiry is encouraging. We have seen an increasing emphasis among many scientists on the participative nature of knowing, and on a multi-leveled, interactive view of reality requiring ways of thinking which go well beyond exclusively mechanistic and reductionistic models and assumptions. At the same time we have also seen that older ways of thinking remain strong and often continue to dominate in many areas of science, making it difficult for many of the new perspectives to receive a real hearing. Nevertheless, the central importance of the imagination in science is receiving more and more recognition.

As John Davy has pointed out, the work of the imagination in science is most apparent when it becomes necessary to formulate hypotheses or to embody insights and mathematical relationships in models and experimental apparatus to test hypotheses. All science that becomes experimental, he stresses, must rely conspicuously on the image-making capacity of the imagination. Image making does not come into play in the purely formal mathematical relationships of theoretical physics (though we have attempted to show that imagination in the larger sense of insight as developed by Bohm is at work also at this level), but, when it becomes necessary to construct models and experimental apparatus to embody these relationships, image making as such becomes crucial.[47]

At this point in science, Davy says, we begin to get not only "detached observation," but "detached imagination." The scientist uses the image to probe invisible worlds inaccessible to the senses; he begins to draw upon inner experiences as the source of access to an invisible outside world. Thus, in the image-making process the unconscious inner reality of the scientist enters in as the source of the images by which he probes nature. As science begins to deal more and more with dynamic, flowing, interconnected forces and energies, these have to be imaged and pictured in order to deal with them experimentally, but in the imagining process we draw upon our own inner experience.

Two kinds of questions, therefore, become critical: (1) What sources in himself is the scientist drawing on in the creation of his images? Are they drawn from the dimensions of sense experience most appropriate for exploring and working out the kinds of relationships the scientist is discovering? And related to these questions is a second: (2) Is it not essential that the scientist become increasingly conscious of the deep sources of his imagery, if the images he uses are to be freed from the grooves and compartments of old mental concepts and habits of imaginative fancy, if, in other words, his images are really to be infused by deep participative imagination and insight? As science begins to deal more and more, for example, with dynamic, flowing, interconnected forces and energies, these have to be imaged and pictured in order to work with them experimentally. But in the imaging process the scientist draws upon his own inner experience. The scientist must begin to bring to birth commensurate energies within himself to enable him to grasp adequately the energies which he is encountering in his theoretical work. The questions we have raised become crucial, therefore, once, in the image-making work of experimental science, the energies dealt with theoretically are also unleashed into the world of space and time, for they actually change the world we experience.

It is this essentially creative nature of knowing that underscores the importance of these questions. Theory and experiment change the world. For this reason Barfield writes that "what occurs when the imagination is functioning is not simply a subjective event. It is an event in the world, the outside world as well."[48] To illustrate this we can say with the philosopher of science Paul Feyerabend, "All we need to do is to point out how often the world changed because of a change in basic theory."[49] And, with the images that embody theory in experiment new phenomena result that were not available and present to us previously—the energies get embodied and come to expression, in nuclear bombs, for instance. A crippled imagination, an unclear, unconscious source of imagery, an application of images drawn from sources inappropriate to the energies and relationships that are being dealt with—all also can produce real changes, even if they are fragmenting and destructive. "It is at this point, of course," says Davy,

> that science also begins to have social consequences: new phenomena emerge, are embodied by means of apparatus which first had to be imagined. If we don't like what science is now embodying into the world, or find it dangerous, or would like it to go away, or are nervous about the extraordinary fertility with which scientists keep on producing new discoveries; if we start asking, "How can we really control the scientists?" we are really saying, "How can we really be responsible in the activity of picture-making?" If we begin to pursue this question further, we then have to ask: "Where does this activity of picture-making come from?"[50]

It becomes crucial that we not remain content with a limited, constricted, and largely unconscious source of imagery, and that we therefore pay heed to the adequate inner development of the human being. What is needed is a new sense of objectivity.

A call at this point for a renewal of objectivity must initially appear inconsistent. Have we not maintained throughout that the mind of the knower is never totally detached from the world he investigates, and that there can never be so-called objective knowledge of a world that exists independently of any inter-action with the mind of the knower? We have called this false sense of objectivity *objectification*, however, to distinguish it from an adequate understanding of objectivity, which is essential to all knowing. Here we can begin to make the distinction more explicit, in order to show that a participative view of knowing does not mean jettisoning objectivity but really entails reclaiming it in its fullness.

Objectification is the fallacy of setting up the notion of a de-tached, independent reality which has no connection whatso-ever with mind and intelligibility, whether we claim that it can be known as it is in itself or maintain skeptically that we can never have any real knowledge of it but can only deal with it and manipulate it instrumentally. Either way a false assumption of objectification is at work. By contrast, objectivity in its positive sense is the ability to discriminate in one's inner life and images between that which is purely personal and that which is, at once, personal and, at the same time, points beyond itself and has wider, perhaps even universal significance. Objectivity in this positive sense is being able to discriminate among one's inner experiences and to recognize which apply to what. Without this ability to discriminate we should have endless confusion in all our knowing. One of the strengths of science has been its in-sistence that we eliminate all personal bias from our judgments about the quantitative aspects of the objects we investigate. Even this, we have seen, is dependent on certain personal value com-mitments of the scientists themselves.

Nevertheless, as Barfield and others have argued, the em-phasis of science on objectivity about "objects" can be the point of departure and good training for developing a much more precise and comprehensive objectivity about one's own inner life. But, Barfield points out, being objective about objects is really no great achievement, and too much ought not to be made of it. "After all," he writes, "it is not so very difficult to eliminate all personal considerations, all subconscious bias, when the mat-ter or process you are investigating is, by definition, one in which you could not possibly have a direct personal concern; when from the beginning to end it is assumed to be absolutely other than yourself. To put it rudely, any reasonably honest fool can be objective about objects."[51] It becomes much more difficult when objectivity includes becoming unflinchingly and accurately aware of the different elements, interactions, and qualities in one's own inner being.

What is involved can perhaps be illustrated by our experience of knowing other people, which, like all knowing, but, perhaps, more immediately apparent as such, is participative. In dealing with other people we grasp quite readily how important an awareness of our own inner life is in coming to know and understand them. The more highly developed our understanding of ourselves—the greater our awareness of our own inner life, our feelings, fears, self-deceptions, foibles, ideals, needs, and so forth—the larger our capacity to understand and enter into the reality of the other. Here, inner knowledge is clearly part and parcel of our knowing another. At the same time, if we cannot be objective in the positive sense, if we cannot discriminate between that in us which makes empathetic understanding possible and that which has its source in personal memories, neuroses, and habitual patterns of reactions, we will simply enshroud the other in a cloak of our own projections and never come to any genuine understanding of him. The alternative to imposing on others our purely personal biases and fantasies is not to objectify and treat them as things, killing empathy and sympathy in ourselves at the same time, but to bring to life within ourselves those personal qualities that lead us to understand the other as also a person.

An adequate conception of objectivity has, then, several dimensions. First, it involves becoming increasingly conscious of one's own inner life and the sources of one's own images and mental concepts. "There is no necessary opposition between clarity and imagination," writes James Hillman, and clarity is essential for the simple reason, as he says elsewhere, that "Ideas we don't know we have, have us."[52] Modern views of the world are saturated with images and conceptions drawn from dim, unknown sources and applied to areas in which they are utterly inappropriate and misleading.

Second, objectivity in its positive sense means bringing to life the full range of the senses and our inner sources of imagery.

John Davy has indicated, for example, the almost exclusive tendency in dealing with nature to draw our images only from inner experience having to do with quantity—images associated, for instance, with the physical sense of touch, the sense that presents the outsidedness of things, their resistance, hardness, and impenetrability, and that tend to give rise to a picture of the world as made up of solid, impenetrable particles moving through space.[53] As physics deals increasingly with energies and interconnecting relationships, the inadequacy of such images becomes more and more apparent.

From where in our inner experience are new, more adequate images to come? We can persist in employing only quantitative images and notions and to ignore those suggested by such other inner experiences as colors, sound and tone, warmth, feeling, and life, but in doing so will continue to get those scientistic pictures of a grey, cold, silent, and dead universe. What would be the result for our understanding of nature if we were to include with our particulate, quantitative imagery, images, and concomitant methods, derived, for instance, from those realms in which, Bohm says, we have an immediate experience of the implicate order—movement, time, music, other persons, and so forth? It would then be possible to envisage a science in which the study of life is as basic as the study of inanimate matter, in which the experience of consciousness is seen to shed light on the phenomena of life and matter, and in which our understanding of the human being is fundamental to our understanding of nature.

Third, objectivity involves a delicate act of balancing: remaining open to all that nature has to reveal to the senses and at the same time staying with thinking in spite of the power that old images derived from sense experience can exert. Only in this way can new dimensions of meaning disclose themselves which at the same time do not do violence to what nature and other persons have to reveal.

Finally, imaginative objectivity means being able to create new energies within ourselves commensurate with the energies revealed in the universe: energies of will, moral energies of imagination and perception, capable of striving for meaning without stopping short or being diverted by lesser energies of narrow interest and desire. The enormously destructive energies released by the fragmenting of the one nucleus—that of the atom—and the similar destruction threatened by the fragmenting of the other nucleus—that of the cell—are not by-products of a neutral knowledge of objective reality; they are the direct consequences of the personal and social interests, images, and energies that have entered into and are part and parcel of that knowledge.

Every act of imagination is, thus, an act—an achievement or failure—of moral imagination. In imagination new meanings and perceptions emerge out of the tension of opposites or polarities. Moral imagination is brought fully into play in maintaining this tension of polarities: recognizing the integrity of self *and* others; striving for clarity *and* meaning; affirming individuality *and* community. In this tension of polarities, everything is not swallowed up in monolithic sameness. The whole pervades and sustains the parts, and the richness of diversity is preserved.

Throughout, we have avoided dealing with the question of morality and values separate from the question of knowing. The main problem with most of the current demands that greater attention be given in our families and schools and other social institutions to values is that these calls frequently serve only to widen further the prevailing split between what is taken to be, on the one hand, moral idealism, and, on the other, cognitive realism. In such a separation, that which is considered cognitive will eventually always triumph (where, for example, the scientistic world view dominates as the cognitive reality, awareness of qualities, and of the meaning they make possible, diminishes and fades); or the cognitive will be swamped in an upheaval of reactionary fears and irrational drives (elements not entirely absent in many present moral emphases). The gap is itself, however, the result of an error in cognition. There is no knowing that does not embody value choices and implications; there are no value commitments and capacities for valuing that do not enter into our ways of knowing and with the forms our knowledge takes. The inner moral development of the individual, the moral qualities of being in the knower, shape the imagination. And the depth and quality of our imaginative knowing-participation determine the realities we perceive, understand, and are capable of entertaining.

The imagination is always powerful. If cut off from the whole or if crippled by convention and mental habit, the imagination will continue to bring into being the world in which we must live, but in this case it will be a fragmented, distorted world. The restoration of wholeness of the imagination is our most pressing task. Through a fragmented imagination we have made the destruction of the world a real possibility. Can we not begin through the enlivening of the whole imagination to envisage the creation of a whole and living world?

Far from being the special concern of a few curricula and pedagogical professionals, the education of imagination is seen to be of utmost importance to us all. What is required for a genuine education of imagination is the urgent question we now address.

Notes

1. See, for example, A. M. Taylor, *Imagination and the Growth of Science* (New York: Schocken Books, 1970); and Gerald Holton, *The Scientific Imagination: Case Studies* (New York: Cambridge University Press, 1978).

2. Mary Warnock, *Imagination* (Berkeley and Los Angeles: University of California Press, 1976). The quotations in this paragraph are from pages 194, 196, and 202.

3. The discussion of Bohm's conception of knowledge and insight is based mainly on David Bohm, "Insight, Knowledge, Science, and Human Values," *Teachers College Record*, vol. 82, no. 3 (Spring 1981), 380-402. Except where otherwise noted, all quotations in the following paragraphs are from this article. Other writings by Bohm dealing directly with insight on which I have also relied are, David Bohm, "On Insight and Its Significance, for Science, Education, and Values," in *Education and Values*, ed. Douglas Sloan (New York: Teachers College Press, 1980), pp. 7-22; and idem, "Imagination, Fancy, Insight, and Reason in the Process of Thought," in *Evolution of Consciousness, Studies in Polarity*, ed. Shirley Sugerman (Middletown, Conn.: Wesleyan University Press, 1976), pp. 51-68.

4. Warnock, *Imagination*, pp. 207-8.

5. See Chapter 3, pp. 117-18, 123-24, and notes 38-41, pp. 133-34.

6. See especially, "The Enfolding-Unfolding Universe: A Conversation with David Bohm Conducted by Renee Weber," *Revision*, vol. 1 (Summer/Fall 1978), 35, 39.

7. Warnock, *Imagination*, p. 202.

8. Owen Barfield, *The Rediscovery of Meaning and Other Essays* (Middletown, Conn.: Wesleyan University Press, 1977), p. 60.

9. Ibid., p. 61.

10. Ibid., p. 30.

11. Quoted in Richard Hocks, "Contemporary Theories of Metaphor: An Overview and Interpretation," *Towards*, vol. 1 (December 1978), 26.

12. Barfield, *The Rediscovery of Meaning and Other Essays*, p. 123.

13. Ibid., p. 42.

14. See Owen Barfield, *Saving the Appearances; A Study in Idolatry* (New York: Harcourt, Brace & World, n.d.).

15. James Hillman, "An Inquiry into Image," *Spring; An Annual of Archetypal Psychology and Jungian Thought* (1977), 68.

16. John Davy, "Science and Human Rights," *The Golden Blade* (annual) (1968), 35.

17. M. C. Richards, "The Public School and the Education of the Whole Person," *Teachers College Record*, vol. 82, no. 1 (Fall 1980), p. 60.

18. Warnock, *Imagination*, p. 180.

19. Quoted in Hocks, "Contemporary Theories of Metaphor," p. 26.

20. John Macmurray, *Reason and Emotion* (London: Faber and Faber, Ltd., 1935), p. 26.

21. Ibid., p. 31.

22. Owen Barfield, *What Coleridge Thought* (Middletown, Conn.: Wesleyan University Press, 1971), pp. 10-11.

23. Macmurray, *Reason and Emotion*, p. 42.

24. Ibid., p. 40.

25. Quoted in Barfield, *What Coleridge Thought*, p. 239.

26. Macmurray, *Reason and Emotion*, p. 76.

27. Paul Roubiczek, *Thinking Towards Religion* (London: Darwen Findlayson, 1957), pp. 109-12.

28. Bohm, "Insight, Knowledge, Science, and Human Values," p. 388; and Barfield, *What Coleridge Thought*, pp. 86-87.

29. Barfield, *What Coleridge Thought*, p. 87.

30. Rollo May, *Love and Will* (New York: W. W. Norton, 1969).

31. Ibid., p. 227.

32. Ibid., p. 236.

33. Ibid., pp. 228-30.

34. Ibid., p. 230. Also extremely helpful on the relation between intentionality and cognition is Ronald Brady, "Goethe's Natural Science: Some Non-Cartesian Meditations," in *Toward a Man-centered Medical Science*, ed. Karl E. Schaefer et al., vol. 1 (Mt. Kisco, N.Y.: Futura Publishing Co., 1977), pp. 137-65.

35. Ibid., p. 291.

36. Barfield, *What Coleridge Thought*, pp. 164, 165; 257, n.24.

37. See Owen Barfield, "Either: Or," in *Imagination and the Spirit*, ed. Charles A. Huttar (Grand Rapids, Mich.: William B. Eerdmans Publishing Co., 1971), p. 40.

38. That Marxist analysis is itself a mobilization of ideas confounds any crude Marxist social-economic determinism, and points toward the need for an even deeper analysis of the evolution of consciousness underlying social, economic, and cultural manifestations.

39. Henry Corbin has commented: "Amongst all the principles of explanation which people make do with at little enough profit to themselves, there is this dogma of a pseudo-causality, as though every ideology were nothing but a superstructure raised on a socio-economic infrastructure, a dogma arbitrarily transformed into a principle of explanation which itself remains unexplained, since it is no less admissible that everything happens in exactly the opposite sense: does not man organise this world, his economic and political office in the world, as a function of the sense he gives his own presence in the world, to his coming into and going out of this world, in short, according to his vision of another world, without which one seeks in vain for a direction in this one? In this case, it is sheer illusion to transform socio-economic evolution into an explanatory principle when it itself is to be explained in as far as it is under the jurisdiction of a superior process." Henry Corbin, *The Concept of a Comparative Philosophy* (Ipswich, England: Golgonooza Press, 1981), p. 10.

40. J. M. O'Connell, "The Poet in the Stream of History: An Approach to Poetry," *Towards*, vol. 1 (Summer 1980), 18.

41. Paul Ricoeur, *The Rule of Metaphor* (Toronto: University of Toronto Press, 1977), p. 246.

42. Quoted in Barfield, *What Coleridge Thought*, pp. 79-80.

43. See Barfield, *The Rediscovery of Meaning*, pp. 171-72.

44. Adolf Portmann, *Animal Forms and Patterns, A Study of the Appearance of Animals* (New York: Schocken Books, 1967), p. 218.

45. "*Towards* Interviews Owen Barfield," *Towards*, vol. 1 (Summer 1980), 10.

46. Owen Barfield, *History, Guilt, and Habit* (Middletown, Conn.: Wesleyan University Press, 1979), pp. 71-72.

47. "Science and Imagination: An Interview with John Davy," *Towards*, vol. 1 (Winter 1980-1981), 17-24. Compare Bohm: ". . . it is my main proposal . . . that we cannot thus dispense with an overall world view. If we try to do so, we will find that we are left with whatever (generally inadequate) world views may happen to be at hand. Indeed,

one finds that physicists are not actually able just to engage in calculations aimed at prediction and control: *they do find it necessary to use images based on some kind of general notions concerning the nature of reality,* such as 'the particles that are the building blocks of the universe'; but these images are now highly confused (e.g., these particles move discontinuously and are also waves)." Bohm, *Wholeness and the Implicate Order,* p. xiii (emphasis added).

48. "*Towards* Interviews Owen Barfield," p. 6.

49. Paul Feyerabend, *Science in a Free Society* (London: NLB, 1978), p. 70.

50. "Science and Imagination," p. 21.

51. Barfield, *The Rediscovery of Meaning,* p. 139.

52. James Hillman, *Re-Visioning Psychology* (New York: Harper & Row, 1975), p. 246, n. 6.

53. "Science and Imagination," p. 20.

5

Living Thinking, Living World: Toward an Education of Insight-Imagination _____

"I have come very strongly to believe," writes the philosopher Mary Warnock, "that it is the cultivation of the imagination which should be the chief aim of education, and in which our present systems of education most conspicuously fail, where they do fail."[1] In the present climate of educational opinions and practice many persons might very well agree eagerly with Warnock's statement—or for that matter disagree–but do so in either case having in mind a very restricted and limited notion of the imagination. In its fullest sense, imagination involves the whole person, and, if it is to be the chief aim of education, it must permeate and be integral to the entirety of the educational undertaking. It cannot be a partial aspect of education, nor something added on that does not suffuse and shape the whole. At a time when the word *imagination* is bandied about with little care or thought, it might be well, to begin with, to keep in mind some elementary cautions about what an education of imagination does and does not imply.

The cultivation of imagination is not the encouragement of

capricious self-expression and indiscriminate spontaneity. Imagination has its own demanding and uncompromising discipline. Playing, dreaming, light-headed musing are all essential to imagination, and where they are not valued, neither is Insight-Imagination. But they do not constitute imagination, and by themselves are prone to the fixations and ruts of undisciplined fancy. Attentiveness, a love and respect for form, and the inner discipline born of these are equally part of insight-imagination. In imagination, dream and attention, play and discipline, novelty and form find their unity, and each leads each to the others. To indiscriminately praise as an exercise in creative imagination, for instance, any mess of white glue and string which some poor child has been induced to assemble out of his inner emptiness, is to demean the child, education, and imagination in one swoop.[2]

The cultivation of imagination does not mean the rejection of hard, lucid, logical thought. It is, rather, the bringing of thought to life, permeating concepts and abstractions with life-giving images and inner energies through which thinking can penetrate and participate in the fullness of reality. Nor does the cultivation of imagination necessarily require a rejection of tradition. Indeed, an education of imagination will value the expression and presence of imagination wherever it manifests in human history. There is a sense, for example, in which the great artistic achievements of tradition are potentially always new, and always radical, because they possess the ability continually to burst the bonds of our ordinary perceptions and ways of thinking. Hence, an education of imagination will view with alarm the alacrity with which traditional wisdom and insight are abandoned by an age convinced that it alone has found the truth and can, therefore, change any and everything at will and with impunity—an age so enamored of itself that in its culture and education it thinks it alone has the key to innovation and change, when so often in reality it is conventional, dull, and philistine through and through.

In short, an education of imagination is a seeking of wholeness in the individual and in the community. How we might begin to conceive in some concrete detail an education of imagination in its wholeness and in our present social, intellectual, and spiritual situation we must now consider.

Education of Persons

An adequate conception of education, an education of imagination, will always strive for that way of knowing which springs from the participation of the person as a total willing, feeling, valuing, thinking being—a way of knowing that leads to the wisdom in living that makes personal life truly possible and worthy. It will have as its prime purpose, as its ground and aim, the complete, harmonious realization of the full capacities and potential of the individual as a whole person. Any conception of education that arises from some other or lesser concern or that fastens on a partial or isolated aspect of the total person will finally abort, delivering only fragments of persons and figments in place of reality. And by its nature, such a lesser education cannot avoid serving purposes that will be basically non-human and ultimately inhuman.

Contemporary education, in theory and practice, has moved steadily away from any conceptions of knowing as involving the participation, harmonizing, and liberation of the whole person. The majority of leading educational theorists, and those parents, teachers, and educational agencies most in touch with the forefront of educational research, are bent chiefly on developing the academic brightness of their students. The literature of educational research is rife with talk about "stages of intellectual development," "academic readiness," "the extension and enhancement of the learner's cognitive structures," and so forth. Deeply concerned parents fret whether they have yet done enough to promote the academic readiness of their two-year old; caring teachers strive to create situations conducive to proper "cognitive growth"; educational researchers are indefatigable in their efforts to discern the earliest traces in young brains of evolving "cognitive structures and conceptual networks" and to establish the "optimal conditions" for them.[3] In all of this there is a good deal of idealism and deeply felt commitment, and if we are to criticize, as we are about to, the dominant notion of cognition at work here, it is not to attack the general good intentions of most of those who have taken it up. However, we must ask about the unintended results.

At first glance, the contemporary emphasis on cognition would seem to be the proper aim of education and to be welcomed by anyone concerned with our ways of knowing. A closer look, however, begins to reveal that at almost every point in modern education the meaning of cognition is exceedingly narrow and limited. Cognition turns out to mean almost exclusively verbal and logical mathematical skills (often as measured by IQ tests). Cognition is narrowly conceived as a matter of discursive knowledge and calculative intellect, and the essence of education is accordingly taken to consist entirely in the imparting and retention of information and the development of logical-mathematical facility. In other words, the narrowing of reason to mean only discursive and technical reason has taken root in the heart of modern education, and has been written into the assumptions of educational research, educational administration, and classroom and family teaching. The results of this narrowing of reason, here, as elsewhere, have been devastating.

One result has been a tendency within education to value children and youth not as persons in their own right and with their own inherent value, but only as potential learners. The problem would not be as serious if learning in turn were not conceived in its most restricted sense as being solely the development of calculative skills and the acquisition of subject matter. A premium is placed on narrow intellectual attributes, while other capacities and aptitudes, personal, social, moral, aesthetic, go unattended. The deep wisdom inherent in the body and in the emotions is neglected. Instead, the natural energies and passions of the child become problems to be dealt with. Discipline then becomes something imposed from without to hold the emotions under control and to contain them. Or in more progressive-minded classrooms the emotions may be used to catch the students' interest, to lure them to the lesson at hand, a kind of candy coating on the bitter pill of learning. In either case the potential for knowing and the wisdom already at work in the whole person are not valued and frequently go unperceived. Aptitudes and qualities in the child essential to a meaningful, satisfying, full, and competent life are overlooked and suppressed.

When the chief goal of education, and with it the whole process of growing up, is defined in such a limited way, the temptation becomes nearly irresistible to bring children into what is called *learning readiness* at an ever earlier age. The slow learner becomes a problem child and is streamed out for special attention, which in that child's case is often a euphemism for systematic neglect—never mind that the slowness may actually be the ripening and flowering of a child unusually endowed with sensitivities unamenable to hothouse intellectual stimulation. The child who shows evidence of precocious mental operations is selected out as gifted. Every bit as vulnerable as the slow child to the machinations of learning specialists, the gifted, if not burned out in the process, stands in peril of finding his human worth measured by his mental brightness, and subjected to the constant temptation to judge the humanity of others by the same standard. As for the special child, for whom acute mental activity, perhaps because of an impairment at birth, is an utter impossibility, there are no grounds whatsoever in such a system for according him or her any worth at all. But these are all extreme cases, the end direction of an education that concentrates on only a part of the human being. Fortunately, in many schools the logic of the underlying educational assumptions is not carried out to its consistent conclusions, and the obtrusive, messy humanity of teachers and students continues to make itself felt. Still, the casualties mount.

Another result of an education tied mainly to the enhancement of mental facility measured by academic achievement is that it reflects and furthers the steady deterioration of the resources necessary for significant cultural criticism and renewal. Put more bluntly, if carried out consistently, it leads to a cultural desert. This is not to say that every experience in modern education is utterly bleak and without social value, for there are many persons at work, teachers, parents, and others, concerned to make education a force for social and cultural renewal. And their efforts, and often successes, need to be recognized and affirmed. The point, is, however, that there is very little in the underlying assumptions of current educational theory and practice to lend support to such efforts, and a good deal that directly undercuts them.

An education that stresses only narrow mental facility offers no foundation for resisting and stemming the relentless contemporary erosion of the communal forces essential to cultural health. A sense of time and place; the cultivation of mutuality; a sense of natural rhythm; celebratory traditions of communal renewal and hope; the pride and beauty of craft; vocation experienced as a genuine summons or calling, *vocatio*, in which the challenge of the task, pride in one's work, and the satisfaction of serving actual human needs are central; a deeply felt, because deeply real, sense of civic responsibility—all that which makes for the sources of significance and cultural richness necessary to a free and vital society is constantly uprooted and dissolved away where an abstract rationality and technical reason dominate. The challenge at hand, it should perhaps be emphasized, is not that of attempting to return to old communal and cultural forms, but of carrying out a search for new possibilities within a situation in which the process of cultural uprooting and erosion is far advanced. But this requires, at the least, an education in which the full dimensions of rationality are recognized and nurtured, for therein lie the sources of humanly meaningful cultural life and activity. An education devoted entirely to the development of abstract and technical mental facility, which lacks any vital connection with human meaning and substance, becomes itself a main agent of cultural impoverishment and the displacement of human concerns.

Moreover, it strengthens all those forces that work to sap the foundations of a democratic society, undercutting the possibilities for sustained public dialogue about cultural goals and effective popular participation in the determination of public policy. An exclusive emphasis on the development of instrumental, technical reason reduces rationality to a consideration only of quantities and quantitative relationships, which in the public sphere means a preoccupation with the lowest common denominator, material elements of society, and with their manipulation, management, and control. The result is to strip public deliberations of all cultural contents and to cripple the capacity of the public and its leaders to deal with the qualitative dimensions of public life. The ensuing cultural impoverishment becomes manifest at nearly every point in the society.

It can be seen in the realms of education, business, and government, for example, where the concept of public policy is steadily reduced to mean mainly the efficient implementation of technique and the smooth management of institutions, rather than the engaged and critical consideration of the larger goals those techniques and institutions are to serve. Concerned observers have frequently noted similar tendencies in political life as the opportunity for informed and sustained dialogue about vital social issues, the *sine qua non* of an enlightened and responsible citizenry, continues to disappear and to be replaced by the management of public opinion and the manufacture of issues and candidates by communications and public relations specialists. The almost complete collapse of a live, meaningful public philosophy and the disappearance of all cultural depth can be seen today particularly in the fact that, as Sheldin Wolin has pointed out, where public dialogue is still pursued, it is increasingly conceived entirely as a matter of economic and cost-benefit analysis. "It is more common practice," observes Wolin, "to rely upon economic categories to supply the terms of discussion in legislature, bureaucracies, and mass media; to frame the alternatives in virtually every sphere of public activity, from health care, social welfare, and education to weapons systems, environmental protection, and scientific research; and to function as a sort of common currency into which all problems have first to be converted before they are ready for 'decision making.' "[4] Where the terms and goals of public policy are wholly set by economic categories and goals, as important as these may be, purely utilitarian and instrumental considerations reign supreme. And crucially important political, moral, aesthetic, and philosophical issues and choices go unattended and decided by neglect. The stage is then set for the further consolidation of control in the hands of the already politically, economically, and technologically powerful, who in the process can appeal demagogically, a la the moral majority, for example, to blind and completely irrational longings for some semblance of moral and cultural sustenance.

Perhaps the most ominous symptom of cultural decay, however, is in the realm of international affairs, where diplomacy, negotiation, mutual cooperation, and the building of strong cultural and political relationships threaten to be overshadowed by an exclusive dependence on military strategy and military technology. For a people who begin to think of national security as resting primarily in military might and supremacy, and based on weapons of a kind whose use would incinerate millions and probably poison the earth irreparably, rather than primarily in the creation of a society committed to justice, to the enhancement of its cultural and natural riches and beauty, and to the dignity and freedom of the human being—for such a people there has been an educational failure of the first order.

A change in education, to be sure, will not be sufficient for a recovery of cultural vitality. But it will be necessary, if the essential resources for personal and communal health are to be nourished and tapped. A purely instrumental education, one based solely on the heaping up of information and the development of narrow mental facility and technical reason, is personally and culturally bankrupt. If given its run, it can only reinforce the powers that be and the most brutish elements in society. As Wendell Berry has said, "to think and act without cultural value and the restraints invariably implicit in cultural value, is simply to wait upon force."[5] An education cut off from the deep rationality capable of sustaining cultural value begins actually to foster increasing reliance on a thoroughly technological understanding of human problems, the greater centralization of social control in the hands of those who possess and manage the technology, the growing homogenization of culture, and the consequent depletion of new cultural possibilities.

Eventually, all come to share and play their parts in this personal and communal impoverishment: the gifted, whose academic careers are successful, as much as those bringing up the rear—not only the outright failures, but the mass of ordinary achievers as well. Those who display the requisite intellectual skills are singled out as special for their proficiency in the use of an aspect of the mind that has no intrinsic relationship to the art of living well as persons.[6] They come to feel entitled, and are expected by others, in time to assume the posts of leadership in society, in education, the corporate world, the government, and the professions. That the majority of them are no more or less wise than anyone else (and that among them may be "gifted" megalomaniacs, moral nonentities, and cultural ignoramuses) becomes increasingly immaterial to their being accorded social leadership. If they bring, as some fortunately do, outstanding personal qualities to bear in their work, these are mostly drawn from sources other than their education and flower in spite of it—unless they have been favored with having had a teacher or a school standing outside the mainstream. Most have been ill-equipped by their education to live well as persons, to find delight in friendship and love, in the joys of sound and touch and color, even in the satisfaction of ideas and the contemplation of ideas. For many, therefore, the temptation is great to immerse themselves totally in their careers in order to ward off the sense of meaninglessness that pervades the modern world—but that is a fearful weight to have to hang upon career and its small ambitions.

Perhaps the most fortunate are those who receive from their education an ability to calculate and successfully infuse this with personal meaning derived from other sources. To them the opportunities still exist for the realization of self-directed and purposeful lives. That this remains the experience of many is a prime ground for hope in the possibility of cultural and educational renewal. Less hopeful, however, are the prospects for the large numbers of students, the non- and under-achievers, marked out for training in what is called minimum competency and functional literacy, an act of resignation by a society that can envisage nothing better to offer them. These are the students who, unable to read, write, or reckon, will be cynically promoted from grade to grade out of desperation and for reasons of social and political expediency. For them, minimum competency and functional literacy mean the lowest-level utilitarian knowledge and literacy skills (the ability to read the want ads, to apply for a driver's license, to check prices at the supermarket, and so on) without which it is feared the students will be unable to survive in modern society. No one would deny the need for survival-level competency, but if that is the highest education can aim for, it is a training in despair. Even when such training succeeds (and that it can by itself is doubtful) the results would more accurately be described as minimum incompetency and functional illiteracy. For these students it is society that has failed its minimum competency examination in education.

To maintain as some so-called social radicals have that the

people need only utilitarian and basic skills to enable them to achieve economic and political power, that they have no need for beauty, for ideas, for personal and social vision, that these are bourgeois delusions, is both condescending and the political *reductio ad absurdum* of instrumentalism. It only betrays how completely immersed the would-be radicals are in the worst assumptions of the society they wish to overturn. A thoroughgoing utilitarian education provides students, whether destined for the labor force or for the professions, with no personal or social leverage on their outer circumstances, something absolutely essential if they are to be effectively critical of the shortcomings of society and to work as committed and concerned citizens for its renewal. A thoroughgoing utilitarianism does not aim for the liberation of the human spirit: It provides individuals with no inner resources for a self-directed life, no basis for distance from enmeshment in the immediate social circumstances, no channels for the creative expression of their own vital energies and insights, no inner resistance to the low-level enticements and sedatives of an entertainment-consumer culture, no capacity for rational criticism of the society or of its leaders. It fits individuals to the given social arrangements. It is not an education for citizens, it is an education for servants. It is a mis-education, a non-education.

Among the most poignant victims of an education without moral, aesthetic, and real intellectual substance are the aged. They are the ones left to wrestle out of the vacuum bequeathed them by an empty education whatever spiritual strength they can muster to maintain their dignity and a sense of fulfillment. Some succeed, but for many others, whose inner resources have never grown, their last years become a plunge into panicky querulousness and depression, rather than the deepening in wisdom, fulfillment, and expectation these years might have been. An education in which skills, narrow intellect, and information have no connection with insight, imagination, feeling, beauty, conscience, and wonder and that systematically evades all engagement with the great, central issues and problems of human life, is a wasteland. It is harmful enough for society in general; for the individual children within the society, and for the old people they will become, it is an unallayed desolation.

And yet we make here what may appear a rather shocking, perhaps contradictory turnaround, to say that, despite all the criticisms we have leveled against it, the emphasis in modern education upon cognition contains a truth of utmost importance. And it is the recognition of this that prevents our criticism from being total rejection and makes of it, instead, an attempt at renewal and regeneration. The emphasis upon cognition, however dimly the fact may be realized by today's educators, begins to define for education its own proper concern and to distinguish it from all that society is constantly tempted to confuse with education and to put in its place. To recognize that education has primarily to do with cognition, knowing and the ways of knowing, sets it off in sharp contrast from those pseudo-educational goals of indoctrination, socialization, certification, or schooling as mere training. To enter into the way of knowing is the beginning of self-determination and personal-communal meaning. But that suggests that it is here, after all, that the most telling indictment of modern education at its most successful is to be found. It fails on its own terms: it does not lead to genuine cognition. It produces, instead, a one-sided caricature; and the more successful it is, the more one-sided and distorted the outcome: a reason without rationality, an intellect without intelligence, a knowledge without understanding. It does not even lead to genuine knowledge of the world, only to an instrumental know-how about the very limited domain of quantity. And from this acquaintance with quantity, it builds up abstracted, phantasmagoric models of a disqualified universe, which in turn feed the spreading blight of an exquisitely stupid cleverness adept at taking the world apart with no grasp of what it is doing, nor apparent concern.

It is, therefore, not the emphasis in modern education on cognition that is to be rejected, but its fallacious conception of cognition, and the mistaken approaches to teaching and learning that result. Some critics of education in their desperation for a change of direction frequently speak as though what is called for is a repudiation of reason. A genuine renewal of education, however, would mean, rather than the repudiation of reason, the redemption of reason. Hard, lucid, logical thought, and instrumental reason itself, would all come into their own as the indispensable companions and helpmeets of insight. And rather than being rejected or diminished in importance, conceptual thinking would be revitalized by the transformation of our rigid, abstract concepts into fluid, living, mobile concepts. Acuity of mind would be joined with the deep wisdom potential in body and feeling. The now vaunted ideals of education—the liberation of the human spirit, a love and search for truth, the seeking of understanding, and the building-up of human community— would have the possibility of becoming the guiding realities of education. It would be an education that would aim to develop persons capable of meeting life's challenges.

An education of imagination in its fullest sense will require a fundamental change of premises about our ways of knowing, teaching, and learning and all that follows thereon. Such a change of premises, of basic assumptions, will be so thoroughgoing, so far-reaching, that it will preclude any quick-and-easy move from theoretical reflection to detailed practical application. Any demand for a ready kit bag of teaching techniques will have missed the depth of change envisaged. And, yet, more is called for than a mere general change of attitude, however "value-laden" such might be. A truly fundamental change of premises will have truly specific and detailed implications for curriculum, pedagogy, and educational setting. But what will be required in such a restructuring will reveal itself fully only in the process of being lived into and worked out. And it will never be a once-for-all accomplishment. It is in this spirit that the following is presented as one beginning attempt to explore in some detail the educational implications of a participative knowing grounded in Insight-Imagination.

An Education of Imagination: The Child

Some preliminary considerations by way of reminder may help to uncover the essential areas in which a fully participatory knowing bears most directly on the educational task. A first consideration has to do with the unity of thinking, feeling, and willing. In clear thinking, we experience ourselves as separated and distanced from other people and the world. This is the experience of the onlooker-consciousness, which we have seen can be said to be the characteristic mode of consciousness of our time, and for which there is also good reason to suppose that it has developed most fully only during the last several centuries of the modern period. Our experience of self-identity, of being separately existing individuals, is closely tied up with our waking, thinking consciousness. It is commonly noted, for example, that stroke victims who have suffered a loss of memory feel the experience most excruciatingly as a blow to their self-esteem and self-image because portions of their lives have sunk from conscious, thinking awareness. With the experience of individual identity, thinking consciousness also carries with it the potential for increased self-determination and liberation from the constraints imposed upon us by others and our environment.

Conscious thinking tends always toward ever-increasing abstraction, which confers with it great powers of generalization. These, together with the capacity in consciousness for detachment and distancing, make possible the exercise of control over an incessant and exceedingly complex flow of experience which would otherwise engulf and sweep us with it. We are able, for instance, to detach ourselves from being totally immersed in the problems that arise constantly in our personal lives and in our workaday tasks. In thinking, we are able to stand back from the problems, identify and isolate them, look them over, break them down, and begin to deal manageably with them, all the while bringing them in the light of consciousness into an identity of their own. Because we have throughout called attention to the aberrant and self-destructive tendencies of an onlooker consciousness severed from a deeper participation with others and in reality, it is perhaps especially important here to affirm and underscore the potential in thinking for the fulfillment of personal identity and self-determination. If it is to escape aberrant development, however, it is a potential that cannot be adequately realized in isolation from other more fundamental sources of knowing and knowledge in the human person.

At the opposite pole from abstract, analytic consciousness there is to be found a form of direct, participative knowing: the knowing contained within intentionality, willing, and bodily activity. We experience an aspect of this form of knowing, for example, in performing skills involving touching, moving, balancing, auditory response, shaping, and so forth that draw upon the infinitely rich store of what Michael Polanyi has called *tacit knowledge*, a knowledge contained in the whole being of the person, extending all the way into the body, muscles, skeletal structure, fluids, cells, and so forth.[7] In any skill involving motor activity, for instance—carpentry, dancing, hitting a ball, any craft—a highly developed, intricately ordered fund of implicit, or tacit, knowledge is brought into play, though it usually remains below the level of conscious awareness—often in the doing must remain unconscious as is indicated in Polanyi's example of the bicycle rider who performs with great finesse until the moment he begins to take thought of what he is doing. While the capacity for abstract, analytic thinking ordinarily emerges only in the maturing adolescent and develops fully in adulthood, the knowing associated with will is present at every stage of life, and is preeminently the knowing characteristic of the infant and young child.

While in thinking we experience a distancing from the world, in willing we enter into it in immediate participation. In touching, moving, and giving shape and form to objects we enter directly into the world of our surroundings, and move with them in a mutual interaction and interdependence. The skilled carpenter feels at one with his tools, his materials, and his tasks. The rider and his bicycle move as one, unless some sense of separateness unhappily intrudes. Similarly, analytical, conceptual knowledge is in a basic sense backward-looking, analyzing what is already given, dissecting what is dead; the knowing in willing and doing is forward-looking, in process, creating what does not yet exist. Through willing, conceptual knowledge can be given actual form and expression in the world. Through it, conceptual thinking can also be saved from its tendency toward isolation, thin abstraction, and rigidity. But in this last task, willing must itself be infused and guided by a living feeling for reality, else it stands in danger of being neglected in its own right and wisdom, or of being pressed into the service of dead concepts and the creation of a dead and death-dealing world of abstractions.

It is, therefore, in the third realm of feeling that the polar movements of willing and thinking are joined and find their unity. Feeling provides a rhythmic connection between participation in the world in volitional activity and detachment from the world made possible in thinking. It is a mediator between the movement of will outward toward identification and the movement of thinking inward toward identity. Without the intermediate realm of knowing in feeling we are sentenced to oscillate between immediate immersion in activity, on the one hand and, on the other, thinking without life and depth.

The knowing in feeling comes to expression in the imaging, picture-making activity of the person. The imaginative picture, the image, invests abstract thinking with life, and brings into consciousness the impulses of body and will. In the absence of living, feeling images we impose abstractions upon life, suppressing and distorting it, and, at the same time, have no way of preventing dim and often dark forces of will from overpowering our brilliant intellect, driving it toward ends that are neither understood nor decided upon. Or when the ability to bring living images to birth out of our own active being is stunted and undeveloped, we resort often to reliance on ready-made, conventional and commercially produced images. The living image, evoked in the realm of feeling, makes possible the development and exercise of a full-bodied, mobile, and creative rationality.

It is in this sense that John Macmurray speaks of imagination, taken in its imaging activity, as the all-important, mediating form of knowing. "Intention," Macmurray writes, "involves knowledge, and knowledge depends on the acquirement of reflective skills. The basic reflective skill, on which the others depend, is imagination; the formation, definition, and coordination of images, especially visual and auditory images. Hand in hand with this there goes the discrimination of feelings, particularly those which are associated with tactual experience; and the coordination of these with sensory images."[8] The feeling, image-making capacity integrates and extends the act of knowing in all its many dimensions. It is the ground of a *conscious participation*. And in keeping with its mediating activity, we find the life of feeling and imaging beginning to flower in late childhood and remaining the dominate mode of knowing until early adolescence—emerging between the volitional activity characteristic of the young child and the sharp, critical analytical thinking of which only the adult is fully capable.

A second area of preliminary consideration has to do with the need for the establishment of rhythm and harmony in the knowing experience and concomitantly in learning and teaching. Volition, emotion, conceptualization—each one requires its own full development in a balanced and harmonious relation to the others. To press upon pre-school children, for example, perhaps through misconceived programs of learning readiness, a demand for conceptual thinking really appropriate only to a much later period in life, does not respect the unique value of childhood, nor does it grasp the fundamental importance of the kind of knowledge implicit in the growth and activity of the young child. Furthermore, it robs the child of just the foundation that will be needed in later years for the sure and healthy development of conceptual thinking. Similar considerations apply to the relation between feeling and conceptualization. We will explore some of these relationships in further detail when looking more specifically at the curriculum. Here it suffices merely to stress the importance of a concern for the harmonious development of all aspects of the person, and for a sensitivity to what is appropriate and required at different points in the person's life and education.

A concern for balance, harmony, and rhythm in education is crucial in thinking about the curriculum and in planning an education in which subjects and activities are integrated and mutually supportive. Throwing children too early upon their own resources, demanding of them decisions they are not yet capable of making, as well as holding them back when they need to be given their reins in spontaneous expression and self-directed exploration stem equally from a deadened sensitivity to the requirements of rhythm and of the appropriate. Submitting students to a chaotic round of random or only tangentially related courses and activities, one short period following another with no real or apparent connection, infests the whole educational undertaking with a practical, palpable, and often insurmountable irrationality. Permitting students to go through the day or the school year or their entire education with no experience of the special qualities of the different periods of the day, of time, month, and the seasons of the year, deprives them of the occasions for developing the sense of anticipation and fulfillment without which a love and delight in learning can never flourish. Play, practical work, quiet rest, the time of calm reflection, concentrated study, discussion and common tasks with others, the celebratory moment and occasion—each has its place and integral relation to the others. Harmonious, balanced personal growth finds its reflection and support in an education that seeks to understand and embody the creative rhythms of life. Dissonance and conflict in the person and in society can only be accentuated by an education lacking its own inner rhythm and balance, and oblivious to their importance.

The final consideration concerns the central importance of the *human presence* in knowing, and, hence, in all of education. Care and conscience are integral to the full development of consciousness. We become aware of ourselves as conscious subjects, as persons, only in relationship to another subject, another person, and the greater the mutual respect and responsibility in the relationship, the more heightened the consciousness of subjecthood, of personal being. This is an ancient insight, and one that in our own time has been put forward by persons as otherwise disparate in their outlooks as Martin Buber, Merleau-Ponty, Michael Polanyi, John Macmurray, and a host of others. "I exist as an individual only in a personal relationship to other individuals," writes Macmurray. And he goes on to say, "The personal is constituted by personal relatedness. . . . This original reference to the other is of a definitive importance. It is the germ of rationality."[9] The presence of the person, and accordingly the relationship of care, respect, and responsibility personal presence entails, is, therefore, not an incidental accompaniment to knowing; it is an essential, integral component of knowing. It can only follow that the presence of caring and responsible persons is equally essential to education. Without the heightening of consciousness that personal relationship makes possible there can be no genuine participative knowing. And there can be no genuine education. At most there can only be the channeling of tropisms, the inculcation of the conditioned response, the honing of mechanical reflexes—the developing of a sub- and anti-human facility in performance. How is it, then, that the central importance of personal relationships and the presence of caring and responsible persons can be ignored in any efforts to educate or to think about education?

Personal presence in education must also be governed by a sense of rhythm and of the appropriate. There are times for nurture, times for authority, times for guidance, times for withdrawing support, and each, including the necessary withdrawal of support, will be an act of respect for the other. Essential to education, therefore, will be a highly developed sensitivity to the rhythmic movements required in the personal relationships of teaching and learning, relationships that will vary, for instance, with the age of the student, the situation, the physical and emotional maturity of the student, and the type of knowing and learning being undertaken. But, while the quality and direction of the relationship must vary, the fact of the relationship must remain constant.

Up to this point we have been speaking, without further elaboration, of relatively distinct educational stages in which the earlier prepares, or fails to prepare, the way for later developments. In this understanding of education what is educationally appropriate at a later stage may prove inappropriate, ineffectual, or even harmful if introduced too early; and, conversely, what is a desirable goal at a later stage may be unattainable if the proper foundations have not been laid during prior educational development. We are now perhaps in a position to look in closer detail at this notion of educational stages and its implications for teaching and learning during the young, adolescent, and adult years.

The distinct concept of childhood, the concept of the child's being in some essential ways qualitatively different from adults, appears to have emerged gradually only during the past several centuries.[10] And, the notion that children's development takes place in relatively distinct, sequential stages has largely gained currency, it seems, only during the past hundred years, as the result primarily of investigations in the fields of psychology, both in the psychoanalytically and the more empirically and descriptively oriented schools of psychology. While attempts have been made to draw educational implications from these psychological theories of child development, the success in doing so has left a good deal to be desired. It has proven extremely difficult to move from theories of child development derived exclusively from psychology to specific directives for actual pedagogical theory and practice and, most notably, for curriculum planning and development. Although important insights have been attained, efforts in these directions have remained, nevertheless, eclectic, unsystematic, and full of holes. That this has been the case need not be surprising, for psychology by itself provides too narrow a basis from which to develop a full-fledged theory and practice of education concerned with the entire human person. The psychological aspects of human development, as important as they are, and education dare never ignore them, constitute, nevertheless, but one dimension of the total human person which an adequate conception of education must take account of.

The one seeming exception to the statement that psychological theories of human development have not been exceedingly productive for educational theory and practice comes from the lifelong work of Jean Piaget, whose studies of the development of intelligence have drawn great attention from educators. The exception appears all the more justified, perhaps, by Piaget's continuing interest in aspects of philosophy that pervaded much of his work in psychology. Piaget's main concern was with the nature of stages of cognitive development in the growing individual. It was in the light of this focus on cognition that Piaget characterized the maturational stages that he discovered.

Cognition, or intelligence, for Piaget, is conceived exclusively as the capacity to perform abstract, logico-mathematical mental operations. One of Piaget's major discoveries was that the capacity for full-fledged, logical, abstract thinking does not appear until about the age of twelve. Only then, from about twelve on, does the growing child begin gradually to develop the ability, one that may never be fully developed even in adulthood, to reason logically and abstractly, to analyze, to handle hypotheses, manipulate variables, and deal inductively and deductively with propositions and so on. Prior to this time the child passes through a number of earlier, distinct developmental phases, each with its own unique characteristics and requirements.

There are many important insights and observations for education to be obtained from Piaget's work. Among the most important is Piaget's insistence that before the last stage of mental development the child is incapable of abstract thinking, and that therefore, to demand intellectualization too early is futile and can be destructive.

However, certain aspects of Piaget's work, and misconceptions and applications of it, have had other, much less beneficial consequences for education. For one thing, Piaget's definition of cognition in purely abstract, logico-mathematical, operational terms has often lent reinforcement in education to the narrowest instrumental conception of human rationality. The curriculum is pushed toward those subjects having to do entirely with mathematical, quantitative relationships as the ones of any real importance, thus further displacing from the center of educational concern all subjects pertaining to quality, meaning, and content. His overriding focus throughout each stage of development on the emergence of operational reasoning skills tends, furthermore, to overlook and to disvalue other dimensions of personal reality. From this point of view a narrow conception of cognition begins to define what is of worth in the human being. Likewise, each early stage in the individual's development is deprived of any intrinsic value of its own and comes to be measured by its contribution to the flowering of abstract thought in the last stage. There is little, therefore, to prevent the great part of childhood from being regarded only as something to be gotten through with no inherent worth in its own right. Although Piaget would have most certainly objected that this last was any part of his own intention, just the opposite in fact, it is difficult to deny that this has been an unfortunate consequence of his thought in the hands of many of his followers.

Finally, the Piagetian emphasis on cognition has induced many American thinkers about education to try to find ways to speed up the development of cognition, to move children more quickly into stages where logical mental operations first begin to appear. Piaget, as we shall see, has cautioned against such efforts, calling them a misinterpretation of his work, but they continue, and there seems to be no end in sight. Despite their misuse by some, Piaget's observations and insights are of considerable importance for aspects of education, and we shall have occasion to draw upon some of them. But the narrow definition of cognition on which they turn prevents their becoming in themselves the basis of an adequate conception of education.

In this chapter an attempt is made to sketch, in a way that is fully intended to be exploratory and suggestive and not doctrinaire and final, a view of education in which the notion of educational stages plays an important part. The entire conception of an education of imagination developed here has been deeply influenced by the insights of the Austrian philosopher Rudolf Steiner, and by the more than sixty years of actual educational experience of the Steiner or, as they are also known, Waldorf schools in attempting to develop, refine, and put Steiner's insights into practice. The view of education presented here, however, is not, nor is it intended to be, an exposition of Waldorf education (and, Waldorf educators would be entirely right in insisting that the views developed here represent in no way an adequate portrayal of their educational theory and practice). Rather, it is simply that Waldorf education contains rich resources for thinking in concrete ways about an education of imagination, and these, along with many others, are taken advantage of here. And while the insights of Waldorf education have been drawn upon in abundance, but in no way exclusively, the effort has always been made to do so critically, and in the doing to make connection with relevant views and insights from many other sources.[11]

An adequate conception of educational stages will take into account the development of the entire person as a thinking, feeling, willing being; it will exemplify an educationally significant harmony and rhythm; and it will seek those environmental conditions and personal relationships most appropriate at each stage of a student's development. It will not get lost in fruitless controversy, for example, between the proponents on either side of discipline vs. freedom, authority vs. anti-authority, work vs. play, structure vs. flexibility, and so forth, but will recognize these as necessary polarities that must be maintained in tension, and will seek the balance and emphasis appropriate at given stages and in given situations, for the full development of the capacities and competences of persons. And it will also see each stage as bringing to life that which is valuable in itself, and not something to be left behind or measured only by its contribution to later developments. If, for example, an ability for abstract thinking fails to develop in a normal person, we would rightly say that here the education has not been complete. But an abstract thinking not grounded in imaginative perception and incapable of active embodiment is, likewise, deficient. Earlier developments are transformed in successive stages, but ought at the same time to be taken up and preserved in them.

Any conception of educational stages must, to be sure, stand constantly ready to be reevaluated and revised in light of new evidence from any field of research, such as, for example, from developmental psychology. New perspectives and information arising from a single field, however, ought not as an isolated body of inquiry and data to dictate changes in education, but must be evaluated and appropriated in relation to a whole host of other interconnected and educationally significant considerations—physiological, psychological, intellectual, and ethical.[12] An adequate conception of educational stages will also contain sources for specific directives for actual curriculum planning and pedagogical practice, directives that are never fixed, once for all, but that, while always open to change, provide more than curricular and pedagogical generalities. Such a conception of education must as a whole remain open and subject to revision, not least because of the human being's potential for new insight and self-revelation.

The Young Child

The first six or seven years of the child's life may be described almost literally as the progressive embodiment of the person in the world. The intelligence is at work, but it manifests itself primarily in the developing of complex patterns and forms of physical growth, sensation, and bodily activity. The child enters the world open and receptive to it, absorbing for good and ill the many influences that work upon him from it. Immersed in his environment, he does not distinguish clearly, and for a time it seems hardly at all, between himself and the world with its objects that surround him. Into this world the child enters actively seeking to assimilate and to digest it for himself, uniting himself with the gestures, attitudes, and expressions of those around him, working to make them his own in the most intimate way. At the same time he seeks to bring to expression his own inner impulses, to lay claim to his body and take possession of it, to orient himself in space and in relation to other people. It is the most formative period in the person's life, during which the foundations are laid for all that is to follow.

A. C. Harwood has called attention to how the child's life during these early years reflects in miniature, and in a crucial way anticipates while preparing for, the whole process and pattern of later childhood development.[13] The first years are a time primarily of physical, sensory activity. The child learns to acclimate himself to his surroundings and, gradually, though actually with astonishing rapidity, learns on his own to stand upright, to walk, and to speak. With the ability to speak, the child enters into a much more conscious personal interaction with others and begins to experience a new quality of feeling. He learns, as Harwood notes, to say "I like" and "I dislike"— to lavish his affections on others and to articulate his displeasures. He acquires an enhanced capacity to enter into mutual communication with others.[14] Sociability and the development of social competences begin to develop. And with this new growth of feeling—which will come fully into its own and will dominate the years of early childhood—fantasy, the forming of images and the recognition of resemblances in forms, gestures, and objects, makes its appearance. Play takes on a new dimension, becoming not merely a form of experience but of self-expression and symbolic exploration.[15] With speech, sociability, and imaging, the child begins to ask questions and to seek meaning (in his own rather than in adult terms). It is the appearance of a new kind of thinking, a concrete and image-filled way of thinking; it is not the generalizing, abstract, logical thinking that the adolescent will begin to discover and seek to master, but it is the latter's anticipation and necessary preparation. Throughout all, however, the dominant note is that of sensory, bodily, willing activity. Imitation, example, mimicry, emulation, and identification are the child's chief means of learning. It is a time in which direct participation is the primary mode of knowing and learning.

The accomplishments of the child during the first years of life are truly remarkable, and their significance for all of education ought never to be neglected or underestimated. Within a relatively short time the child masters an entire range of infinitely complex skills and competences that involve his whole being. In learning to stand, walk, speak, and think the child lays the basis for all later development. And he accomplishes this entirely without a teacher or without instruction. Indeed, deliberate instruction by others hinders and often harms the child's normal, sound development. The child's first and most important learning is in the fullest sense a self-directed learning. The more fully we are able to develop further and to transform throughout our lives this capacity for self-directed learning in total involvement, the more complete becomes our growth and fulfillment as persons. Formal instruction, the acquisition of information and special skills, the development of abstract reason all require for their human significance this larger capacity for the self-directed learning of the whole person established in the earliest years of life.

This can be a chastening thought for us when we are tempted in thinking about education to suppose that the child has not really learned anything of importance until he is subjected to the formal instruction of the school. Philip Phenix has cautioned, for example, against any tendencies to underestimate the importance of the child's own earliest learning and to regard the child as mere "raw material" waiting to be shaped by the imparting of "real" knowledge—discursive and conceptual knowledge—at school. Phenix writes:

> Far from being a piece of clay ready for the potter, the child who enters school for the first time is a veritable prodigy of knowledge of the most important kind. He is a walking miracle, a talking phenomenon, an incredible genius of social subtlety in an untold variety of circumstances. He possesses the astounding ability to live, and to do so well. His knowledge is incarnate in his dynamic being. His amazing ability to live successfully is the evidence of what he knows. The great and enduring wonder is this bundle of life, for which the only fitting response is reverence and thanksgiving. The teacher should know that he also is just such a wonderful, awe-inspiring being and should behave accordingly in relation to the other prodigies of knowledge with whom he is associated in the school experience.[16]

The child in his own self-directed personal knowing brings within himself the context, the goal, the standards—and the source of inspiration—for all education.

The awakening of intelligence through imitation and will in these early years has been stressed, for example, by Piaget, who very early in his work wrote that, "At this most imitative stage, the child mimics with his whole being, identifying himself with his model."[17] And Rudolf Steiner, writing many years earlier, and with the actual implications for education much more in the center of his concern, pointed out that in his earliest years "the child is one great sense organ. . . . Everything from without is reproduced in his inner being. . . . He imitates his whole environment. . . . He does not merely shape his nature according to our words and actions, but in accordance with our whole attitude of heart and mind."[18] An awareness of how deeply the child in his early years enters into the world around him through imitation, emulation, and play is of utmost importance for education. It suggests that the primary task of education during these years is to provide activities, an environment, and the presence of persons worthy of the child's imitation.

Creative activities and a secure environment can enable the child to bring into play his own vital formative energies in entering into and making the world his own. Playing with blocks, digging in the sand, modeling with clay, joining in rhythmic, active games, playing house, performing small useful tasks, crayoning and painting in vivid colors, singing, planting and tending potted plants or little gardens, observing and caring for small animals, experiencing the changing seasons, listening to fairy tales and acting them out, reciting verses, and lighting candles at snack times—such as these offer activities that can encourage the child's healthy physical growth, and help form the basis for continued growth in wonder and delight in living.

Essential to an environment, whether in the family, playroom, or kindergarten, that provides the stability, harmony, and order required by the growing child is the presence of engaged, caring persons. That the child is sensitive not only to external surroundings, but perhaps in an even more intense and immediate way through tone and gesture, emotional and physiognomic expression, to the intention and attitudes of those in his presence, underscores the crucial importance of the quality of persons to whose care the child is entrusted. It is a modern commonplace that a life-long sense of security and confidence is established in the earliest years of childhood. It is here also that the foundations are laid for the anxiety-free, firm sense of self-identity from which stems all moral action that is not merely conventional and fear-ridden. The later capacity for moral imagination, which derives from the ability to recognize and to accord respect to the other as a person in his or her own right, is found in this primal trusting relationship with trustworthy persons.[19] Do we know the extent of harm done by efforts to substitute television, tapes, machines, and so forth in place of an actual living, caring, human presence? The real threat to the growing child in such surrogates for human presence may not lie so much, as many fear, in the content they convey as in their coldness.

Efforts to speed up the child's intellectual development through accelerated learning programs that aim to develop abstract reasoning as early as possible really represent attempts to force the young child into an adult model of learning—and usually a model that is itself deficient in the portrayal of adult learning and knowing. Most such attempts would seem to be not only premature, but counterproductive. The issue is not whether children can be induced to adapt themselves to such tasks as reading and writing and other intellectual feats that require abstract reasoning abilities. Many can; and many well-intentioned parents and schools eager to speed up the intellectual growth of their children point with pride at the ever younger virtuoso reading and writing performances of their three-, four-, and five-year olds. But serious questions can be raised about these efforts at acceleration.

Piaget, for example, spoke out more than once against what he considered the misunderstanding and misappropriation of his research to justify ever earlier intellectual training for children—a misuse of his research to which he thought American educators especially prone.[20] And Piaget has been joined in these warnings by increasing numbers of others.

In the first place, many of the children's early performances seem to be but the semblance of abstract reasoning. David Elkind, a leading student of Piaget's, has observed that ". . . it must be remembered that while young children do learn easily, they learn by rote and imitation rather than by rule and reason. Their learning is capricious, non-selective, and arbitrary; it is not the kind upon which formal learning should be based."[21] In the second place, there is little or no evidence to show that early formal instruction has any lasting effects in encouraging later mental development.[22] On the contrary, a mounting body of research indicates that early formal instruction correlates negatively with later intellectual attainments. In other words, an early emphasis on academic reasoning skills fails in its own goal of promoting strong, clear thinking capacities in later life. The evidence suggests, Elkind writes, that "the longer we delay formal instruction, up to certain limits, the greater the period of plasticity and the higher the ultimate level of achievement."[23] Dorothy and Raymond Moore of the Hewitt Research Center in Berrien Springs, Michigan, have recently reviewed an extensive body of research on early childhood from neuro-physiology, developmental psychology, and other fields that points overwhelmingly to the deleterious effects of early formal instruction on both the individual's intellectual growth and, equally serious, on the individual's later physical and emotional health.[24] By not permitting the development of the child's whole physical, emotional, and social capacities, by diverting the vital, formative energies of normal growth into prematurely fixed and narrow channels, an early academic emphasis may do untold damage to the individual's personal-intellectual fulfillment. Evaluating current research, the Moores conclude that children

> need time to develop the physical and sensory abilities necessary for the full blossoming of their intellectual capacities. . . . Students of human development are well aware all children do not grow and develop at the same rate, but there is a similar sequence or pattern that appears in each individual. Time must be allowed for this orderly sequence of development, just as we allow a flower to blossom naturally, rather than pull down the petals. To force or even unduly encourage one aspect of development out of sequence, such as intellectual stimulation when the social-emotional and sensory aspects have not yet progressed sufficiently, is to invite havoc for the individual, and eventually for society.[25]

The School-Age Years

Any sensitive parent or friend of children recognizes the vivid life of feeling and pictorial imagination that begins to quicken in the child by the time of elementary school. It is a time when children delight in vivid sense experiences—colors, rich and strange sounds, textures, movement; it is a time when they enter into rhythmic games and games of adventure with gusto; a time when they will sit spellbound to hear a favorite story again and again, or enthusiastically take the characters of the story into themselves and act them out. It is a time when the child begins to know the world around it and its own inner world in pictures and images born of a feeling-awareness. The life of feeling becomes more and more the dominant way of knowing for the school-age child. And from about the age of seven until puberty, the life of feeling and fantasy deepens, acquires layers of nuance and subtlety, and gradually gains in focus and control—all, that is, if the child's feelings are not frittered away, scorned, or snuffed out by the indifference of others or their conviction that more important things should occupy children's lives. Apathy, pointless dreaming, rage, and calculating indifference are often the remnants of feelings that through abuse have never found root and form.

The life in the children's lives is feeling. And this feeling is the source of the images and pictures in which the children's knowledge of the world lights up. In the picture-making and imaging consciousness, it is qualities that above all are known, and they are known in an active and creative way. Without the picture-making element in consciousness, logical, conceptual thinking becomes empty, lifeless, and disembodied—"disqualified." The primary task of education during these years is to nourish the feeling, imaging powers of the child, and to lead them over into the development of strong, conceptual abilities grounded in the capacity for a living-thinking which the image makes possible.

Many persons, aware of the emotional, feeling life of childhood, have, like Alfred North Whitehead, John Macmurray, and Rudolf Steiner among others, urged that art can be the center of all educational work during the elementary school years. Calls for an emphasis on art in education and for an artistic education are greeted sometimes with enthusiasm, more often with little or no interest, but in either case almost always in the assumption that art has only the most tangential relation, if any, to the tasks of intellectual development. That such reactions betray a lack of understanding of both art and intellect is true, but they often seem well justified in light of the almost universal separation that exists in most schools, even where much instruction in the arts is exemplary, between the arts and the rest of the curriculum and teaching activities. And where the assumption reigns that subjects in the arts and subjects having to do with knowledge and cognitive development have no integral connection, it can be little surprise to find that art instruction is often the least esteemed, the most neglected, and the first to go in times of financial exigency.

The first step in grasping the major place of the arts in a valid conception of education is to begin to understand the cognitive nature of the arts and the essential importance of the kinds of knowledge that the arts and artistic activity make possible. The range of activities recognized explicitly as making up the arts includes painting, modeling, carving, movement, dance, gymnastics, handcrafts, pottery, music, poetry, story telling, recitation, drama, and still others. Despite their many differences, all of them share certain things in common. They all demand the development of active, practical skills, a knowledge of the most basic kind: an engaged, participative active knowing, a doing-knowing. Technique and technical knowledge are central to the arts, but not as detachable skills. They are a part of the artist, an embodied know-how. Moreover, this participative doing-knowing of will-activity is taken up and guided by feeling-perception, and finds expression in the creation of meaningful patterns, forms, and image. And, finally, all of the arts require a joining of skills, form, and individual style in one interrelated, unbroken whole. At every point in the artistic process there is the potential for an integrated knowing of the most important kind. It should also be added that the arts seek to call forth a wholeness of response in appreciation that is itself a union of intelligent feeling-perception and willing-participation.

The arts can be a primary way through which we gain and

nourish a heightened awareness of our own inner being. Color, tone, rhythm, figure, proportion, beauty arouse and sharpen our senses, and bring feeling to life. Our capacity to be moved by the world around us and by others depends on our feeling awareness. Personal delight and interest in life, empathic understanding of others, and compelling self-expression all spring from the strength and variegated nuances of our emotional life.

The neglect of those things that nourish the emotions begins quickly to have a dulling and deadening effect on the whole person. There is, for example, little to prevent a premature or total immersion in abstract thought severed from all artistic feeling from producing a dessicated and joyless experience of life. And once deadness sets in, a vicious circle arises from which it is difficult to escape. Charles Darwin has provided a well-known and vivid example. In the later years of his life he expressed his deep regret at his loss of the "higher aesthetic tastes." Until after the age of thirty he took an intense delight in "poetry of many kinds," the plays of Shakespeare especially, painting, and music, but afterward these lost their attraction for him entirely. He wrote:

> My mind seems to have become a kind of machine for grinding general laws out of large collections of facts, but why this should have caused the atrophy of that part of the brain alone, on which the higher tastes depend, I cannot conceive. . . . If I had to live my life again, I would have made a rule to read some poetry and listen to some music at least once every week; for perhaps the parts of my brain now atrophied would thus have been kept active through use. The loss of these tastes is a loss of happiness, and may possibly be injurious to the intellect, and more probably to the moral character, by enfeebling the emotional part of our nature.[26]

An education conceived and pursued with no central place for the life of feeling can hardly be expected to be appealing to children, for whom feeling is the element in which they live. It can be expected even less to produce a society of individuals capable of being moved by the real needs of the earth and the others around them. In this fundamental sense the arts provide the cornerstone of moral education, far more than any special course in ethics or value clarification.

Art provides a primary way not only of discovering and cultivating the emotions, but also of educating the emotions. Overwhelming surges of passion and uncontrolled jerks of feeling are only a little less destructive of personal development than lack of feeling. Artistic activity requires and provides the means for achieving disciplined and discriminating powers of feeling. Artistic creativity arises from a balance in polarity between spontaneity and discipline. When this has been forgotten in the modern obsession with spurious views of novelty and self-expression, art, whether in the classroom or in sociey, has suffered both in repute and reality. But insight, of which artistic creativity is a principle manifestation, does not come easily. It requires, as we have seen, a sustained attentiveness, a disciplined awareness, and a heightened personal objectivity even more demanding than the vaunted objectivity of the onlooker consciousness. And it is precisely in these that artistic activity can provide indispensable schooling.

Art confronts the artist at every point with resistances that must be overcome, sometimes by submitting to them and transforming them, sometimes by diverting or overpowering them. Technique must be developed, usually through long and arduous practice. The constraints of tradition must be acknowledged and a saturation in the tradition must take place before the truly innovative breakthrough can occur. And the recalcitrance of the artist's materials and medium must be respected; they do not yield to immediate manipulation, they are not formed on a whim. At every point intelligent, discriminating, disciplined powers of feeling and will must be developed. At the same time it must never be forgotten that technique and discipline are themselves dead apart from the vitality of feeling. In these polarities of artistic activity there appears at the most elemental level that *emotional rationality* of which Macmurray speaks.

What is discovered through the arts, however, need not remain a purely subjective or inner discovery. The arts make possible the awareness of qualities as an inherent aspect of reality, as both subjective and objective. The arts, in other words, have a genuine cognitive power in their ability to reveal a dimension of the world, as well as of the self, entirely denied to an exclusively quantitative way of knowing. Without the arts, a major source of access that ordinary awareness has to the qualitative and to the qualitative relationships that form the matrix of all meaningful knowledge is closed.

The power of the arts to open up deeper dimensions of reality than we are ordinarily aware of manifests in different ways. Many have described the effect on them of a poem, or a piece of music, for example, as a heightening or intensification of consciousness. In the response to the work of art new depths of reality, not apparent to ordinary sense experience, may be disclosed, if only for a time. This sense of a transcendent dimension beyond the immediately given may be very subtle: a new-found sensitivity to delicate nuances of meaning and perception. Or, for some, it may be awesome and overpowering. In his autobiography, Bertrand Russell, for example, describes how he first heard of Blake when a friend recited to him the entirety of

> Tyger! Tyger! burning bright
> In the forests of the night. . . .

while they were standing "in the darkest part of a winding college staircase. . . . The poem affected me so much," wrote Russell, "that I became dizzy and had to lean against the wall."[27]

The inner pictures and images, which constitute the stuff of artistic experience, are the bearers of the qualitative. The capacity to be moved by the inner pictures and images, with which the imagination in the artistic experience works, is to find a connection within ourselves to the qualitative dimensions in reality, to the source of life and meaning in the world. Moreover, as we observed earlier, the images present themselves as wholes. In the images of imagination more meaning is always presented than can ever be stated, and the greater a work of art, for instance, the more inexhaustible the things that can be said, analytically and discursively, about it. The arts require and help cultivate, therefore, the development of an ability to respond creatively to the global nature and interrelatedness of experience.

The real cognitive potential in the arts inheres in this possibility of a twofold disclosure of the hidden dimensions of self and world and of their interconnectedness. The pursuit of the arts demands the cultivation of the image-making abilities and powers of the mind through which alone these disclosures take place. To speak of the arts as central to the education of children is to seek for children at once the gift of a rich, deeply felt, and meaning-filled experience in growth, and to cultivate those deep powers of rationality whereby they can keep that experience alive and make it truly their own.

Making the arts in this sense the center of education means above all summoning up the image of the whole of education itself as involving as artistic approach and sensitivity. It then becomes more accurate to describe education as an art than to speak, as we have until now, of the arts in education. In this conception there is no place for that separation between the arts and the rest of the educational curriculum and experience common in many schools in which the arts are consigned to special periods—often degraded to little more than periods of relaxation or, in some of the better schools, to a few weekly hours of enrichment activity—or to special tracks, as in the highly professional courses in the arts sometimes provided for the exceptionally talented. What all of these have in common, from the best to the worst, is a separation of artistic activity from the totality of the rest of education.

At this point a few reflections on the relation between the image-making activity of the mind and the images supplied by television may also be in order. There continues to be much concern about the effect of television viewing on children, especially in light of the staggering amount of time many spend in front of the television screen. Much of this concern has centered on the low quality—the banality and violence—of the content of television programming. As many people are beginning to realize, however, there is a more important question to be asked of television that goes beyond the problem of content. Assume for a moment that the content of television programming has been made unobjectionable: Is there, nevertheless, something about the act of television viewing in itself that may be physically, emotionally, and educationally harmful, especially for children?

A number of considerations make this a pressing question. In the first place, there is nearly universal agreement that physical activity is essential to healthy child development, and to the acquisition by the child of a deep-seated, tacit knowledge of self and world. In the passivity demanded by sitting before the television set, how is the necessary activity, the doing so important to the child, to take place? Where are the opportunities for the exercise of eye and limb and for the development of motor skills and dexterity, which some researchers have also seen related directly to the emergence of mental strength and subtlety later in life?[28] Furthermore, the education of the senses is also of utmost importance in the child's development of full, responsive awareness. This requires, on the one hand, that all the senses be engaged—touch, movement, balance, smell, taste, sight, hearing, and so forth—and, on the other hand, particularly important amidst the steady and chaotic bombardment of the senses in modern society, that order and harmony and self-direction in sensory experience be established. In television viewing, however, both conditions for sensory experience are sabotaged. Most of the senses are blocked out, and the two that do remain, the visual and auditory, are employed at their most minimal—except that for children sitting long hours before the television set, sight and hearing are subject to a relentless, cacophonous assault.

Finally, and perhaps most important of all, the imaging, picture-making capacity of the mind, precisely at an age when it is most susceptible to being formed and most in need of self-activation and self-forming, has its images provided for it. And the television image is inserted, willy-nilly, directly into the mind of the viewer. A foremost critic of the effects of television, Jerry Mander, has pointed out that in looking at television "the mind is never empty, the mind is always filled. What is worse it is filled with someone else's obsessive thoughts and images."[29] How much permanent damage is done the child's imagination by substituting the processed images of someone else for the child's own active, creative image making, at just the time of life when it most needs to be exercised? Television would raise the most serious educational questions if all the images on the screen were of the finest and noblest, to say nothing of the violent, jejune, and stereotyped images that constitute the usual television offerings. In an age of the ubiquitous, ready-made image, the arts in education and education as an art become all the more crucial.

The issue at stake is not the denigration of television in all its forms, but the need to think rigorously and responsibly about its proper place in education—particularly during the formative years of the child's life, when the image-making capacity of the mind so crucial to a living, creative thinking is developing.

Similar considerations apply to the introduction of the computer in education, although it poses, perhaps, even more complex problems. Again, the task is not to stand, Canute-like, before the incoming tide of electronic technology, but rather, to be responsible educators in its adoption and use. Responsibility in this sense means much more than enthusiastically trying to come up with as many new ways as possible in which the computer can be used for teaching, which has so far been the main response of educationists. Responsibility here does mean raising the critical questions about which ways of understanding and using the computer are humanly—and, therefore, education-ally—beneficial and which are harmful. It also means, despite the risk of a loss of funding and status, to refuse to run with the crowd, if doing so requires blinking the educationally harm-ful. In the enthusiasm for computer teaching and learning now becoming apparent, a certain inchoate uneasiness can be de-tected beneath the surface, but very little sustained effort in raising the hard questions is yet evident. Justice cannot begin to be done to the problem in the space available here, but a few of the questions that seem worthy of careful consideration can be listed:

1. How can the computer be introduced and used in education in such a way that the illusion is not fostered that all important human problems are computable?
2. How can the computer be introduced and used in education in such a way that the illusion is not fostered that the human brain and mind are to be understood solely in terms of electrochemical information processing?

3. How can the computer be used in education without furthering the tendency, already pronounced, to cut off and isolate the student even more completely from the direct experience and knowledge of living nature?
4. How can the computer be used in education without furthering the disintegration of language and of words, sound, and tone as the bearers of meaning (especially the fine-textured meanings that often mark the difference between the human and the non-human)?
5. What is the effect of the flat, two-dimensional, and externally supplied image, and the lifeless, though florid, colors of the viewing screen, on the development of the child's own capacity to bring to birth living, mobile, creative images of his or her own?
6. What effect does viewing the computer screen have on the healthy development of the growing but unformed mind—and body?[30]

Impressed with the vast powers of the computer, are we in danger of beginning to surround ourselves increasingly with intelligences that are powerful in certain important areas and—gradually subduing our own thoughts, actions, and visions to them—to sacrifice those less specialized and seemingly weaker, but more supple, flexible, creative, and ultimately more intelligent and powerful capacities of ourselves?

When education is itself conceived as an art, several things of fundamental importance must follow: First, a concern for the beauty, harmony, and wholeness of the entire educational setting must be paramount. Harmony and proportion in the physcial and emotional environments will be sought as essential. Ugliness, coldness, or chaotic clutter in educational architecture and classroom arrangements will be recognized as hurtful, and not matters of little educational consequence. The therapeutic nature of appropriate color—on the classroom walls perhaps more than on the art pad—of a rhythmically balanced day, of an aesthetic, warm, and calm architectural, social, and teaching environment will be seen as crucial to education.

Second, the arts will not be confined to special periods or courses isolated in their own curricular compartments. Instead, they will be seen embodying the perspective and mode of approach for presenting and understanding all the subjects of the curriculum. An artistic outlook and activity will pervade the teaching of all subjects and the ordering of the school days and years. It is from this perspective that M. C. Richards, poet, potter, and educator, writes:

> From the beginning of school, artistic expression should infuse cognitive learning. Colored pencils and crayons should not be restricted to an hour of art each week (as is often the case in public schools), but should be used as a matter of course in all lessons, such as arithmetic, writing, social studies, biology. Pupils should make their class books and decorate them with drawings. They should express their feelings in poems and pictures and collage. Information should always keep its connection with life rhythms and imaginative examples, enabling the children to continue their inner picturing in relation to what they are learning. Bodily activity in relation to numbers and letters and speech and music can be a part of daily practice right from the beginning, as well as specific instruction in gymnastics and dance. Working in the arts—singing, playing an instrument, knitting, dramatic acting—should insure the balance of the days. The direction is toward the child's growing wholeness.[31]

Third, making the arts the center of education looks toward a reenlivening and elevation in importance of much of the traditional subjects of study. Literature, history, foreign languages, and, contrary to what might superficially be supposed, mathematics and natural science all receive emphasis from the earliest years. The approach, however, is one in which artistic feeling and a sense of the whole is pervasive, and in which the integration of the entire curriculum becomes a reality. Not only is the inner approach to the traditional subjects artistically undertaken, but the so-called arts subjects proper are never divorced from the other studies. The so-called arts subjects—painting, modeling, movement, music, handcraft—are worked into the entire curriculum throughout, and become indispensable in the teaching of every subject. The artistic element in every subject begins to glow.

Indeed, recognizing the role of imagination in knowing will lead to a corresponding recognition of the role of the arts as revealing, par excellence, what is fundamental to all knowing—scientific, philosophic, religious, and practical—as well as in achieving the basic goal of all knowing: to discover intrinsic meaning.

Fairy tales, fable, and myth can offer, perhaps, the most obvious and powerful starting point for education. Children take a natural delight in fairy tales, and the reasons are not hard to find. During the early school years especially, children live in a world permeated with feeling and moral qualities. Everything in the world of the child is endowed with life and purpose. The child is immersed in a magical world and looks for a living, purposive response from everything encountered. This is the world that comes to imaginative presentation in the fairy tale. In myth the world of the fairy tale persists, but undergoes transformations consonant with changes and revelations of further aspects of human consciousness.

Fairy tales told imaginatively by teachers (not simply read from books) and acted out by children in movement, drama, painting, and song can provide a familiar, alive world within which the children can begin to explore and express their own inner natures and gradually come to terms with reality. Bruno Bettelheim has recently dealt with the uniqueness of fairy tales, "not only as a form of literature, but as works of art which are fully comprehensible to the child, as no other form of art is."[32] In fairy tales children can begin to encounter and deal with the enduring issues and questions of humankind which they in their own way are intensely interested in: good and evil, heroism and villainy, reward and punishment, life and death, the self and others, and so forth. And the fairy tales deal with these questions in exciting, vivid, compelling ways which engage the child's own inner feeling.

However, as A. C. Harwood has pointed out, "Fairy tales not only see the world as the child sees it, they contain much of the nature lore, the moral lessons, and practical wisdom of our ancestors."[33] Because fairy tales are based on a time-tested primeval human wisdom, there is in them a depth and substance, layers of meaning upon meanings, which cannot be exhausted by neat explanations, and which can continue to light up in the understanding even into adulthood and old age. By comparison, much contemporary reading fare for schools, which seeks to bring children as soon as possible into a modern, grown-up, real world—often itself presented as a scrubbed, smiling, and utterly monotonous world—seems trivial. "Fairy tales," Bettelheim writes, "unlike any other form of literature, direct the child to discover his identity and calling, and they also suggest what experiences are needed to develop his character further."[34]

Above all, fairy tales call forth from children an imaginative activity of their own. The picture-forming, image-making activity of the mind, essential to the development of a thinking capable of insight, is engaged and brought into play from the very first hearing and acting out of the fairy tales. The images evoked need not be only visual, they may be auditory, kinetic, and spatial as well, but they provide the connections between inner and outer meaning. Here can be sought, in the modest fairy tale, the beginnings and basis of a living-thinking.

In the first year, moreover, fairy tales can provide a point of departure and actual materials for an imaginative teaching of other subjects. Fairy tales supply a wealth of pictures for letters, reading, counting and arithmetic, plays, songs, painting, and modeling. Fairy tales foster in children the building up of their own inner imaginative activity, and at the same time provide them with stories and images having substance, content, and meaning. From fairy tales can follow a natural introduction to myths, the great wisdom stories of world cultures, and from there to history, the social sciences, and a deepening in literature—accompanied by a constantly developing, imaginative appreciation and observation of nature.

Let us look briefly at three important areas of study from this point of view: language and literature, history, and natural sciences.

The meaning and power of language are recognized and made central. The student is immersed in stories, images, and words that are meaningful and that strike a deep, active connection with the student's own inner being. A living feeling for the inherent meaning of words, a respect for the potency and integrity of words, can grow naturally. From the outset the strong modern tendencies toward the degradation and impoverishment of language are countered. Where the integrity and vital connections of words with human meaning, which is the essence of language, are recognized, all studies can retain their essential human significance. All subjects will preserve their human interest in every sense of the term: they will be interesting to the students and important to their lives.

To take one basic example, the teaching of reading, which is of considerable concern to many parents and teachers today: Where children can delight in the sounds of words, and in the movements and gestures they inspire, and when they themselves are actively engaged in using words in the hearing, telling, and dramatizing of stories, then reading can occur on its own. Where the context of living language has been established, it makes more sense to begin not with the teaching of reading but with the teaching of writing.[35] The nature and different qualities of letters can be explored in movement, sound, painting, and picture—the "S" walked through, snaked out, on the floor; the "M" of the mountain range traced with brush and crayon in vivid colors and towering size; the "W" of the waves expressed in rhythmic dance; the *buzz* of the "B" sounded and felt—and all dramatized through the characters and pictures of fairy tales. Again the intelligence is first awakened in the doing and comes to consciousness in the fluid image and mental picture. A love and sense for language are grounded in the activity and feeling of the child. As reading occurs there will already be established a delight and meaning in words and desire to avail oneself of them, never mind that actual reading may come a little slower than the accelerated reading programmer might like.

In a climate saturated with a natural delight in the experience of words and language, the learning of foreign languages can begin in the very earliest school years, with the first experiences again being sound, movement, singing, chanting, games, plays, all being followed only gradually in later years with formal grammar, for which a solid basis will by then have been laid. To approach reading as though it were solely the mastering of technical, functional recognition skills, and the building of a vocabulary of the two or three hundred most used words, is an impoverishment of language and of life which leaves children with only the husks of literacy. It is no wonder that reports mount of children who have been trained formally to read, that is to recognize words, but have no understanding of what they read. Such a miscarriage of education has little opportunity where understanding is established and present from the start.

The study of history, a crucial subject for human understanding, exemplifies the importance of an education of imagination. History requires an imaginative activity of the mind that must be at once participatory, synthesizing, and critical.

The study of history for many people is frequently ruined irremediably before they reach high school because it has not been presented in a way in which the past has been made to come alive. Or history has been made trivial in an ill-conceived effort to liven it up by turning it into just another version of the present.

In the most general terms history is concerned with development in time, with the fact and meaning of change and persistence through time. One of the most important tasks of history is to present the past in such a way that the essential otherness of the past is fully respected, and at the same time to make the past, in Phenix's words, "available for sympathetic participation by persons now living."[36] The important thing in history is not to garner "facts" about the past, because by themselves the facts are worthless; nor is it to learn lessons from the past applicable to the present, always a dangerous undertaking at best because the lessons, so-called, are constantly changing with the movements of time. Rather, the prime task is to recover and enter into the meaning of the past with understanding. In this primary task the study of history and the arts are at one in their fundamental attitude of respecting the otherness of things, allowing them to be what they are, yet participating imaginatively in them.

History thus becomes indispensable to an understanding of other persons, other times, to recovering ways of thinking about the world and experiencing the world lost to our age, but often of no less validity for that. History pursued in this spirit can be a chief safeguard against that chronological snobbery and temporal provincialism that so constrict the modern mind set. And, positively, history can be a primary source of insight, inspiration, and consolation, which the present by itself does not contain and cannot supply.

History, if it is not studied merely academically, can lead to a deeper awareness and understanding of the polar tensions of human life: the general and the particular, the universal and the unique, essential freedom and limitations.[37] Furthermore, the moral dimension at the heart of the study of history can here be seen clearly in the obligation to render an account that does full justice to the times, circumstances, and assumptions of others in the past, which is at the same time an obligation to become fully aware of the degree to which they can rightly be held responsible for their actions. To give an account is to hold accountable. Objectivity is, thus, seen in the study of history to be much more complex than mere neutrality and unengaged looking on.

The imaginative, participative capacity required in the study of history can grow naturally out of the child's experience and immersion in the living language nourished by the imaginative pictures of fairy tale and myth. In this way, beginning in the later elementary years and from their engagement with language and myth, children can find that the past speaks to them and they can take up a study of ancient cultures with great interest. As a more pronounced sense of time develops in the child during the later elementary school years, the sense of otherness also required in the study of history will itself find reinforcement in the artistic experience. In reconstructing the past, for example, the student as historian encounters resistance in a way directly analogous to that of the artist in working with his medium: the recalcitrance to yield their meanings of the documents, the artifacts, and other evidence from which the past is imaginatively recreated. Just as the artist struggling with his materials may be led to a new insight, so in the study of history, the encounter with the evidence may give rise to new questions in the student's mind, which in turn may even generate new kinds of evidence. But all rests, if history is to live, upon a fluid, mobile, imaginative mind.

Also as with the arts, history attempts to recreate the past in its wholeness. The story that is told must hold together, the connections among events and persons must all be there. This is one reason why narrative, the telling of the story, is so important in history. Analysis and explanation are also extremely important in history, but they depend on the prior narrative, whose presence may sometimes, to be sure, be largely covert and only suggested. And at times the narrative itself may become the main form of explanation and analysis, for often only in the telling of the story can the intricate interweaving of historical relations and meanings be grasped. History, then, depends on a living language and a respect for the ability of words to reveal the nuances of meaning, the qualitative distinctions, and the complex, often delicate interconnections among people and events that constitute the uniqueness of history. The possibility of historical understanding and respect for language depend upon each other in the closest possible way.

Natural science occupies a central place in an education of imagination. It has, unfortunately, become all too possible for students to study science—physics, chemistry, biology—with little interest in nature or experience of her. Science instruction then often seems of a kind that dulls rather than enhances the student's appreciation of living nature. The study of science becomes easily occupied with the components and physical properties and effects of nature, but lacks, in the words of the biologist George K. Russell, "genuine experience of living plants and animals, stars, clouds and the weather, and the entire natural world."[38] Despite the great technological prowess that it may, thereby, attain, such a science actually serves to increase man's alienation from nature. In biology, for example, there can arise the kind of situation described by the naturalist R. D. Lawrence, in which "the average non-biologist remains singularly ill-informed where nature is concerned, while those young people who elect to pursue a career in biology become programmed to think of life as expendable, something that can be clinically analyzed with scalpels and microscopes."[39] The passion for truth, which animates all true science, fades. And science becomes peculiarly vulnerable to the crassest instrumentalism and utilitarianism, which ask only how nature can be used. Against its own best spirit, science can do little to hinder and may actually contribute to that coarsening of sensitivity to the real needs of living creatures, including the human.

The basis for a meaningful study of natural science is formed even during the pre- and early elementary school years. Through handcraft activities and working with physical objects in a shaping of the senses through experiences with colors, textures, sounds, and materials; in the engaging pictures of nature contained in fairy tales, myth, and art; and, above all, in the experience and observation (which early on can be very acute) of nature and natural processes, a direct acquaintance with plants, animals, the seasons, the sun and wind—in all of these, and in their many possible combinations, the study of science is actually begun. Before the end of elementary school botany and zoology can be taken up, followed shortly by such subjects as geography and mineralogy. Physics can be introduced with experiments in acoustics and optics, heat, magnetism, electricity; chemistry, nutrition, and physiology can also begin. In short, a solid study of science can be entered upon from the start to the great delight and interest of the child.

Three things, however, will be of utmost importance during these years: The study of science will be situated within the context of a direct experience, observation, and appreciation of nature. And, second, abstract, analytic thinking will not be pushed on the child too quickly. It will, instead, be permitted to emerge naturally and in due course from a sound imaginative, experiential foundation. Abstractions will not be lifeless and empty that are anchored in a vigorous, disciplined imagination, a developed accuracy in observation, and a practical knowledge attained in healthy growth, personal relations, and the disciplines of craft.

Finally, throughout there will be an intermingling and intermeshing of art, literature, and science. Selections from poetry may illuminate and vivify the child's study of plants and animals. A unit in geography or arithmetic may begin with an apt reference to the child's concurrent studies in ancient history. The children will illustrate their observations of nature with their own colorful paintings, drawings, and geometrical constructions. A class in woodworking, may, for example, be an occasion to combine as a unity the handcraft skills in making, say, a recorder, with a lesson in music as the students learn to tune and play their own instruments, and with a lesson in physics as they study the nature of harmonics. And all will be done with great care and accuracy. An experience of the wholeness of knowledge will be for the student a reality, as will the awareness, in the words of the psychiatrist Iona Ginsburg, that "beautiful imagery and vivid color are part of life in general and are not limited to the painting lesson or to any one small corner of living."[40] The experience of science as part of a larger and always human enterprise will not be wanting.

During the high school and college years students begin to experience the awakening of the full powers of analytic and abstract conceptual thought. They begin to want to test, to call into question, to criticize, and to compare what they read and are told to see if it holds up in the light of their widening experience. If at this time concepts are experienced as rigid and lifeless and basically foreign to the person's own being, they will be employed ruthlessly and without feeling. Or they will be accepted dully and grudgingly, but without real comprehension. And, not infrequently, if concepts are experienced as dead and alien, the same powers on which conceptual thinking depends may be turned against it in anxious defense and become destructive aberrations of themselves—criticism becomes carping, questioning rebellion, and analysis a resentful tearing apart— phenomena many teachers will recognize all too readily. Abstract, conceptual thinking, however, need not be experienced as dead and foreign.

A deep sense of personal confidence, a robust and disciplined picture-forming consciousness, a grasp of connectedness—together these imbue abstractions and concepts with life. Grounded in imagination, in other words, conceptual thinking becomes the fulfillment of participative knowing; not its opposite, but its completion. The full abilities for abstract, analytic conceptual thinking that begin to stir during these years will be eagerly embraced by the student for the new powers of exploration they afford—provided, that is, that they are experienced as the outgrowth of an adventure in personal knowledge and development the student has been engaged in from the beginning.

From this basis, the study of science at its most advanced can be taken up during these years in earnest. But the connection of science with the whole of knowledge and of the human being will be maintained, and the possibilities strengthened for further progress in a genuinely participative knowing. The development of quantitative skills and modes of thinking, which can be pursued during these years in remarkable depth and complexity, will be accompanied by the exploration of the qualitative realities also manifest in natural phenomena. The study and analysis of the mechanics of nature will be carried out hand in hand with an awareness of organic wholeness, rhythm, and inward relatedness. The powers of conceptual modeling will be explored and enjoyed and infused with the tentativeness and flexibility that can make of the model a precursor to further insight, rather than its procrustean curtailment. The onlooker consciousness will be cultivated as indispensable for certain essential kinds of knowing. It will also be recognized as a limited, special expression of a larger participative consciousness, and not the sole or determining mode of all knowing. The detachment required by the onlooker consciousness will thereby not be set in opposition to the involvement and responsibility required of a more complete knowing in participation.

Beauty will be held together with the practical and the abstract. As students, for example, move further into the pure symbolism and abstract nature of mathematics, there can also be a deepening of their awareness of symmetry and beauty as the qualitative realities at the heart of mathematics. It can perhaps then become possible for students to discover early what David Bohm has called the poetic and metaphorical, as distinct from the strictly logical, quality of mathematics in its highest forms.[41] It is for good reason that from earliest times mathematics has been regarded as an integral part of the humanities, and not merely as a powerful calculative accessory to utilitarian and technological purposes. The abstractions by which we grasp the outwardness of nature will be infused with the inner pictures through which alone we can apprehend the inwardness of nature revealed in living form and rhythmic pattern. Above all, it will not be forgotten that the reach and compass of scientific, as with all knowing, is inseparable from the personal qualities of the knower.

The central role of imagination in knowing points to the possibility of a genuine integrating principle for what is widely acknowledged to be a fragmented modern curriculum. The deep insight-imagination present in scientific discovery is the same activity at work in art, poetry, and in the perceptions of ethical vision. A fundamental unity joins scientific insight, artistic insight, and moral insight. Here lies the possibility of a unified cross-fertilizing curriculum that promises to go well beyond the vagaries of so-called interdisciplinary courses without losing the conceptual powers of the individual disciplines.

Concluding Reflections: The Communal

An education of imagination, and the total transformation in our ways of knowing which it involves, will have profound and, for many, unsuspected social dimensions. As long as the need for a transformation of knowing and, with it, the possibility also of new cultural insight and creativity are ignored by educational reformers, they are condemned to deal only with the secondary political and economic aspects of education, in the vain hope that from political-economic change, cultural-educational renewal will follow. Unfortunately, however, the primacy of culture thereby sinks from view, and the autonomy of education is also undermined. The whole question of what kind of education is of most worth is submerged and disappears in a swamp of political-economic theorizing and political-economic power struggles. Furthermore, when the same positivistic assumptions about knowing and the world are shared alike by educational reformers and their opponents, political-economic change can only bring about a shift in power. It cannot usher in a permanent change in the quality of education or in the emergence of fundamentally new and creative cultural possibilities and impulses.

An education based on a predominantly utilitarian and technical reason will oscillate periodically between an emphasis on excellence, defined as the mastery of discursive, logico-mathematical skills, and an emphasis on equality, conceived as equal opportunity for all academically gifted, irrespective of background, or as the provision of fundamental, survival skills for the masses—or as some politically palatable combination of the three. A large part of educational reform during the past hundred years has consisted of just such pendulum swings between now an emphasis on "excellence," now on "equality," with the former frequently devolving into a mean meritocracy and the latter into a destructive demand for the abandonment of all excellence in the face of a single-track reward system geared only to academic excellence narrowly defined. In this situation there also arises from time to time great anxiety over the loss of common social values and the breakdown of personal morality that increasingly seem to tarnish this scramble for opportunity. A furious search then gets under way for some basis within the prevailing technical rationalism for a reinstatement of "the moral component"—the missing piece in the machinery—and moral education in the curriculum. Many a bevy of experts in ethical education, all duly certified, appear on the scene. All the while, the increments of inner emptiness and confusion and outer barrenness and disintegration show a relatively steady rate of increase.

An education of imagination, however, which is itself grounded in a transformation of our ways of knowing, embodies also, therefore, the beginnings of a cultural transformation. And it will demand for its fulfillment commensurate political and economic changes. In the first place, it will foster an appreciation of a diversity of excellences, a diversity of gifts—logical, mathematical, technological, musical, linguistic, artistic, personal excellences—each deserving reverence and capable of revealing important dimensions of reality. What then becomes required is a diversity of institutional supports for a diversity of excellences. A basis would thus also be laid for the rebuilding and reenlivening of community, and for the recovery of the richness of cultural and communal diversity. An appreciation of cultural diversity would be rooted, not in irrational assertions of social preference and group superiority, but in genuine recognition of a diversity of communal, as well as of personal, excellences. And recognizing such diversity will link education directly with a concern for a just global society, for it will demand a world in which diversity in wholeness is cherished. A holistic education demands a just and caring society.

Second, a recovery of the objective aspect of qualities relates education directly to the quality of the environment, the economy, the social structure. It jars to lecture authentically on aesthetics in barren classrooms and ugly neighborhoods. And it would jar to continue to treat the earth as a machine or a dead slag heap while increasingly coming to know it as a living being. The unrelieved despoliation of the earth and the continued amassing of weapons of destruction that threaten the future of all living things would be seen to stand in intolerable incongruity with the educating of individuals to be free, creative persons with a joy in life and a feeling for beauty and love of all existence. By contrast, every program for political and economic change that does not issue from a personal, cultural, and cognitive transformation can no longer be considered very radical.

Third, a transformation of knowing and an education of imagination are essential to the education of the public. They make possible a renewed sense of civic pedagogy and the formation of an enlightened and committed public. Only when the connections among knowledge, education, and human values are recognized is it possible to sustain effective public dialogue about the kind of society desired. The erosion of genuine community by a narrow technological rationalism and the consequent spinning off of a multitude of conflicting interest groups is, as we noted earlier, both socially fragmenting and simultaneously homogenizing in its effects. All the groups tend to conflict and struggle for power with one another, and yet they all begin to look very much alike in that they all lack roots in time and place and personal commitment, and all share a common fascination with power and status.

There are increasing numbers of concerned persons today who seek to mitigate the fissiparous, socially fragmenting effects of technical reason by calling for a renewed devotion to "common social values." But the calls for common social values are almost never accompanied with the demand for a critical questioning of the dominance of technical reason in modern society as the only recognized source of knowledge. When the knowledge base of modern society goes unchallenged and untransformed, the call for common social values can come to mean only one of two things (though it may lead to a worst-case combination of both): Either it comes to a mean a heavy-handed imposition of the values of one or a few powerful groups on all the others, á la a moral majority, for example; or it means accepting as the basis for commonality the dominant, underlying technological, positivistic orientation of the society and the translating of all issues of public policy and social purpose into technological questions. Thus, the call for common social values, often against the intentions of those concerned, simply furthers the centralization of social control in the hands of those who control the technology. A transformation of our ways of knowing is essential if questions regarding the quality of communal life are to be recognized as just as real and ultimately more basic than those having to do with quantitative growth and technological efficiency. The genuine public dialogue about public issues that make a vital difference to the quality of life then becomes possible. The educational responsibilities of the media, the family, churches, political groups, and a variety of other institutions become manifest. And it can also become possible to begin to embody in new communal forms and associations those perceptions of quality, meaning, purpose, and value essential to human dignity and a living world. Politics and political organization will remain important; indeed, they will acquire their true significance in existing for the sake of something beyond themselves. An education of imagination can become a new education in political imagination.

A Final Reflection: The Personal Once Again

Clearly, education is not solely a matter of the upbringing of children. That is the point of departure. Nor can it be entirely a matter of family and school education. Those are obvious and useful points of reference. Education relates to the whole of life; and it is for life. Education, and thinking about education, must, therefore, look to the end as well as the beginning of life. A culture that can conceive of nothing more worthy for its children than a purely utilitarian, achievement-oriented education, will in all probability have little better in store for its adults. There is a deep sense in which insight and understanding come only in the shaping and fulfillment of an entire life. A real test of the education offered by a culture will be seen, as we suggested earlier, in the place accorded to its old people: Does the culture value the presence and wisdom of its old people, and have its old the understanding which is granted only them to attain? Recall Walt Whitman's

> To get the final lilt of songs
> To penetrate the inmost law of poets—to know the mighty ones,

Job, Homer, Eschylus, Dante, Shakspere, Tennyson, Emerson;
To diagnose the shifting-delicate tints of love and pride and
    doubt—to truly understand,
To encompass these, the last keen faculty and entrance-price,
Old age, and what it brings from all its past experiences.[42]

Whitman's reference to the poets is surely meant to be taken
seriously, both straightforwardly (and on this level ought not to
be passed over too lightly) and also as symbols of all that fills
life with the substance of which it is worth "to truly understand," a substance which immediate experience and calculative
reason can never exhaust. An education of imagination aims to
enable us to bring a love of truth and feeling for beauty, a sense
of meaning and fresh wonder into the myriad practicalities and
routine of every day. It seeks a deepening of awareness and
insight that can affect and transform the trivial ambitions, fret-
ting and conniving about career, and frenetic busyness with
which under the best of circumstances we are wont to fill our
days. For these calculative reason will suffice, but for a love of
ideas, a concern for truth, a sense of meaning, the delights of
color, sound, and beauty, the satisfactions of personal competence, and the company of friends—a deeper rationality and
grasp of vital priorities is needed. The final test of an education
comes in whether it has nourished or sapped our ability to bring
out of our own inner resources the strength and hope needed
to meet the challenges, difficulties, and vicissitudes of life.

The future of the human being and of all the earth now hang
upon our recovery of imagination—of a thinking imbued with
life and love. The warning of Albert Einstein underscores our
unprecedented and perilous situation: "The unleashed power
of the atom has changed everything save our modes of thinking,
and we thus drift toward unparalleled catastrophes."[43] A dead
thinking and failed imagination have not relieved us of our central position among the creatures; but they have given this unique
centrality a nightmarish and deadly turn. Having spurned our
vice-regal potential, with its life-filled and life-giving privileges
and responsibilities, we now threaten each other and all the beau-

teous, wonderful life on earth with extinction—final and irrevocable. But to bring our situation to full consciousness without flinching may be our first act of imagination by which we can begin to halt the drift and open a new way into the future—the first step in joining our thinking with the life, the love, the freedom, the sensitivity, the warmth, the courge, and the infinite reach of meaning that are our true human reality. Never before has it been made more apparent that only a living thinking can give us a living world. Despair, therefore, and the numbed indifference and business-as-usual attitude born of despair, are unworthy of our true being. And perhaps, also as never before, we face the possibility, as well as the necessity, of recognizing and realizing our true being.

Notes

1. Mary Warnock, *Imagination* (Berkeley and Los Angeles: University of California Press, 1976), p. 9.

2. At the same time, the discipline of form demanded by imagination has nothing in common with that arbitrary imposition of order that is often meant when the cry goes up for stricter discipline in the schools. When the only alternative to complete chaos seems to be a militaristic crackdown, in the society and the school, all amidst a welter of mingling calls for more police on the streets and in the corridors of our schools, for corporal punishment in the classrooms and capital punishment in the prisons, and so on, then we may be sure that we are nearing the end of a process in which there was no love of form and no imagination from the beginning. Chaos and iron rule alike are symptoms of the loss of imagination—and are equally hostile to it.

3. "Cognitive structures," along with the myriad other little creatures that they seem to have spawned—"cognitive constructs," "cognitive maps," "cognitive frames," "cognitive sets," "'cognitive networks," "cognitive schematas," "cognitive scripts," the fecundity is awesome—all appear in the research literature as though possessing an almost tangible, palpable substantiality. A literalistic reader might be forgiven for supposing that were the skull of the hapless learner to be opened, albeit at the right stage of development, one would find the brain infested with cognitive structures, a bit like maggots in cheese, or, less dynamic, steel webs in concrete. Of course no cognitive specialist would for a moment intend or tolerate such naiveté, but the fact remains that these putative cognitive entities are named in the literature

with such a matter-of-factness and tangibleness as to discourage questions about their actual existence. Is there really such a thing as a cognitive structure in even a figurative sense? Or do we have in this whole menagerie of cognitive creatures a kind of latter-day bestiary of the brain?

4. Sheldon S. Wolin, "The New Public Policy," *Democracy*, vol. 1 (October 1981), 28.

5. Quoted in Steven Hahn, "Agriculture and Political Culture," *Democracy*, vol. 1 (October 1981), 104.

6. The central importance of the "art of living well as persons" is discussed by Philip H. Phenix, "Promoting Personal Development Through Teaching," *Teachers College Record*, vol. 84, no. 2 (December 1982), 301-16. See also John Fentress Gardner, *The Experience of Knowledge: Essays in American Education* (Garden City, N.Y.: Waldorf Press, 1975), pp. 103-18.

7. Ibid. See also Michael Polanyi, *The Tacit Dimension* (Garden City, N.Y.: Doubleday, 1966).

8. John Macmurray, *Persons in Relation* (Atlantic Highlands, N.J.: Humanities Press, 1979), p. 56. See also Maurice Merleau-Ponty, "The Child's Relations with Others," in *The Primacy of Perception*, ed. James M. Edie (Evanston, Ill.: Northwestern University Press, 1964), pp. 95-155; Martin Buber, "Education," in Martin Buber, *Between Man and Man* (New York: Macmillan Co., 1965), pp. 83-103; and David Michael Levin, "Moral Education: The Body's Felt Sense of Value," *Teachers College Record*, 84 (Winter 1982), 283-300.

9. Macmurray, *Persons in Relation*, pp. 25, 61.

10. Philip Ariés, *Centuries of Childhood: A Social History of Family Life* (New York: Alfred A. Knopf, 1962).

11. The first Waldorf school was founded in Germany in 1919, and others soon thereafter began to be established. Closed by Hitler, the schools reopened after World War II, and since then the movement has spread throughout Europe and to the United States, Canada, South America, South Africa, Australia, and New Zealand. Based on a holistic understanding of the human person and a detailed view of child development, Waldorf education offers a comprehensive approach to teaching and to the curriculum. Despite the existence and growth of Waldorf education in Europe for decades, the presence of the Rudolf Steiner School in New York City for half a century, and the founding of several new Waldorf schools throughout the country during the past decade or so, Waldorf education remains to become better known to Americans. Other educational movements, much less thoroughgoing in their attempts to integrate art, science, and an appreciation of the

fully human at every level of education, have, curiously, been given much more attention. A movement that is today one of the largest independent educational movements in the world, and one with its own unique understanding of the child, a comprehensive and detailed curriculum, and more than sixty years of teaching practice and institutional experience deserves the *informed* consideration of those genuinely concerned with education and the development of human wholeness. That few American educators know about Waldorf education, and often then on only the flimsiest of hearsay, is something of a professional scandal. See the bibliographic essay for basic literature on Waldorf education.

12. In this sense the educational stages set forth by A. N. Whitehead are in many respects educationally more useful and significant than many derived, for instance, from the fields of psychology. More intuitive and seemingly less rigorous empirically than many educational theories based on psychological research, Whitehead's phases, nevertheless, encompass more educationally relevant considerations than almost any of the former. Alfred North Whitehead, *The Aims of Education and Other Essays* (New York: Macmillan, 1929).

13. A. C. Harwood, *The Recovery of Man in Childhood; A Study in the Educational Work of Rudolf Steiner* (London: Hodder and Stoughton, 1958), pp. 47-58.

14. Compare Macmurray, *Persons in Relation*, p. 60.

15. Ibid., pp. 55-56. See also Jean Piaget, *Science of Education and the Psychology of the Child* (New York: Viking Press, 1971), pp. 155-57.

16. Phenix, "Promoting Personal Development through Teaching."

17. Howard E. Gruber and J. Jacques Vonèche, *The Essential Piaget* (New York: Basic Books, 1977), p. 71, also pp. 481-514.

18. Rudolf Steiner, *A Modern Art of Education* (London: Rudolf Steiner Press, 1972), p. 106.

19. John Davy, "The Social Meaning of Education," *Teachers College Record*, vol. 81, no. 3 (Spring 1980), 345-59.

20. See the long statement by Piaget on how disturbing he found American efforts to accelerate children intellectually, printed in David Elkind, *Children and Adolescents, Interpretive Essays on Jean Piaget* (New York: Oxford University Press, 1981), p. 28.

21. Quoted in Raymond S. Moore and Dorothy N. Moore, "Caring for Young Children: Danger of Early Schooling," in *A New Image of Man in Medicine: Individuation Process and Biographical Aspects of Disease*, vol. 3, ed. Karl E. Schaefer et al. (Mount Kisco: Future Publishing, 1979), p. 52.

22. Says Elkind: "What is the evidence that pre-school instruction has

lasting effects upon mental growth and development? The answer is, in brief, that there is none." Elkind, *Children and Adolescents*, p. 152.

23. Ibid., p. 153.

24. See Moore and Moore, "Caring for Young Children," pp. 37-70.

25. Ibid., p. 63.

26. Charles Darwin, *The Autobiography of Charles Darwin, 1809-1882* (New York: Harcourt, Brace, 1958), pp. 43-44, 138-39.

27. Quoted in Charles Davy, "Art for Whose Sake?" *The Golden Blade* (annual) (1980), 76.

28. Elkind writes: "What children acquire through active manipulation of the environment is nothing less than the ability to think." Elkind, *Children and Adolescents*, p. 53.

29. Jerry Mander, *Four Arguments for the Elimination of Television* (New York: William Morrow, 1978), p. 214.

30. The range of such questions requiring careful, sustained attention can be multiplied.

31. Mary Caroline Richards, "The Public School and the Education of the Whole Person," *Teachers College Record*, vol. 82, no. 1 (Fall 1980), 67, 68.

32. Bruno Bettelheim, *The Uses of Enchantment: The Meaning and Importance of Fairy Tales* (New York: Alfred A. Knopf, 1976), p. 12.

33. Harwood, *The Recovery of Man in Childhood*, p. 98; Bettelheim makes the same point.

34. Bettelheim, *The Uses of Enchantment*, p. 26.

35. Elkind writes: "Writing as preparation for reading makes good theoretical as well as pedagogical sense. . . . Obviously, reading involves much more than the ability to motorically reproduce letters, but motoric reproduction is a good example of an appropriate pre-reading activity for young children who are not yet ready for formal instruction in that skill." Elkind, *Children and Adolescents*, p. 54.

36. Phenix, "Promoting Personal Development Through Teaching."

37. Trygve Tholfsen, "The Ambiguous Virtues of the Study of History," *Teachers College Record*, vol. 79, no. 2 (December 1977), 245-58.

38. George K. Russell, "Introduction," in R. D. Lawrence, *The Study of Life: A Naturalist's View* (New York: Myrin Institute, 1980), p. 7.

39. Lawrence, *The Study of Life*, p. 12.

40. Iona H. Ginsburg, "Jean Piaget and Rudolf Steiner: Stages of Child Development and Implications for Pedagogy," *Teachers College Record*, vol. 84, no. 2 (Winter 1982), 327-37.

41. David Bohm, Lecture at the Charles F. Kettering Foundation, Dayton, Ohio, March 20, 1981.

42. [Walt Whitman], *The Complete Works of Walt Whitman*, vol. 2 (New York and London: G. P. Putnam's Sons, 1902), p. 307.

43. Quoted in Jonathan Schell, *The Fate of the Earth* (New York: Alfred A. Knopf, 1982), p. 188.

Bibliographic Essay ─────

The central argument of this book is that in an adequate grasp of Insight-Imagination a fundamental transformation in our ways of knowing is not only a necessity for the future of civilization but is, indeed, a genuine possibility. While it makes no claims to being a complete or definite survey of the relevant literature, a vast and probably impossible task in any case, this brief essay is an attempt to provide a useful guide to some of the main readily available sources for the argument of the book. It is presented here in the hope that readers will find in it points of departure for their own explorations in Insight-Imagination.

Preface

The importance of the connections among knowledge, education, and human values, and many of the crucial issues and problems involved, are examined from various perspectives in the essays in Douglas Sloan, editor, *Education and Values* (New York: Teachers College Press, 1980), and in the articles in the special issue of *Teachers College Record*, 82 (Spring 1981) devoted to the topic "Knowledge, Education, and Human Values: Toward the Recovery of Wholeness."

1. Fragmented Thinking, Broken World

Among the many treatments of the history, philosophy, and nature of science, three especially are classic works and indispensable in beginning to understand the development, the conceptual basis, and the influence of science. They are H. Butterfield, *The Origins of Modern Science, 1300-1800* (London: G. Bell and Sons, 1958); Thomas Kuhn, *The Structure of Scientific Revolutions*, 2d ed., enlarged (Chicago: University of Chicago Press, 1970); and Alfred North Whitehead, *Science and the Modern World* (New York: Macmillan Company, 1925).

The nature of scientific positivism and its cultural consequences are succinctly and penetratingly described in Alan Bullock, "The Future of Humanistic Studies," *Teachers College Record*, 82 (Winter 1980), 173-90, and in Owen Barfield, "The Rediscovery of Meaning," in Owen Barfield, *The Rediscovery of Meaning and Other Essays* (Middletown, Conn.: Wesleyan University Press, 1977), pp. 11-21. Ernst Lehrs's *Man or Matter* (New York: Harper & Brothers, 1950) depicts the onlooker consciousness characteristic of the modern mind, and Frederick Ferré's *Shaping the Future: Resources for the Post-Modern World* (New York: Harper & Row, 1976) analyzes the notion of scientism and its inadequacies as a way of knowing and viewing of the world. Huston Smith's *Beyond the Post-Modern Mind* (New York: Crossroad, 1982) demonstrates the hold of scientistic assumptions within nearly every field of modern scholarship. Each of these authors provides rich resources and insights for the development of a participative way of knowing, which is the subject of the remaining chapters.

Some of the most telling criticisms of scientism and its exclusive reliance on detached and reductionistic conceptions of knowledge have come from outstanding scientists. Few have been more important than the chemist and philosopher Michael Polanyi in showing that all scientific investigation, including reductionism and detached analysis, is based on ways of knowing that are holistic, integrative, and personally committed. Polanyi's major work is *Personal Knowledge, Towards a Post-Critical Philosophy* (Chicago: University of Chicago Press, corrected edition, 1962). Important in its own right, and also a useful introduction to his thinking, is Polanyi, *The Tacit Dimension* (Garden City, N.Y.: Doubleday and Company, 1966); and the same holds for the book jointly authored by Polanyi and Harry Prosch, *Meaning* (Chicago: University of Chicago Press, 1975). The biochemist Erwin Chargaff provides many trenchant observations on the limitations and dangers of an exclusively reductionistic science in *Voices in the Labyrinth: Nature, Man, and Science* (New York: Seabury Press, 1977), and in *Heraclitean Fire: Sketches from a Life before Nature* (New York: Rockefeller University Press, 1978). The renowned physicist David Bohm, in *Wholeness and the Implicate Order* (London: Routledge & Kegan Paul, 1980), demonstrates the failures of an exclusively reductionistic thinking in modern physics, as well as its fragmenting consequences for our world and our personal lives. The physicist Werner Heisenberg provides important reflections on the problems and possibilities of modern science in *Across the Frontiers* (New York: Harper & Row, 1974).

From the field of philosophy, two perceptive and succinct descriptions of the loss of meaning and the destructive narrowing of human reason, which result from a purely quantitative, scientistic world view, are to be found in Owen Barfield, "Language, Evolution of Consciousness, and the Recovery of Human Meaning," *Teachers College Record*, vol. 82, no. 3 (Spring 1981), 427-33, and in Philip H. Phenix, "Teilhard and the Uses of Reason," *Forum for Correspondence and Contact*, vol. 11, no. 4 (March 1981), 37-39. And C. S. Lewis's classic, *The Abolition of Man* (New York: Macmillan Publishing Company, 1947), demonstrates the ominous consequences for education of the modern narrowing of reason.

Discussions of the problems of technology and technicism are myriad. All writers on the subject are indebted to the work of Jacques Ellul, particularly to his masterpiece, *The Technological Society* (New York: Alfred A. Knopf, 1965), to which he has added his *The Technological System* (New York: Continuum, 1980). Langdon Winner's *Autonomous Technology* (Cambridge, Mass.: MIT Press, 1977) is an extremely valuable discussion of the problems of technology, which draws upon, and frequently summarizes, most of the important writings on the subject. Frederick Ferré's *Shaping the Future*, mentioned above, contains a penetrating analysis of *technolatry*, and David Ehrenfeld's *The Arrogance of Humanism* (New York: Oxford University Press, 1978), is an eloquent and wide-ranging analysis of the destructive consequences of technolatry.

The technolatrous erosion of human community and of nature are movingly examined by Wendell Berry in *A Continuous Harmony: Essays Cultural and Agricultural* (New York: Harcourt Brace Jovanovich, A Harvest Book, 1975) and in *Unsettling America: Culture and Agriculture* (New York: Avon Books, 1977). The political problems of technology are discussed in their many dimensions in Richard J. Barnet, *The Lean Years: Politics in the Age of Scarcity* (New York: Simon and Schuster, 1980). The political and social responsibilities of scientists are considered in Jonathan King, "Scientists in Society," *Anticipation*, no. 25 (December 1980). The socially destructive influences of a narrow rationality are also discussed in Robert N. Bellah, "Cultural Vision and the Human Future," *Teachers College Record*, vol. 82, no. 3 (Spring 1981), 497-506. One of the most important treatments of the human issues posed by the computer is in Joseph Weizenbaum, *Computer Power and Human Reason: From Judgment to Calculation* (San Francisco: W. H. Freeman and Company, 1976). A useful, brief statement of Weizenbaum's concern is his article, "Limits in the Use of Computer Technology, Need for a Man-Centered Science," in *Toward a Man-Centered Medical Science*, vol. 1, edited by Karl E. Schaefer et al. (Mt. Kisco, N.Y.: Futura Publishing Company, 1977), pp. 83-97. The biochemist Liebe F. Cavalieri deals with the pressing human and social problems posed by the new genetic science and technology in *The Double-Edged Helix: Science in the Real World* (New York: Columbia University Press, 1981). A treatment of the religious and ethical dimensions of modern science and technology, J. Robert Nelson's *Science and Our Troubled Conscience* (Philadelphia: Fortress Press, 1980) is especially useful in discussing the ethical issues of the life sciences. The ethical and metaphysical issues of modern technology are analyzed in Hans Jonas, "Toward a Philosophy of Technology," *The Hastings Center Report*, 9, no. 1 (February 1979), 34-43.

2. Toward the Recovery of Wholeness: The Radical Humanities and Traditional Wisdom

The crucial importance of the evolution of human consciousness from an original sense of undifferentiated communal, cosmic oneness toward the sharp awareness of separate individual selfhood characteristic of the modern period is introduced in this chapter. Few thinkers have discussed with greater insight the evolution of consciousness and all that it entails for modern human beings, both negatively and positively, than has Owen Barfield. See especially Owen Barfield, *Saving the Appearances: A Study in Idolatry* (New York: Harcourt, Brace and World, n.d.); idem, *History in English Words* (Grand Rapids, Mich.: William B. Eerdmann Publishing Co., 1967); idem, *The Rediscovery of Meaning and Other Essays* (Middletown, Conn.: Wesleyan University Press, 1977); idem, *Romanticism Comes of Age* (Letchworth, England: Rudolf Steiner Press, 1966); idem, *World's Apart* (Middletown, Conn.: Wesleyan University Press, 1963); idem, *Speaker's Meaning* (Letchworth, England: Rudolf Steiner Press, 1967); idem, *Unancestral Voice* (Middletown, Conn.: Weslyan University Press, 1965); and idem, *History, Guilt, and Habit* (Middletown, Conn.: Wesleyan University Press, 1979). See also Shirley Sugerman, "A Conversation with Owen Barfield," in *Evolution of Consciousness, Studies in Polarity*, edited by Shirley Sugerman (Middletown, Conn.: Wesleyan University Press, 1976), pp. 3-27.

Other important treatments of the evolution of consciousness from various perspectives include: Karl Jaspers, *The Origin and Goal of History* (New Haven, Conn.: Yale University Press, 1953); Erich Neumann, *Origins and History of Consciousness*, Ballinger Series, vol. 42 (Princeton, N.J.: Princeton University Press, 1970); Nicholas Berdyaev, *The Meaning of History* (London: G. Bles, 1949); L. L. Whyte, *The Unconscious before Freud* (New York: Basic Books, 1960); idem, *The Universe of Experience* (New York: Harper Torchbooks, 1978); Charles Davy, *Towards a Third Culture* (London: Faber and Faber, 1961; revised edition, Edinburgh: Floris Books, 1978); Walter Ong, *Interfaces of the Word: Studies in the Evolution of Consciousness and Culture* (Ithaca: Cornell University Press, 1977); Ernst Cassirer, *Language and Myth*, trans. Susanne K. Langer (New York: Dover Publications, 1946); and Julian Jaynes, *The Origin of Consciousness in the Breakdown of the Bicameral Mind* (Boston: Houghton Mifflin, 1976).

Those humanistic studies which view qualities as being as much a part of reality as quantity are explored in this chapter as the radical humanities. Works especially helpful in developing the concept and sense of the radical humanities include George Steiner, *In Bluebeard's Castle: Some Notes toward the Redefinition of Culture* (New Haven, Conn.: Yale University Press, 1971); John Lukacs, *The Passing of the Modern Age* (New York: Harper & Row, 1970); Huston Smith, "Flakes of Fire, Handfuls of Light: The Humanities as Uncontrolled Experiment," *Teachers College Record*, vol. 82, no. 2 (Winter 1980), 191-206; Alan Bullock, "The Future of Humanistic Studies," *Teachers College Record*, vol. 82, no. 2 (Winter 1980), 173-90; E. F. Schumacher, *Small Is Beautiful: Economics as if People Mattered* (New York: Harper Torchbooks, 1973); J. Robert Nelson, *Science and Our Troubled Conscience* (Philadelphia: Fortress Press, 1980); Wendell Berry, "Standing by Words," *The Hudson Review* (Winter 1980-1981), 489-521; Jacques Ellul, *The Technological System* (New York: Continuum, 1980); idem, *The Betrayal of the West* (New York: Seabury Press, 1978); and William Barrett, *The Illusion of Technique* (Garden City, N.Y.: Doubleday, Anchor Press, 1978). In addition to all his works already mentioned, which bear directly on the radical humanities, see also Owen Barfield, *Poetic Diction* (London: Faber and Faber, new ed., 1952); and idem, "Language, Evolution of Consciousness, and the Recovery of Human Meaning," *Teachers College Record*, vol. 82, no. 3 (Spring 1981), 427-33.

Particularly valuable for understanding the nature and importance of traditional wisdom are Huston Smith, *Forgotten Truth: The Primordial Tradition* (New York: Harper Colophon Books, 1976), and idem, *Beyond the Post-Modern Mind* (New York: Crossroad, 1982). A major work from the perspective of traditional wisdom is Sayyed Hossein Nasr, *Knowledge and the Sacred*, The Gifford Lectures, 1981 (New York: Crossroad, 1981). Also helpful is Huston Smith, *The Religions of Man* (New York:

Harper & Row, 1958). Other important resources for the recovery of traditional wisdom are provided by Gai Eaton, *King of the Castle: Choice and Responsibility in the Modern World* (London: Bodley Head, 1977); E. F. Schumacher, *A Guide for the Perplexed* (New York: Harper & Row, 1977); Jacob Needleman, *Consciousness and Tradition* (New York: Crossroad, 1982); Frithjof Schuon, *Light on the Ancient Worlds* (London: Perennial Books, 1965); Catherine Roberts, *Science, Animals, and Evolution* (Westport, Conn.: Greenwood Press, 1980); Henry Corbin, "*Mundus Imaginalis* or The Imaginary and the Imaginal," *Spring; An Annual of Archetypal Psychology and Jungian Thought* (1972), 1-19; and Kathleen Raine, "Towards a Living Universe," *Teachers College Record*, vol. 82, no. 3 (Spring 1981), 458-74. Robert N. Bellah's "Cultural Vision and the Human Future," *Teachers College Record*, vol. 82, no. 3 (Spring 1981), 497-506, deals with the reappropriation of traditional wisdom in ways suitable to the modern mind. Catherine Roberts's *The Scientific Conscience* (New York: George Braziller, 1967) relates the radical humanities, traditional wisdom, and modern science.

3. Toward the Recovery of Wholeness: Another Look at Science

Michael Polanyi's works cited in connection with Chapter One are indispensable in understanding the ethical foundations of science. Also useful are Jacob Bronowski, *Science and Human Values* (New York: Harper & Row, 1956) and Werner Heisenberg, *Across the Frontiers* (New York: Harper & Row, 1974).

Michael Polanyi's writings are also essential for grasping the participatory nature of knowing in science. Owen Barfield's *Saving the Appearances*, already cited in connection with the evolution of consciousness, is also one of the most original and probing investigations of participation. John Archibald Wheeler's "The Universe as Home for Man," *American Scientist*, vol. 62 (November-December 1974), 683-91, and Bernard d'Espagnat's "The Quantum Theory and Reality," *Scientific American*, vol. 241 (November 1979), 158-81, discuss the fundamental importance of participatory knowing in modern physics. Errol Harris's "Testament of a Philosophic Dissenter," *The Carlton Miscellany*, vol. 17 (Spring 1979), 48-73, and Michael Polanyi's *The Tacit Dimension*, already cited, both discuss participatory knowing in science as well as the hierarchical relationships of knowledge and reality. A. R. Peacocke's *Creation and the World of Science*, The Bampton Lectures, 1978 (Oxford: Clarendon Press, 1979) also contains a valuable summary discussion of "nature's hierarchies." Important insights on various aspects of knowing in modern science are contained in Charles Davy, *Towards a Third*

Culture (Edinburgh: Floris Books, 1978). The primacy of the unmanifest dimensions of physical reality and of human personality are discussed respectively in Michael Polanyi, *Scientific Thought and Social Reality* (New York: International Universities Press, 1974) and in David Bakan, *The Duality of Human Experience* (Skokie, Ill.: Rand McNally, 1966).

Forceful statements of the central importance of human experience and consciousness to an adequate understanding of the world include John Archibald Wheeler, "The Universe as Home for Man," cited above; Alan Howard, "Education and Our *Human* Future," *Teachers College Record*, vol. 81, no. 3 (Spring 1980), 337-44; Owen Barfield, "Historical Perspectives in the Development of Science," in *Toward a Man-Centered Medical Science*, vol. 1, edited by Karl E. Schaefer (Mt. Kisco, N.Y.: Futura Publishing, 1977), 121-36; and Charles Birch, "Nature, God and Humanity in Ecological Perspective," *Christianity and Crisis* (October 28, 1979), 259-66.

Systems theory in biology is developed in Paul A. Weiss, *The Science of Life: The Living System—A System for Living* (New York: Futura Publishing, 1973); idem, "The System of Nature and the Nature of Systems: Empirical Holism and Practical Reductionism Harmonized," in *Toward a Man-Centered Medical Science*, cited above, pp. 49-50; and in Ludwig von Bertalanffy, *A Systems View of Man*, edited by Paul A. La Violette (Boulder, Colo.: Westview Press, 1981). Ilya Prigogine's theory of dissipative structures is deftly and succinctly discussed by A. R. Peacocke, *Creation and the World of Science*, cited above, pp. 97-100. Marilyn Ferguson's *The Aquarian Conspiracy: Personal and Social Transformation in the 1980s* (Los Angeles: J. P. Tarcher, 1980) surveys usefully, though often uncritically, many new developments in science. Walter J. Ong's *Interfaces of the Word: Studies in the Evolution of Consciousness and Culture* (Ithaca: Cornell University Press, 1977), discusses systems theory in many different fields.

Critics of Darwinian and neo-Darwinian theories of evolution represent many different perspectives. Revisions of neo-Darwinism by scientists who, nevertheless, affirm natural selection as the primary evolutionary mechanism include: Stephen Jay Gould, "'Evolution's Erratic Pace," *Natural History*, 86 (1977), 12, 14, 16; and S. J. Gould and R. C. Lewontin, "The Spandrels of San Marco and the Panglossian Paradigm: A Critique of the Adaptationist Programme," *Proceedings of the Royal Society of London. Series B. Biological Sciences*, 205 (1979), 581-98. See also Niles Eldredge's demolition of the neo-Darwinian synthesis in "Gentleman's Agreement," *The Sciences* (April 1981), 20-23, 31.

Philosophical and scientific criticisms of Darwinism and the development of non-Darwinian approaches to evolution are presented in

Marjorie Grene, *The Knower and the Known* (London: Faber and Faber, 1966); Sir Alister Hardy, *The Living Stream: Evolution and Man* (Cleveland: World Publishing Co., 1968); W. H. Thorpe, *Animal Nature and Human Nature* (London: Methuen, 1974); and Charles Birch, "Nature, God and Humanity," cited above. Succinct statements of *non*-Darwinian approaches to evolution by leading philosophers and scientists (mainly, though not entirely, from a Whiteheadian perspective) may be found in David R. Griffin and John B. Cobb, Jr., eds., *Mind in Nature, Essays on the Interface of Science and Philosophy* (Lanham, Md.: University Press of America, 1977).

For a thoroughgoing criticism of the scientific adequacy of Darwinism, see Norman Macbeth, *Darwin Retried* (New York: Dell Publishing, 1971), and the review of Macbeth's book by E. O. Wiley, "Book Review," *Systematic Zoology*, 24 (June 1978) 269-70. See also the fascinating "Darwinism: A Time for Funerals, A *Towards* Interview with Norman Macbeth," *Towards*, 2 (Spring 1982), 18-29.

John Davy has presented a penetrating summary of the work of the biologists Gareth Nelson and Norman Platnick, Brian Goodwin, Gerry Webster, and others and their challenges to neo-Darwinism in his "Review," *The London Observer* (August 16, 1981). See also the report by Anne C. Roark, "A 'New Synthesis' in Evolution," *The Chronicle of Higher Education* (March 23, 1981), 3.

The indeterminateness of the theory of natural selection is thoroughly discussed by Ronald H. Brady, "Natural Selection and the Criteria by Which a Theory is Judged," *Systematic Zoology*, 28 (1979), 600-621. Owen Barfield, "The Evolution Complex," *Towards*, 2 (Spring 1982), 6-16, probes fundamental inadequacies in the underlying premises of modern evolutionary theory.

New and unorthodox perspectives on mind and brain research are developed in Wilder Penfield, *The Mystery of the Mind* (Princeton, N.J.: Princeton University Press, 1975); John C. Eccles, *Facing Reality: Philosophical Adventures of a Brain Scientist* (New York: Springer-Verlag, 1970); idem, *The Human Mystery*, Gifford Lectures, 1977-1978 (New York: Springer-Verlag, 1979); idem, *The Human Psyche*, Gifford Lectures, 1978-1979 (New York: Springer International, 1979); and idem, "The Self-Conscious Mind and the Meaning and Mystery of Personal Existence," *Teachers College Record*, vol. 82, no. 3 (Spring 1981), 403-26.

David Bohm's important work in physics is presented in his classic *Causality and Chance in Modern Physics* (London: Routledge & Kegan Paul, 1957), and in his recent *Wholeness and the Implicate Order* (London: Routledge and Kegan Paul, 1980). Also extremely helpful and important, and fully understandable to the non-physicist, are the following interviews: "The Enfolding-Unfolding Universe, A Conversation with David Bohm," *Revision*, vol. 1 (Summer/Fall 1978), 24-51; "The Physicist and the Mystic—Is a Dialogue between Them Possible? A Conversation with David Bohm, Conducted by Renee Weber," *Revision*, vol. 4 (Spring 1981), 36-52; Bohm and Weber, "Nature as Creativity" and Rupert Sheldrake and Bohm, "Morphogenetic Fields and the Implicate Order," both in *Revision*, 5 (Fall 1982), 35-48.

Fritjof Capra's *The Tao of Physics: An Exploration of the Parallels between Modern Physics and Eastern Mysticism* (Boulder, Colo.: Shambala Publications, 1975) discusses many new dimensions of modern physics. For some critical questions about Capra's approach see Chapter Three, note 53, and the references cited there.

4. Insight-Imagination

A. M. Taylor's *Imagination and the Growth of Science* (New York: Schocken Books, 1970) and Gerald Holton's *The Scientific Imagination: Case Studies* (New York: Cambridge University Press, 1978) present the importance of imagination in the development of science. Mary Warnock's *Imagination* (Berkeley and Los Angeles: University of California Press, 1976) is a major history of philosophical conceptions of imagination.

The concept of Insight-Imagination developed in this chapter draws primarily on the work of David Bohm and Owen Barfield. David Bohm has written explicit on the nature of insight and knowing in three articles, "Imagination, Fancy, Insight, and Reason in the Process of Thought," in *Evolution of Consciousness, Studies in Polarity*, edited by Shirley Sugerman (Middletown, Conn.: Wesleyan University Press, 1976), pp. 51-68; "On Insight and Its Significance, for Science, Education, and Values," in *Education and Values*, edited by Douglas Sloan (New York: Teachers College Press, 1980), pp. 7-22; and "Insight, Knowledge, Science, and Human Values," *Teachers College Record*, vol. 82, no. 3 (Spring 1981), 380-402. Moreover, the interviews with Bohm referred to in connection with Chapter Three also contain much of relevance to Bohm's understanding of insight.

Again, all of Owen Barfield's work is fundamentally and deeply concerned with imagination as the involvement of the whole person in knowing. In addition to his other works already mentioned, Owen Barfield, *What Coleridge Thought* (Middletown, Conn.: Wesleyan University Press, 1971), is a profound discussion of Coleridge and essential to understanding the nature of imagination. Also valuable is Owen Barfield, "Either: Or," in *Imagination and the Spirit*, ed. Charles A. Huttar (Grand Rapids, Mich.: William B. Eerdmans Publishing Co., 1971), pp.

25-43. In connection with Barfield's conception of metaphor the reader may find useful Richard Hocks, "Contemporary Theories of Metaphor: An Overview and Interpretation," *Towards*, 1, (December 1978), 22-28; Paul Ricoeur, *The Rule of Metaphor* (Toronto: University of Toronto Press, 1977); and J. M. O'Connell, "The Poet in the Stream of History: An Approach to Poetry," *Towards*, vol. 1 (Summer 1980), 16-24.

Three articles that shed light on the wholeness of imagination are: James Hillman, "An Inquiry into Image," *Spring; An Annual of Archetypal Psychology and Jungian Thought* (1977), 62-88; John Davy, "Science and Human Rights," *The Golden Blade* (annual) (1968), 24-40; and M. C. Richards, "The Public School and the Education of the Whole Person," *Teachers College Record*, vol. 82, no. 1 (Fall 1980), 47-75.

In his *Reason and Emotion* (London: Faber and Faber Ltd., 1935) John Macmurray explores the interconnection between thinking and feeling as does Paul Roubiczek in *Thinking towards Religion* (London: Darwen Findlayson, 1957), Chapter 5, pp. 99-116. Similarly, Rollo May examines the deep connection between thinking and willing in *Love and Will* (New York: W. W. Norton, 1969). The primacy of consciousness and imagination is dealt with by Henry Corbin in *The Concept of a Comparative Philosophy* (Ipswich, England: Golgonooza Press, 1981).

In "*Towards* Interviews Owen Barfield," *Towards*, vol. 1 (Summer 1980), 6-12, and in "Science and Imagination: An Interview with John Davy," *Towards*, vol. 1 (Winter 1980-1981), 17-24, respectively, Barfield and Davy explore many of the deep interrelationships between imagination and the world of nature.

5. Living Thinking, Living World: Toward an Education of Insight-Imagination

The development of autonomous, free persons as the aim of education is set forth eloquently, and with concrete indications for teaching and curriculum, in Philip H. Phenix, "Promoting Personal Development through Teaching," *Teachers College Record*, vol. 84, no. 2 (December 1982), 301-16. John Macmurray's classic *Persons in Relation* (Atlantic Highlands, N.J.: Humanities Press, 1979) argues that personal existence depends on trustworthy relations with other persons in community. Also emphasizing the importance of trustworthy personal relationships for the development of authentic selfhood are Maurice Merleau-Ponty, "The Child's Relations with Others," in *The Primacy of Perception*, edited by James M. Edie (Evanston, Ill.: Northwestern University Press, 1964), pp. 95-155; Martin Buber, "Education," in Martin Buber, *Between Man and Man* (New York: Macmillan Company, 1965), pp. 83-103; and David

Michael Levin, "Moral Education: The Body's Felt Sense of Value," *Teachers College Record*, 84 (Winter 1982), 283-300. The implications for education are manifold.

Philip Ariés, *Centuries of Childhood: A Social History of Family Life* (New York: Alfred A. Knopf, 1962), looks at changing conceptions of childhood in Western culture. Jean Piaget's research on the stages of child development has been made readily accessible in Howard E. Gruber and J. Jacques Vonéche, *The Essential Piaget* (New York: Basic Books, 1977). The reader will also find a succinct statement of Piaget's views in Jean Piaget, *Science of Education and the Psychology of the Child* (New York: Viking Press, 1971). A helpful discussion of Piaget is provided by his student, David Elkind, in *Children and Adolescents, Interpretative Essays on Jean Piaget* (New York: Oxford University Press, 1981). For a different view of educational development and its curricular requirements see Alfred North Whitehead, *The Aims of Education and Other Essays* (New York: Macmillan, 1929). A large body of research on early child development is surveyed and its implications for education are explored in Raymond S. Moore and Dorothy N. Moore, "Caring for Young Children: Danger of Early Schooling," in *A New Image of Man in Medicine: Individuation Process and Biographical Aspects of Disease*, vol. 3, edited by Karl E. Schaefer et al. (Mount Kisco, N.Y.: Futura Publishing, 1979), pp. 37-70.

There are several sources for the reader who wants to learn more about Steiner (or Waldorf) education. Rudolf Steiner's writings are voluminous, but his introductory treatments of education include Rudolf Steiner, *The Education of the Child*, 2d. ed. (London: Rudolf Steiner Press, 1974); idem, *The Roots of Education* (London: Rudolf Steiner Press, 1968); and idem, *A Modern Art of Education* (London: Rudolf Steiner Press, 1972). For many readers the best place to start may be with the excellent introductions by Mary Caroline Richards and A. C. Harwood: Mary Caroline Richards, *Toward Wholeness: Rudolf Steiner Education in America* (Middletown, Conn.: Wesleyan University Press, 1980); A. C. Harwood, *The Recovery of Man in Childhood: A Study in the Educational Work of Rudolf Steiner* (London: Hodder and Stoughton, 1958); and idem, *The Way of a Child: An Introduction to the Work of Rudolf Steiner for Children*, 4th rev. ed. (London: Rudolf Steiner Press, 1967). See also Ekkehard Piening and Nick Lyons, *Education as an Art—Essays on the Rudolf Steiner Method—Waldorf Education* (New York: Rudolf Steiner School Press, 1979). A major case study of Waldorf education, carried out and published by UNESCO, is George Rist and Peter Schneider, *Integrating Vocational and General Education: A Rudolf Steiner School, Case Study of the Hibernia School, Herne, Federal Republic of Germany* (Hamburg: UNESCO Institute for Education, 1979). A collection of articles introducing the basic concepts and practices of Waldorf education is contained in "Special Section: Waldorf Education, An Introduction," *Teachers College Record*, 81 (Spring 1980), 322-70. Iona Ginsburg, "Jean Piaget and Rudolf Steiner: Stages of Child Development and Implications for Pedagogy," *Teachers College Record*, vol. 84, no. 2 (Winter 1982), 327-37, is an introductory comparison of Jean Piaget and Rudolf Steiner on the education of the child.

Insights on the indispensable place of art in education are contributed by Charles Davy, "Art for Whose Sake?" *The Golden Blade* (1980), 61-79, and by Mary Caroline Richards, "The Public School and the Education of the Whole Person," *Teachers College Record*, vol. 82, no. 1 (Fall 1980), 45-75. Bruno Bettelheim's *The Uses of Enchantment: The Meaning and Importance of Fairy Tales* (New York: Alfred A. Knopf, 1976) can be profitably read in connection with the Waldorf use and understanding of fairy tales. Jerry Mander's *Four Arguments for the Elimination of Television* (New York: William Morrow, 1978) is provocative and should be consulted by readers interested in the educational effects of television. Trygve Tholfsen's "The Ambiguous Virtues of the Study of History," *Teachers College Record*, vol. 79, no. 2 (December 1977), 245-58, is a brief and masterful analysis of the importance of the study of history. The case for a direct and caring experience of nature in science education is developed in R. D. Lawrence, *The Study of Life: A Naturalist's View* (New York: Myrin Institute, 1980).

Index _____

About the Author

DOUGLAS SLOAN, a specialist in the history of religion and education in American culture, is Professor of History and Education at Teachers College of Columbia University, Adjunct Professor of Religion and Education at the Union Theological Seminary in New York City, and editor of the *Teachers College Record*. His books include *The Scottish Enlightenment and the American College Ideal*, *The Great Awakening and American Education*, and *Education and Values*. His most recent articles have appeared in *ISIS*, *The Teaching of Ethics*, and *Teachers College Record*.